Globalizing Collateral Language

STUDIES IN SECURITY AND INTERNATIONAL AFFAIRS

Globalizing Collateral Language

FROM 9/11 TO ENDLESS WAR

Edited by John Collins and Somdeep Sen

THE UNIVERSITY OF GEORGIA PRESS   ATHENS

© 2021 by the University of Georgia Press
Athens, Georgia 30602
www.ugapress.org
All rights reserved
Set in Adobe Garamond Pro by Melissa Buchanan

Most University of Georgia Press titles are
available from popular e-book vendors.

Printed digitally

Library of Congress Control Number: 2021939572
ISBN: 9780820360539 (hardback)
ISBN: 9780820360522 (paperback)
ISBN: 9780820360515 (ebook)

Contents

Globalizing Collateral Language

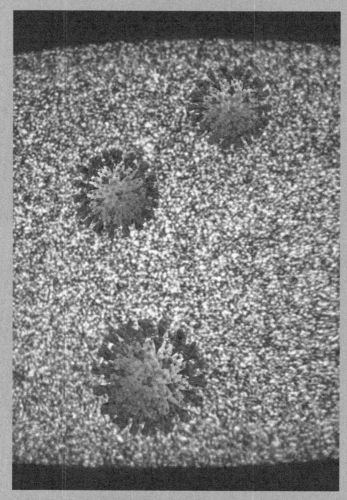

Catherine Tedford, *Introduction*.
Reprinted with permission of the artist.

Introduction   JOHN COLLINS AND SOMDEEP SEN

Language is never just a means of communication. It can also function, as the original *Collateral Language* volume argued, as a "terrorist organization." Its vocabulary, especially in times of war, has the ability to "target civilians" and "generate fear" as a means of producing specific political outcomes, most notably the passive and active acceptance of state violence itself.[1] For this reason, the critical examination of language must be a central part of any effort to fight imperialism, militarism, demagoguery, racism, sexism, and other structures of injustice.

When Collins and Glover coined the concept of "collateral language" in their 2002 volume, they noted that during wartime, new terms enter our lexicon and already existing terms find new/additional meanings.[2] While in some ways a collateral effect of war, this linguistic process is ultimately an important part of war itself. Just as war increasingly unfolds in areas populated by noncombatants, it also takes place in spaces of public discourse where military efforts are promoted, discussed, critiqued, and debated. The concept of collateral language consciously plays on and critiques the innocuousness of the idea of collateral damage, a military term and quintessential example of Orwellian "doublespeak" designating civilians who are killed and maimed as a supposedly collateral effect of violence directed at combatants.

This book continues the work of analyzing collateral language but argues that this language has proliferated both within and beyond the United States since the attacks of September 11, 2001. Several of the chapters explore how the collateral language lexicon now permeates debates in the country over immigration, race, policing, news, and fascist movements. Other chapters reveal how the lexicon has also found global resonance in a further extension of the "collateral" process.

In framing our approach to these dynamics, this introduction integrates terms from the original volume, other terms that emerged in the years immediately following 9/11, as well as the terms we have chosen to cover in the chapters that follow. While we recognize that no list of terms can be fully exhaustive, we do want to help readers see that all of these terms are part of an organic and evolving whole. In addition, we have included chapters that utilize a range of stylistic approaches in order to illustrate the flexibility of this growing lexicon.

Finally, we want to emphasize that this volume is more than just a scholarly exploration of the subject. It is also a principled and polemical intervention in the public sphere at a time when, faced by the tyranny of collateral language, the need for such interventions is greater than ever.

Approaching Collateral Language

Putting together a lexicon of collateral language in the immediate aftermath of the 9/11 attacks was essential because it was necessary to politicize the process of naturalization by which the post-9/11 political rhetoric had become everyday language. Moreover, the history and politics of the use of the fourteen terms included in the 2002 volume also allowed us to better understand how and why "we" consented to the way the "global war on terror(ism)" (hereafter abbreviated GWOT) targeted civilians and generated an environment of fear.[3]

In exploring this lexicon, Collins and Glover identified five analytical angles, each of which highlighted a key aspect of how language affects us as citizens:

1. **Manufacturing consent.** This phrase was coined in 1922 by Walter Lippmann and utilized brilliantly by Edward Herman and Noam Chomsky in their influential 1988 book *Manufacturing Consent: The Political Economy of the Mass Media.* When applied to the realm of collateral language, the concept of "manufacturing consent" shows how wartime language that is often vague, yet powerful, can assist governments in developing "democratic" consent for acts of brutality.

2. **What you hear is what you see.** The Austrian philosopher Ludwig Wittgenstein once said that language defines the limits of the world. In times of war and conflict, the effect of language on our cognition of the world is critically visible in the way it shapes our perception of specific social groups. In the immediate aftermath of the 9/11 attacks, preexisting forms of anti-Arab and anti-Muslim bigotry were further encouraged through language that securitized Arab and Muslim people, as well as those who "look" Middle Eastern, as potential sources of insecurity, violence, and barbarity. Similarly, the rhetoric of "cowardice" (Egan, 2002 volume) in reference to those attacking the United States provided an opportunity to shore up a binary system of gendered identification that made a violent (and masculine) U.S. response against the cowardly (and feminine) enemy feel inevitable.

3. **The real effects of language.** Beyond its role in shaping perception, collateral language directly paves the way for actions that have immediate, material effects on real individuals and communities. Much of the military and broader national security apparatus's own euphemistic terminology, such as "targets" (Neisser, 2002 volume) and "vital interests" (Singer, 2002 volume), is designed precisely to hide these effects from view. In addition to keeping U.S. citizens in the dark as to the real motivations and objects of U.S. actions, this language also silences critical voices and erases the experiences of those whose communities are in the crosshairs of those actions.

4. **Language and history.** Language doesn't simply fall from the sky. Understanding collateral language requires that we examine the history of particular words and phrases. The use of the term "evil" (Rediehs, 2002 volume) to refer to al-Qaeda, for example, draws on an entire history of applying this black-and-white, metaphysical label to a wide range of official enemies, implying that the perspectives and grievances of these groups should never be given serious consideration.

5. **The possibility of language.** The original *Collateral Language* volume also sought to emphasize that while language can serve the purposes of those seeking to justify state brutality, it can also be an essential tool of dissent and resistance. Language, in other words, is always an arena of struggle. Some terms may need to be jettisoned forever or replaced in favor of more accurate terms (e.g., "excessive destruction" instead of "collateral damage"). In other cases, however, we may wish to challenge the efforts of hegemonic elites to monopolize the process of assigning meaning to language. For example, we might seek to use terms such as "freedom" (Van Alstyne, 2002 volume) and "justice" (McCarthy, 2002 volume) as rallying cries against war and exploitation rather than as manipulative calls for more of the same.

As any number of recent examples illustrate, all five of these analytical angles remain directly relevant today to the growing and changing lexicon of collateral language. President Donald Trump's regular use of terms such as "infestation" when referring to immigrants and communities of color, for instance, belongs to a lineage of racist discourse and imagery that includes Nazi Germany, thereby revealing the need to put language in its historical context. Similarly, "democracy" (Saccarelli, this volume), often presented as a universal aspiration, continues to be the pretext for consenting to violent and exploitative interventions in the Global South. In this way, many of the terms analyzed in this volume demonstrate how collateral language continues to generate real effects throughout the world. At the same time, in the way in which this language is employed, it serves to limit the ability of citizens to understand what is happening and fathom the real consequences of the politics to which they have consented.

With all of this in mind, it is essential to recognize that there have been important changes in the two decades since the 9/11 attacks. On the one hand, while politicians continue to invoke 9/11 periodically for a variety of reasons, it may appear that the attacks have receded, to some extent, into the background of the nation's consciousness. Yet a more critical look indicates that, if anything, the lexicon of collateral language has expanded dramatically and has undergone a fundamental process of globalization alongside the globalization of the GWOT itself in a way that doesn't require constant references to a two-decades-old attack. The first volume was prepared in immediate view of the Bush administration's particular response to 9/11 on behalf of "America" (which is its own term in the lexicon of collateral language). The intervening two decades, however, have revealed how these linguistic terms can exist and find relevance somewhat independent of the collective memory and trauma of 9/11, which is rooted in a particular American experience.

This process of globalization extends the geographic reach of collateral language's basic logic: cultivating fear and targeting civilians. Accordingly, this new volume provides close analysis not only of the development of America's own lexicon but also of other cases from around the globe. These include full chapters devoted to the cases of Spain and Sri Lanka, respectively, but other chapters contain discussions of collateral language as it manifests in cases demonstrating rising forms of authoritarian populism (e.g., in Hungary or India), media and information manipulation (e.g., in Brazil or the Philippines), and debates over multiculturalism (e.g., in Denmark) and security (e.g., in Israel). These examples reveal how such language has found wider resonance, shaping political dynamics in a range of societies that are confronting their own past and present experiences of violence. Even here, however, the long shadow of 9/11 remains visible, particularly insofar as 9/11 itself, far from a singular or isolated event, was always embedded in a complex and transnational set of historical processes.

9/11, Myth, and the Freezing of History

Any critical assessment of the past two decades of post-9/11 language politics must take account of what French semiotician Roland Barthes would call the "mythologizing" of the event itself. In his 1957 essay "Myth Today," Barthes famously applied the insights of structural linguistics to the study of nonverbal signs we see every day. Barthes describes a second-order system of signification through which particular signs are emptied of their original content (as one would empty water out of a glass) and then refilled with new content, thus creating a second sign whose articulation and circulation serves the interest of the ruling class.[4] We can thus say that myth is a particularly ideological form of communication: it reveals the link between discourse and power.

While many of Barthes's brief case studies accompanying the essay concern what might appear to be mundane examples from the worlds of advertising, tourism, film, and consumer products, his core example speaks directly to the role of myth in shaping geopolitical identities and interpretations. Barthes discusses a 1955 *Paris Match* magazine cover showing a Black soldier saluting the French flag. In what we would call the first order of signification, we recognize what the printed page contains—a photograph, nothing very remarkable. In the second order, however, something quite different happens. Through the operation of ideology, the first sign takes on a particular meaning having to do with French "imperiality," namely, the implied claim that France is a great empire that treats all its subjects equally regardless of race or ethnicity. In order for this second meaning to be conveyed, a great deal of history having to do with the actual practices of French imperialism must be gathered and consolidated in a single image; much of it has to be discarded (or allowed to "haemorrhage" away, in Barthes's terms); and the rest must be reduced to a single signifying function. This second operation, through which the sign becomes more explicitly ideological, Barthes calls "myth." His work reveals that myth works by fixing meaning in place and hiding what it is actually constructing; in his words, it "transforms history into nature."[5]

Barthes's discussion of myth provides an important tool with which we can begin to assess the deeper social effects of our post-9/11 language politics. Consider how the event itself was perceived inside the United States. In their initial reactions to the attacks, many Americans said the horrifying images coming out of lower Manhattan looked "like a movie," suggesting that the primary frame of reference available to them was the one provided by Hollywood blockbusters such as *Independence Day* (1996) or *The Siege* (1998).[6] For others, the attacks simply came from "out of nowhere," as if Americans had been living in a two-dimensional world and thus were only able to see the giant hole that suddenly appeared on the surface of that world. The causes of the event itself, coming out of a third dimension, remained invisible.

The third dimension is history, in particular the history of suffering in places such as the Middle East and the relationship of that suffering to U.S. foreign policy and militarism. For Americans who have personal connections to those places, that history is always present. So how did it become so invisible to the rest of the country? How was it allowed to "haemorrhage" away? Why is it so difficult for Americans to understand the role of this history in producing the global conflicts in which the country is perpetually embroiled?

One answer is that the United States, with its twin traditions of intellectual isolationism and ideological exceptionalism, has never been adequately aware of history. Another answer is that we are actively encouraged to forget or to focus our attention elsewhere. Consider how quickly the September 11 attacks, with all of the deep history behind them, were consolidated to the point where they could be seen as a single event: "9/11." Imagine an hourglass into which humanity has poured an infinite amount of historical material related to U.S. foreign policy, the complex relationship between Islam and "the West," the creation of the state of Israel and the destruction of Palestine, the rise and fall of empires, the dynamics of the oil economy, and so forth. The middle point of the hourglass here represents the moment of the 9/11 attacks. It's a frozen, Barthean moment, symbolized by the temporary bottleneck that occurs when too much sand pours through at once.

When the sand finally spills out the bottom, we must actively work to reconstruct the history that it represents. The problem is that something happened in the middle of the political hourglass, something that is both natural and unnatural. The natural part is that it's hard for anyone to process fully the complex array of historical factors behind an event like 9/11. The unnatural part is that powerful individuals and institutions (the state, corporations, the mass media, universities, think tanks) intervened in the bottleneck in order to frame the meaning of the event for us—that is, to mythologize it—through the use of collateral language and the circulation of powerful images. Consequently, even as we try to grab onto the grains of sand and understand what they mean, we find that they have been transformed. Someone has altered them so that they bear the mark of the bottleneck: they refer inevitably back to that traumatic moment in September 2001.

The Growth and Analysis of Collateral Language

In the weeks and months immediately following the 9/11 attacks, a series of stale but evocative symbols ritually displayed on the airwaves—the burning and falling towers, the face of Osama bin Laden, the letters FDNY, President

Bush standing in the rubble with a bullhorn—came to signify what was in fact a complex historical event. A similar process took place with collateral language. The event of 9/11 created a kind of explanatory vacuum, and the Bush administration quickly stepped in with a series of words and phrases designed to give a limited, easily comprehensible, but politically loaded set of meanings to 9/11 and the U.S. response: "terrorism" (Collins, 2002 volume) "fundamentalism" (Renold, 2002 volume), "jihad" (Church, 2002 volume), "unity" (Stoddard and Cornwell, 2002 volume), and "civilization vs. barbarism" (Llorente, 2002 volume), to name a few. The corporate media immediately adopted much of this language, but in a way that stripped it of much of its relevant context, thereby contributing to the process of constructing what amounted to a powerful and ubiquitous national soundtrack. Terms such as "blowback" (Thornton and Thornton, 2002 volume), which had the potential to open up a more critical reading of this context, were heard much less often.

Some collateral language phrases functioned as master frames for the new situation in which the nation found itself. Within nine days of 9/11, for example, we were introduced to "homeland security" (Varadarajan, this volume), which fostered a culture of fear and suspicion and played on American patriotism in order to generate support for the reduction of civil liberties. The following month saw the entrance into the lexicon of "war on terrorism," a phrase that added a new object to the construction of "the war on _____" (Glover, 2002 volume) in an effort to label the country's latest open-ended, self-justifying, and self-perpetuating war. In much of public discourse, "war on terrorism" subsequently morphed into "war on terror," oddly implying that the United States was leading a fight against an emotion rather than a type of political violence.

For a brief period in October–November 2001, the word "anthrax" (Egan, 2002 volume) occupied the public's consciousness, suggesting an immediate connection between the 9/11 attacks and the emergence of new cable media-friendly "threats." In January 2002, presidential speechwriter David Frum coined the phrase "axis of evil" for the 2002 State of the Union address in an attempt to link a new set of official enemies (Iran, Iraq, and North Korea) with Adolf Hitler and his allies. The president and other members of his administration invoked the image of a "mushroom cloud" (Alimagham, this volume) and the broader specter of "weapons of mass destruction" (WMDs) to justify preemptive military strikes in the Middle East. As Barnard (this volume) notes, major establishment media outlets amplified this discourse, repeating inaccurate claims regarding Iraq's possession of WMDs.

Since much of this language quickly became second nature to many

Americans, several scholars and public intellectuals noted how we uncritically adopted the post-9/11 lexicon in our everyday communication. Sandra Silberstein and Jeff Lewis, for example, considered the dynamics of physical conflict as replicated in the field of language. In *Language Wars*, Lewis urged readers to look beyond "simple polemics—good against evil, the west against the east." Instead, he insisted, "language wars" draw on the past to rationalize contemporary discussions in a way that stimulates "contentions both within particular social groups and between social groups," all in order to fulfil the "human propensity for forming community, culture and meanings."[7] Specifically referring to the GWOT, Silberstein noted that iconic and historic events like the attacks of 9/11 undertake a "linguistic trajectory" after their occurrence. On this trajectory, the discourse that was inspired by the event uses it as "raw material to (re)create a national perspective" in a way that the polemics of "good vs. evil or the west vs. the east" become commonsensical. When the "'enemy' is positioned as 'evil,'" she argued, few (patriotic) citizens would be willing to question the consequences of the war, especially for civilians.[8]

In a 2005 series of interviews, Noam Chomsky noted that while language has always been used to "shape attitudes and opinions and to induce conformity and subordination," the current proliferation of collateral language is an outgrowth of the way propaganda "became an organized and very self-conscious industry" in the twentieth century.[9] In this sense, the contemporary brand of collateral language is not unlike the propaganda that originated in the British Ministry of Information—the first of its kind—during the First World War. While its official purpose was "to direct the thought of most of the world," the ministry was especially focused on American citizens (particularly intellectuals) as Britain wanted to convince them "of the nobility of British war efforts" and, by extension, to secure U.S. support for the war.[10]

In *Horrorism*, Adriana Cavarero similarly reveals the politics associated with the very act of naming. She writes that naming an act of violence in a certain way supplies a particular "interpretive framework" for understanding (violent) events, which in turn shapes the public perception of such acts.[11] In this sense, the "interpretive framework" becomes an integral facet of the conflict itself as its ability to shape public opinion makes it a valuable tool for garnering public support for the GWOT, including the kinds of "collateral damage" to which many would not have consented otherwise.

In an important 2006 intervention, media and cultural studies scholar Douglas Kellner critically examined the use of binary, good versus evil discourse both by jihadist groups and by the U.S. state as part of the larger linguistic architecture used to create a sense of inevitability around the idea of a violent U.S. response to 9/11.[12] Noting how the post-9/11 discourse drew on earlier constructions such as Samuel Huntington's famous "clash of civilizations" thesis, Kellner focused attention on terms such as "axis of evil," media frames such as "America Strikes Back" and "embedded reporters," and the broader emergence of what he called "Bushspeak" (an early twenty-first-century version of Orwellian "doublespeak"). Equally important, Kellner demonstrated how this language worked hand in glove with the kinds of "media spectacles" that characterized not only the 9/11 attacks themselves but also key moments in the U.S. war on Iraq. These include the initial "shock and awe" bombings, the carefully staged pulling down of the Saddam Hussein statue in Baghdad, the made-for-TV "rescue" of Private Jessica Lynch, and George W. Bush's infamous "Mission Accomplished" proclamation aboard an aircraft carrier.

9

Other scholars carried forward the critical analysis of language and the GWOT by digging deeply into the language used to construct U.S. cities as "homeland" spaces and Middle Eastern cities as "target" spaces; the role of "elite political discourse" in generating public consent for torture; and the "intertextual" construction of the so-called Bush Doctrine through the 2002 National Security Strategy document and its close relationship to earlier documents that had framed U.S. policy after the end of the Cold War.[13]

The Globalization of Collateral Language

While there was a great outpouring of global solidarity with the United States immediately following the 9/11 attacks, it is also true that the trauma and experience of 9/11 were not as immediately or tangibly felt elsewhere. Yet the globalization of collateral language in the subsequent two decades is undeniable. In some cases, this reflects the globalization of the GWOT itself via the actions of the United States and its allies. In other cases, however, we see how the discursive logic of the GWOT can influence a much broader range of political projects as global elites seek to develop consent for their actions.

Many of the chapters in the current volume reveal the blurred lines between the GWOT and these broader global dynamics at a time when we are witnessing an intensification of state repression and right-wing intimidation against migrants, women, sexual minorities, environmental defenders, indigenous people, and activists for racial justice. How is it, for example, that walls (Sen, this volume) emerge as material and symbolic markers of both

Israel's fight against "terrorism" and President Trump's fight against "illegal immigration"? In the increasingly polemical debates on immigration in the United States and Europe, how does the racist language of the immigrant "threat" play upon the traumatic memory of 9/11? How does it extend the binary logic ("either with us or against us") of Bush's borderless war while stoking new fears of what nonwhite "invaders" (Berry, this volume) are plotting to do to "us"? Similarly, the case of "internally displaced people (IDPs)" in Sri Lanka (Jayman, this volume) calls us to ask, how does collateral language function in a context of proto-fascism, ethnic cleansing, and cultural genocide?

These evolving constructions of Self and Other are also reflected in national and transnational struggles over "women" (Segal, this volume), "victims" (Collins, Elvira, and Llorente, this volume), and even "life" itself (Singer, this volume). In such a context, one wonders, how should we understand the emerging discourse of "populism" (Kapoor, this volume)? Who benefits from the coining, circulation, and weaponization of the term "eco-terrorism" (Buck, this volume) at a time of escalating environmental crisis? How is it that the modes of disinformation used in the immediate aftermath of the 9/11 attacks find resonance, under the pretence of "fake news" (Barnard, this volume), in all corners of the world?

All of these examples illustrate how the institutionalization of collateral language into our collective lexicon and its growing tendency to flow across national borders continue to influence contemporary political realities. While the U.S. national security state and its allies once deployed this language for purposes of justifying the U.S.-led GWOT, it has now become a self-sustaining discursive machinery that shapes the way we think about politics in general, even when "terrorism" is not the primary focus.

In this sense, to return to our earlier metaphor, we now see that the bottom half of the hourglass has become a kind of hyperbaric chamber of self-evident truths. With 9/11 established as a mythical (history-free) origin story grounded in collective trauma, collateral language continues to operate in a way that discourages any effort to look beyond the "truths" that it provides. In the U.S. context, this allows for a particular way of doing politics—highly securitized and grounded in malignant constructions of Otherness—to continue, even though the event that led to the proliferation of this brand of politics has receded into the past. Globally, this same process allows others to adopt collateral language despite not having any direct experience of 9/11. Here we see the colonizing impulse of this language: it seeks to incorporate all of humanity into its seductive, binary, good versus evil logic.

Fascism or Global Apartheid?

Why would powerful individuals and institutions want to return us, over and over again, to the moment of trauma? And why would they find it useful to construct and maintain a globalized framework of collateral language that defines the horizon of politics itself? These questions take us directly into the long and rich literature on the cultural production of political obedience. Consider, for example, the words of Walter Lippmann, who first wrote about the "manufacturing of consent" in 1922. In the same text, Lippmann discussed the ease with which elites can manipulate public emotions through the flexible use of emotions, images, and vague concepts: "There are no end of things which can arouse the emotion, and no end of things which can satisfy it. This is particularly true where the stimulus is only dimly and indirectly perceived, and where the objective is likewise indirect. For you can associate an emotion, say fear, first with something immediately dangerous, then with the idea of that thing, then with something similar to that idea, and so on and on."[14]

Just over a dozen years later, Walter Benjamin famously argued that fascism is a product of a systematically aestheticized form of politics. Fascism seeks to render politics aesthetic, he noted, because it cannot offer people what they really want: economic justice. Consequently, it embraces the project of giving the people something else: "a chance to express themselves."[15] While the rise of Donald Trump provided an obvious illustration of this process, it would be a mistake to view the aestheticized politics of Trumpism as somehow separate from the dynamics that produced it. Rather, as Naomi Klein points out in *No Is Not Enough*, Trump's ascendance to the political stage was "less an aberration than a logical conclusion" to a period marked by the politics of branding and spectacle, the growth of corporate and executive power, and the stoking of xenophobic and misogynistic rage across the globe.[16] All of this, it is important to acknowledge, has taken place in response to rising demands for justice on the part of those representing the global majority.

Language plays a fundamental role in this process. As many critics have noted, contempt for and manipulation of language is an inevitable component of all fascist projects. In his influential 1995 essay detailing the fourteen characteristics of what he called "Ur-Fascism," Umberto Eco concluded his list by referring to the "impoverished vocabulary" of fascism, a vocabulary designed to "limit the instruments for complex and critical reasoning."[17] Building on this idea as part of his examination of the Christian Right in the United States, Chris Hedges writes of the "logocide" (killing of words) carried out as part of an incipient Christian fascism that promotes a radical vision of theocratic militarism.[18]

The drift toward fascism is inseparable from the growing urgency of climate crisis. Indeed, the operation of collateral language in recent years reveals a great deal about how global elites themselves understand this crisis: as a new reality that is likely to require increasingly draconian measures to protect the haves from the have-nots in a world of intensifying social inequality. We need look no further than the swirl of racist terminology surrounding state efforts to fortify borders, criminalize migration, curtail the admission of refugees and asylum seekers, and remove protections from populations deemed "disposable." It is no accident that the term "global apartheid" has become a popular way of describing these emerging realities.

On the Afterlives of 9/11

In the end, our exploration in this volume of the story of collateral language and its expansion during the past two decades is instructive for a number of reasons. First, it invites us to consider the long shadow of an event such as the 9/11 attacks: its implications for democracy, for the role of the media, for American exceptionalism, for social movements, for the fight against militarism and imperialism. Second, it reveals how processes of globalization shape, and are shaped by, the use of language in the political realm. Third, it reminds us that the fundamental questions concerning the politics of language—questions about manipulation, emotion, myth, and the "manufacturing of consent"—remain as relevant as ever, even (perhaps especially) in the age of social media and instantaneous, global information flows.

Perhaps most urgently, however, the ongoing story of collateral language provides us with a stark choice between two paths. One of these paths would see us allowing the continued mythologization of events such as 9/11 in ways that have urgent, often troubling implications both within and beyond the United States. The other path would involve recovering history as a tool for bringing a more liberating set of social and political arrangements into being. In other words, the receding of 9/11 into history provides us with a chance to avoid repeating the same mistake. Language is like other aspects of culture: we use it, but it also uses us. We have allowed collateral language to use us for too long. We can begin to reassert control, however, if we connect the history of 9/11 with the intolerable realities we see around us today. Being attentive to language and its role as a "terrorist organization" must be a fundamental part of our ongoing struggles for justice, locally and globally.

CHAPTER I

LATHA VARADARAJAN

Homeland Security

> We will work to ensure that the essential liberty of
> the American people is protected, that terrorists will not
> take away our way of life. It's called Homeland Security.
> —Tom Ridge, the first Homeland Security "czar," 2002

> We are witnessing historic changes across the entire threat landscape.
> . . . The result is a world where threats are more numerous, more
> widely distributed, highly networked, increasingly adaptive, and
> incredibly difficult to root out. The "home game" has merged with
> the "away game" and [homeland security] actions abroad are
> just as important as our security operations here at home.
> —Kirstjen Nielsen, former secretary of Homeland Security, 2019

The language and idea of "homeland security" is today firmly entrenched in mainstream American popular culture and political discourse. Whether in presidential tweets and debates or ratings-winning television shows, the notion that the American "homeland" is under threat and has to be secured by any means necessary is both taken for granted and, paradoxically, constantly reiterated. This development is not merely in the realm of fiction or fevered rhetoric. Homeland Security has been institutionalized, most obviously in the form of a federal agency with vast resources at its disposal and as an academic discipline with centers and departments sprouting across universities.

What makes this development striking is its relative novelty. At the turn of the century, the language of "homeland" was hardly— if at all—used by American policymakers, and the institutions that dealt with security issues were those entrenched in the conventional military-industrial complex. Given the current embeddedness of the term in American political lexicon, it might be hard to believe that the first time any president used the term "homeland" in an address to Congress was in 2001. Or that the term is historically quite alien to the political discourse of the American republic. Or that it has been less than two decades since the American government oversaw the biggest reorganization of federal agencies since the end of the Second World War to create the Department of Homeland Security. At one level, the timing of this development is not particularly surprising.

After all, the attacks of 9/11 were presented as, treated as, and considered by many to be paradigm altering when it came to the question of national security.

For the first time since Pearl Harbor, foreigners attacked U.S. territory, and this time around, the attack was not even carried out by a conventional military force. The new threat and the world it portended, according to the prevailing bipartisan consensus and the mainstream narrative that has gained momentum since, required a reorientation of American security strategy, and hence a new language and new institutions. This chapter aims to undermine those claims.

I argue that the 9/11 attacks presented the American ruling class with an opportunity to reassert its power in a new century, following a decade of seemingly unfocused military adventures in the aftermath of the collapse of the Soviet Union. This reassertion, however, was not intended to be limited only to the global arena, in which the much-heralded "unipolar moment" hadn't quite unfolded in the manner anticipated by American policymakers. The "dividends of peace" that were supposed to accrue after the "end of history" had taken the form of escalating social inequality and recurring economic crises, threatening to bring to the political center stage an increasingly discontented and potentially militant working class. It is in this context that the language and the developing apparatus of "homeland security" has proved to be a critically useful—and, in fact, essential—tool for the ruling elites.

A Nation by Any Other Name . . .

On September 20, 2001, George W. Bush addressed a joint session of Congress in what was presented as the defining moment of his presidency. In the aftermath of the most devastating attack in U.S. history, the American president was about to provide his attentive worldwide audience with not just an explanation of what happened, but also the blueprint for the path ahead. While the sweeping claims about Islam, the terrorists who hate "us" and "our" values, the creation of a new federal agency, as well as the ominous proclamation of the beginnings of an endless war, drew much deserved attention, one small detail was almost overlooked. In proclaiming that "dozens of federal departments and agencies . . . have responsibilities affecting *homeland* security," and that their "coordination at the highest level" required the creation of the "Office of *Homeland* Security," Bush was slipping into the political lexicon a term that had been seemingly consciously avoided by every prior president.

Given that rhetoric about American exceptionalism is par for the course for politicians, and that the twentieth century in particular witnessed a series of presidential wartime speeches aimed at bolstering public morale and support, why was the language of "homeland" not cultivated as part of American political discourse for much of this period, and how do we account for its sudden appearance? To answer these questions, it is worth scrutinizing the reaction to the historical parallel usually touted by advocates of homeland security—the attack on Pearl Harbor.

Much like the narrative surrounding 9/11, the Roosevelt administration presented the Japanese attack on Pearl Harbor as an unprovoked and unexpected act of aggression by hostile forces against a peaceful people. This attack also led to a declaration of war and the United States officially joining a global conflict that FDR declared would be fought to the victorious end. Over the course of the next four years, as much of the world became a bloody battlefield, FDR and his successor, Harry Truman, had plenty of opportunities to lay out the rationale for war and why the nation was sending young Americans to die in European and Asian battlefields. And each time, they did not hold back from explaining that the sacrifices being demanded and made were to safeguard not just foreign territories and peoples but the United States itself. While the language of "American values," the "American people," and even the "home front" was very much part of this rhetoric, the one term that was conspicuously absent was "homeland." The reason for that is not so much that the term was unknown, but rather that American policymakers were conscious of where and by whom this language was actually being deployed.

Across the Atlantic, the Nazis were certainly not hesitant in their usage of the term. In the Third Reich, the notion of *heimat* (homeland) was one to be celebrated, a central axis around which its policies of racial purity revolved. From the 1920s onward, the homeland defense forces in Austria and Germany were in fact known as Heimwehr or Heimatschutz. Tasked with securing the *vaterland* (fatherland), these troops became the face of the Nazis' brutal response to groups ranging from communists and homosexuals to the Roma and Jews—all of whom were regarded as an existential threat to the German homeland. Given that the Nazis were the principal enemy the Allies were supposed to be fighting, it is not surprising that speechwriters for American presidents stayed as far away as possible from this language. Even in Germany itself, the decades following the end of Second World War saw an active avoidance of the terms, given their hypernationalistic and xenophobic connotations. But that began to change by the turn of the century.

15

In post–Cold War reunified Germany, there was a gradual attempt to reintroduce those terms into political discourse by shrugging off the connections to the Nazi past, while highlighting the presumably desirable trait of patriotism. "Heimat," a U.S. government representative claimed, "was misused by the Nazis," for all it means is to declare one's pride in one's roots, "the region where you grew up, your identity, where you belong," to declare that one is proud to be a "native of Germany."[1] The defensive yet self-conscious use of the term by the German political mainstream presented a distinct contrast to its American counterpart.

When questioned about the origins of his agency about a year after its establishment, Tom Ridge, the head of the Office of Homeland Security at the time, declared, "Etymology unknown, don't have a clue." Ridge's no doubt genuine and honest cluelessness was in response to reporters' questions about the fact that the term "homeland security" was being used primarily by bureaucrats, had failed to make its way into common usage, and in fact had provoked complaints about it sounding "un-American." Acknowledging that he had "heard that comment," Ridge merely reiterated one of his favorite soundbites: "We keep saying when the hometown is secure, the homeland is secure." Despite the non sequitur, Ridge would not have had to look too hard to find out how and when the term made its entry into U.S. policymaking documents. It was in 1997 that the Quadrennial Defense Review mandated by Congress included a recommendation to shore up "homeland defense." Its authors acknowledged being aware of the "Germanic implications" and "unfortunate baggage" associated with the term, but they still inserted it, insisting on descriptive prowess. Shortly after, in 1999, the Pentagon contemplated the establishment of the office of a "homeland defense command" but stepped back after criticism by civil rights groups that feared a growing military influence.[2] The events of 9/11, however, provided a different scenario for policymakers to reintroduce the term into circulation.

The *New York Times*, which reported on Ridge's interview along with musings about the "jumble of reasons . . . some rational, others rooted in the mists of confused history and memory" that might cause discomfort, suggested that it might merely be a matter of rebranding. If the American public "was yet to embrace" the term, maybe what was needed was a different term. After all, it wasn't too long ago that Donald Rumsfeld had changed the name of the Afghanistan war operations from "Infinite Justice" to "Enduring Freedom."[3] Thankfully, and in no small measure due to the valiant efforts of the establishment media including the *New York Times* in drumming up support for the limitless "war on terror," there was no need to expend any creative energy on new nomenclature. The Office of Homeland Security transitioned into the Department of Homeland Security; new academic programs with the same name proliferated in academic institutions across the country; Hollywood and television screenwriters deftly incorporated the terminology into their scripts; the media blithely repeated the bureaucratic language even as it purported to critically report the ongoing war; and within a short span of time, the "mists of confused history . . . and memory" seemed to evaporate, giving way to an acceptance, at least of the term, if not about the policies and institutions associated with it.

Notwithstanding its apparently seamless integration into American political discourse today, it is worth asking, what could account for the initial widespread feeling of discomfort, the notion that there was something "un-American" about homeland security? The answer lies in the whole host of unstated assumptions that are smuggled in along with the term. Even setting aside the Nazi connotations, the idea of a "homeland" has been used historically to highlight one's native status, a connection to an ethnic group that is essentially homogeneous, and a particular territory that is claimed to be the historical patrimony of said group.[4] Initially gaining popularity during the heyday of nationalism in the late nineteenth century, the notion of *patria*—of a sense of belonging rooted in a fixed territory, and by extension ethnicity—acquired a new lease in the aftermath of the Cold War, particularly with the wave of what Benedict Anderson designated as "long-distance nationalism."[5] Whether it was already established nation-states or aspiring secessionist movements, ruling elites across the board deployed the language of "homeland" in order to seek material and moral support from those identified as an essential part of the national community, even while living abroad. The term, it should be clear by now, is tied not just to a supposedly well-defined territory but also a shared mythic past. Thus, it can paradoxically accommodate demands for both fidelity toward an established nation-state and mobilization in support of a nationalist movement seeking a state. In other words, "homeland" can act as a rallying cry for the defense of the Nazi Third Reich, the Zionist movement demanding a state, the Palestinian movement seeking a return, as well as Kosovars and Tamils involved in secessionist struggles. Exported wholesale to the American context, this presents a new set of conundrums.

Historically, American nationalism, while very much tied to a notion of exceptionalism, has not rested on explicit appeals to a shared mythic past tied to specific territory. To the contrary, the language of nationalism in the United States has tended to speak to a whole different imaginary, whether the idea of a melting pot, of manifest destiny, of new frontiers, or a classless society of immigrants. Relying as they do on metaphors of spatial mobility, these notions provided the space for a broader and potentially more inclusive vision of belonging. The notion of "homeland," however, is set up to perform exactly the opposite function. For immigrants living in the United States, what counts—or should count—as a homeland? Should the fact of residence in a particular country provide the obvious answer, or should the term always refer to the land of origin? Furthermore, does the answer differ depending on whether the immigrant is first, second, or third generation and beyond? Traditional scholarship on immigration and the diaspora literature has tended to make a distinction between the "host" and "home" countries, but as a way to highlight both the mobility of populations and the limitations of the territorial nation-state form. In the context of the institution of "homeland security," however, this distinction cannot be purely technical.

If an immigrant is a person for whom—regardless of citizenship status or place of birth—the United States can never count as a "homeland," what does that imply regarding their position vis-à-vis its security? Is their essential foreignness an unchangeable fact that makes immigrants a natural threat to homeland security, or are there specific conditions under which they can be drafted to bolster its defenses? Regardless of actual immigration policies in place, spokespersons for various administrations over the past two decades have tended to reiterate their allegiance to the idea of the United States as melting pot, a land that has historically been home to multiple nationalities. In that sense, immigrants need not necessarily pose an existential threat to national security. However, given the presumption of divided loyalties, an immigrant's position will always be one characterized by a radical uncertainty, susceptible to exploitation at any given point in time.

Moreover, it is not just immigrants who bear the burden of this uncertainty. Essential to the process of securing the homeland is the defining of who or what constitutes this space. In the American case, the evocation of a "homeland" has to go beyond gestures toward a shared mythic past, native roots in a territory, or even common ethnicity. It is in this context that the notion of "American values" come to play a critical role. Defending the American homeland becomes not merely a matter of stationing the appropriate police forces at the borders (though that is an essential component), but rather protecting certain values, the "American way of life," of "liberty and the pursuit of happiness" understood as a very specific project, from all that is foreign. Within this framework, security threats to the homeland take the form not just of those armed with guns and bombs but also political ideas that might challenge the ruling class's notion of what constitutes the "American way."

Aimed at omnipresent threats defined, redefined, and still to be defined, the state apparatus that has sprung up under the broad purview of "homeland security" is perennially incomplete and in need of resources and refinements. It promotes the idea of a nation under threat from a constantly evolving cast of enemies, bolstering the smoke and mirrors that surround the true nature of the wars being waged at home and abroad. Far from being a weakness as claimed by some policymakers, this haziness is what makes the concept of homeland security such a potent weapon in the hands of the ruling class. This becomes apparent if one takes a quick look at the ways in which the mission of securing the American "homeland" has been articulated and rearticulated in strategic documents over the past two decades.

Strategies and Missions

The Homeland Security Act (2002) heralded the most sweeping reorganization of federal agencies since the creation of the Central Intelligence Agency and the National Security Agency as a result of the National Security Act of 1947. The newly created cabinet-level agency, the Department of Homeland Security (DHS), subsumed within itself twenty-two existing agencies, including Immigration and Naturalization Services, U.S. Customs Services, Federal Emergency Management Agency, U.S. Border Patrol, and the Transportation and Security Agency. While many of these agencies would undergo some structural changes, the most critical one was carried out almost immediately. As the DHS took over the two immigration-related agencies, it reorganized them into two new separate agencies meant to focus specially on enforcement and services, respectively: Immigration and Customs Enforcement (ICE) and Citizenship and Immigration Services (CIS). Three other agencies were consolidated into the U.S. Customs and Border Protection (CBP), while the investigative branches of the old immigration services were merged to form Homeland Security Investigations.

The massive reorganization of federal agencies, as well as the question of budget allocations, meant that there was a need, at least at the level of policy documentation, to lay out the strategic priorities of the new department and to define what "homeland security" meant. However, as a survey of the seven major DHS-related strategic documents in its first decade of existence makes clear, there is no consistency even in how the various U.S. administrations have formulated the main tasks of this agency.[6] For instance, while the terrorism angle is repeated almost by rote, natural disasters show up as a potential threat to homeland security in only five of the seven; maritime security, borders, and immigration are highlighted as priority areas in only three, a curious fact considering more recent developments. Other documents seem to aim for a bigger-picture definition. The Quadrennial Homeland Security Review (2010), for instance, defines "homeland security" as "a concerted national effort to ensure a homeland that is safe, secure, and resilient against terrorism and *other hazards*, where *American interests, aspirations, and ways of life can thrive*," while the DHS Strategic Plan (2012) opts for a more succinct version, incorporating in its definition all "Efforts to ensure a homeland that is safe, secure, and resilient against terrorism and *other hazards*" (italics mine).

To highlight this openness (for the want of a better term) is not merely to quibble over technicalities surrounding the definition of strategies and missions. Supporters of the DHS and all that it entails have acknowledged the vagueness, with some critics even suggesting a need for more precision. However, others have tended to double-down on the imprecision, arguing that given the "constantly evolving and interdependent" nature of the "threats to [U.S.] national security and strategic interests," it only makes sense that "the efforts to ensure the security of our Homeland reflect these same characteristics."[7] This latter claim has the virtue of honesty, though perhaps not in the intended sense.

Vagueness in definition is in fact critical to the mission of "homeland security," since it facilitates the creation of an expansive and constantly expanding network of state institutions and apparatuses that are designed to surveil the population, stifle any hint of opposition, and generally function as a bulwark of the status quo. This expansion, in turn, serves to justify demands for the allotment of a significant proportion of the national budget to concerns that are broadly framed as being within the purview of the DHS.

According to official reports, the president's fiscal year (FY) 2020 budget included a request to allot $51.7 billion to the DHS. This number, however, is misleading, because it does not include an additional $19.4 billion requested for FEMA, an agency that is part of the DHS. Taking into account various other fees and funding requests, the gross budgetary authority requested for the DHS is actually closer to the $92 billion mark, an increase of 24 percent from the budget that was approved for FY 2019. This increase, former DHS secretary Kirstjen Nielsen argued, was absolutely essential given that the department needed to adapt in order to deal with a plethora of new actors—"a spider web of terrorist groups, emboldened transnational criminals, resurgent and hostile nation-states, *and more*" who all aimed "to disrupt our way of life."[8]

These developments underscore the reality of a powerful, well-funded and still-growing state apparatus that seamlessly crosses the civil-military divide, one with the power to target whomever it pleases under the guise of protecting the homeland. This power, moreover, is not merely "potential" in the sense that it will take a few years before the DHS is harnessed against the "new actors" threatening "our way of life." Such reorientation has already been set into motion, and in the final section of the chapter, we look briefly at two "threats" to "homeland security"—one already identified as a clear and present danger, and the other just beginning to be evoked.

A Threat Is a Threat, Is a Threat . . .

The nineteen hijackers who carried out the attacks of 9/11 were all foreign nationals who had made their way into the United States. It was therefore not surprising that the notion of "terrorism" was almost immediately conflated with "immigrants," particularly from certain parts of the world, who were adherents of a particular faith. The racial and ethnic profiling that followed, which saw the singling out of Muslim men and women by those tasked with securing the homeland, has been well documented by critical scholarship. What has also been exposed is the plethora of policies smuggled in, first through the PATRIOT Act and then through various Homeland Security initiatives, that were aimed at depriving immigrants and noncitizens of basic human rights. These included broad preventive detention authority, closed immigration hearings, wiretaps and searches, deportations, and the creation of military tribunals to try noncitizens on charges of terrorism.[9] The very visible onslaught on immigrant rights provoked a furious response from organizations concerned with civil liberties, but their protests were drowned under the drumbeats of patriotic rhetoric issuing from the Bush administration and its supporters. The genuine shock and outpouring of sympathy for the victims following the 9/11 attack was channeled by the administration into the crafting of a very peculiar notion of what counted as "American" and "un-American." Even as it pushed through policies that included calling over five thousand immigrants from countries suspected of harboring large number of terrorists for voluntary interviews, the Bush administration simply reiterated its claim of taking necessary steps to secure the homeland. Anyone who questioned these policies was not only unpatriotic but was also, as Attorney General John Ashcroft suggested in a Senate hearing, actively "aiding and abetting terrorism."[10]

From the very beginning of the "homeland security" project, therefore, the conflation of "terrorism" with "immigration" meant that immigrants were perceived as and treated as a threat to American "interests," "way of life," "aspirations," "values," or whatever phrase was in vogue. It set the stage for a series of extralegal and extraconstitutional measures including detention of asylum seekers and the use of immigration law to hold foreign nationals when there wasn't evidence to detain them on the original planned criminal charges. In the early stages, these measures seemed to be limited to a certain religion (Islam), certain regions (the Middle East, South Asia), and even a certain gender and age group (men, sixteen to forty-five years), all of which were portrayed as a pragmatic response to the demands of the ongoing "war on terror." That situation, however, has changed quite dramatically in the past few years.

Donald Trump's shock victory in the 2016 elections brought to the White House a man who had never held any kind of public office, had created a larger-than-life persona as a skilled entrepreneur despite numerous bankruptcies, was best known for a television show and a tag line, and promised to "Make America Great Again." While resting on the acknowledgment of what was a reality for much of the America population—that their lives had become significantly and noticeably worse particularly after 2008—Trump's promise was built on sweeping, xenophobic claims about the cause of the crisis. The root of the problem, as he repeated in rally after rally, was that the Washington insiders had lost sight of the real interests of real Americans and how to protect them. These interests—jobs, safety, and security of American families—were under threat from outsiders, the immigrants who were swarming across the borders of the United States (see Berry, this volume).

In his very first address to Congress, Trump declared that his administration was determined to ensure the success of all Americans, but that this "could not occur in an environment of lawless chaos." Citing the series of attacks within the United States and around the world since 9/11, Trump claimed that there was clear evidence to show that terrorist attacks were generally carried out by immigrants and that it was "not compassionate, but reckless" to allow people to come in from places where proper vetting was not possible. To do so would lead "our nation to become a sanctuary for extremists."[11] His administration, Trump promised, would not "allow a beachhead of terrorism to form inside America." And for that reason, one of his goals would be follow-through on his campaign promise to deal with the immigration "problem."

The irony of the "rule of law" being cited by a man whose tenure has been marked by utter contempt toward the American constitution, as well as established international legal norms, cannot be lost on the reader. Space constraints preclude me from engaging in detail with the numerous measures that were put into practice by the Trump administration. Suffice it to say, these policies—zero tolerance, family separations, unlawful detentions, mass raids carried out by ICE, systematic abuse of immigrant children, ban on asylum seekers coming in through the southern border, persecution of humanitarian agencies seeking to aid immigrants making the border crossing, to name but a few—have been characterized by a callous disregard for basic human rights.

Since all these policy changes have taken place under the rubric of homeland security, it is not surprising to find a distinct shift in the priorities and mission statements of the DHS. In her response to the administration's FY 2020 budget, the then DHS secretary Nielsen was clear that "Border security *is* national security." In addition to the $92 billion being requested, there have been moves to get congressional support for a proposal to create a new "Border Security and Immigration Enforcement Fund" to provide resources beyond discretionary funding. In the meantime, in 2019 alone, the DHS moved the funds between its agencies under its purview to provide ICE and Border Patrol an additional $227 million for their operations.[12] What these developments make clear is that by now the "war on terror" has now quite literally morphed into the "war on immigrants." The process of zeroing in on what threatens the homeland, however, is far from having run its course.

While the question of what other threats can be configured in the coming year remains an open one, there are some hints as to what the future might hold. And strangely enough, it looks very much like the past. In February 2019, in a speech given to groups of Cuban and Venezuelan exiles, Trump laid out the main danger in the path ahead: "Socialism, by its very nature, does not respect borders. . . . It's always seeking to expand, to encroach, and to subjugate others to its will." Nonetheless, he promised his audience that "the twilight hour of socialism has arrived in our hemisphere."[13] A month later, in a speech to the Conservative Political Action Conference that began with the president hugging an American flag, he declared, "We believe in the American dream, not the Socialist nightmare. . . . I've said it before and I'll say it again, America will never be a socialist country."[14] A few months later, while addressing the UN General Assembly as part of a distinguished lineup that included Jair Bolsanaro and Abdul Fatah Al-Sisi, Trump reiterated the claim about the U.S. never "becoming Socialist," adding that "socialism and communism are not about justice, they are not about equality, they are not about lifting up the poor, and they are certainly not about the good of the nation. . . . They are about one thing only: power for the ruling class."[15] Setting aside Trump's confusion about not just socialism but also his own class position, it is worth noting that this speech followed a familiar pattern. It moved from insisting on the primacy of nationalism and safeguarding American interests to specifying "foreign" threats that include not just other states (China, Iran) but also a particular group of people ("illegal immigrants" used interchangeably with "criminals," "drug traffickers," etc.) and finally, a specific political ideology.

It has been nearly three decades since the end of the Cold War and the declaration of American victory, the "end of history." What then, one wonders, would prompt an American president and his coterie of advisers to start ratcheting up anticommunist sentiment with the kind of rhetoric that would have made Joseph McCarthy proud? The answer lies in two interrelated recent developments: a growing revulsion for the violent, right-wing populism being openly fanned by the administration (see Kapoor, this volume) and a developing interest in the idea of socialism, particularly among the younger generation. In a preemptive move, while piously disavowing the spate of violent right-wing attacks around the world, Trump and his coterie attempted to establish a moral equivalence between all forms of "extreme ideologies." This would enable the existing state apparatus to turn its attention to groups that might be espousing said ideologies, particularly the dangerous, foreign ones, as a legitimate move to secure the homeland. Such a move is already underway.

On September 20, 2019, the DHS released a new strategic document entitled "Framework for Countering Terrorism and Targeted Violence." Putatively aimed at extreme right-wing groups, the document claims that "anti-authority and anti-government violence" can easily swing from one end of the spectrum to the other. In his introduction, acting DHS secretary Kevin McAleenan insisted that while the old threat "posed by foreign terrorist organizations like the Islamic State and al-Qaeda [still] persists," there was a new and potentially even more dangerous one on the horizon. This was "the growing threat from enemies, both foreign and domestic, who seek to incite violence in our Nation's youth, disenfranchised, and disaffected, in order to attack their fellow citizens and fray at the seams of our diverse social fabric."

The "homeland," it appears, now has to be defended from its own "disen-franchised and disaffected" youth.

It is perhaps a self-evident truth that xenophobia, once let out of the bot-tle, is hard to contain. However, the problem that we face is an even bigger one. Under the rubric of "homeland security," xenophobia is carefully nur-tured and harnessed in a calculated manner in support of specific political projects. These projects—historically and in contemporary settings—have always tended to take the form of movements that appeal to the lowest com-mon denominator, a supposedly instinctive patriotism that is suspicious of and antithetical to all that is foreign. Latching onto real issues—whether it is the lack of jobs, systematic undermining of healthcare, education, bene-fits, and so on, or the sense of disempowerment felt by a majority even in supposed democracies—these movements, from the perspective of the ruling class, can act as very useful channels to distract any deeper questioning of the real roots of such problems. The danger, however, is that such elements, once brought to the political center stage, will not politely return to the background. The last time the language of "homeland" played a vital role in justifying a regime's raison d'être, the world was dragged into a catastrophic war that ended with the deployment of nuclear weapons. Compared to the arsenal that the United States has today, those weapons appear to be almost quaint. As reports of a vast network of detention camps and photographs of concrete walls (see Sen, this volume) become increasingly commonplace, and as fascistic rants about the homeland under siege become part of the daily news cycle, we would do well to remember some of the lessons from the twentieth century.

Mushroom Cloud

As the creator of the nuclear bomb, the United States has a special connection to the visual outcome of its detonation—the mushroom cloud. At once, a nuclear detonation invokes awe for its immensity, scientific ingenuity for its groundbreaking achievement, and life for having saved countless soldiers in the Pacific Theater of World War II when the United States dropped atomic bombs on Hiroshima and Nagasaki, thereby precipitating the end of the war and forestalling further American casualties.[1] To be sure, it also speaks to a dread for its capacity to end all life on the planet via a nuclear holocaust.[2] That dread is best captured in the words of one British sailor who saw a nuclear test: "To say it was frightening is an understatement. I think it shocked us all into silence. When the flash hit you, you could see the x-rays of your hands through your closed eyes. . . . Then the heat hit you. That was just as if somebody my size had actually caught fire and then walked through me. It was an experience that was absolutely unearthly. It was so strange. There was no comprehension that anything like that could even exist. It was immense." Other witnesses observed, "All I saw was this rising fireball. A colossal fireball just going up, and thunder, lightning, you name it . . . it's a sight to see, but I never want to see it again."[3]

Despite the range of reaction that it invokes, and the fact that many countries now possess nuclear arsenals, the mushroom cloud is uniquely part of America's visual heritage from 1945 to the present day. Nowhere is this more apparent than in a video that chronicles the "Top 10 Nuclear Bomb Scenes in Movies," which has amassed fourteen million online views.[4] In the list, *The Sum of All Fears* (2002) is the only movie that underscores America's post-9/11 anxieties of nuclear terrorism.[5] The film contrasts with its antecedent, *The Peacemaker* (1997), to demonstrate visually America's angst about nuclear terrorism after September 11, 2001.

This chapter unpacks *The Peacemaker* and *The Sum of All Fears* as artifacts that attest to those anxieties and then proceeds to underscore how 9/11 affirmed and intensified those fears. Only then can we understand the insecurity that Americans felt and how the U.S. government augmented and harnessed those vulnerabilities to push the population to support its rush to war. That is, the mushroom cloud, the corollary to the nuclear bomb, was a powerful discursive and imaginative symbol of terror that the government utilized with great success to launch a war of choice in Iraq that was otherwise devoid of any real justification. The clouds of dust at the World Trade Center (WTC) were the real cloud, while the Bush administration conjured a fake one from imagery rooted in the collective psyche of the American people to serve a political objective that predated 9/11.

The Peacemaker (1997)

Cinematic films not only visualize on screen the imagination of their screenwriters or the authors of books on which they are based, but also reflect the society's values and cultural norms that inform that writer's outlook. They are the products of their time and place, providing a window into that milieu's politics, aspirations, sexual mores, racial norms, and anxieties. For instance, when tensions between U.S. president Ronald Reagan and Libyan president Muammar Qaddafi rose in the mid-1980s, real-world fears about Libyans seeped into Hollywood films. This was evident in the 1985 film *Back to the Future*. In it, Emmet "Doc" Brown built a time machine that needed plutonium to power its "flux capacitor" in order to travel through time. To obtain the rare material, he agreed to work not with Russians, the typical Cold War silver screen villain, but with Libyan terrorists to build a nuclear bomb. Instead of enabling America's enemies, however, he stole the plutonium for his time machine. The fact that Libyans appeared in the film as adversaries in this iconic 1985 film and not before speaks to America's acrimonious international relations with Libya at that very moment. That is, movies create, alter, depict, and reaffirm a society's wider value-laden lexicon, ensuring that certain words and phrases conjure distinct images. In the 1980s, *Back to the Future* helped render "terrorist" synonymous with "Libyans" much the same way a catalog of American films throughout the Cold War rendered "foe," "adversary," and "totalitarianism" synonymous with "Russia" and "the Soviet Union."

In the same way, *The Peacemaker* serves as the quintessential action adventure film of the post–Cold War 1990s that provides a visual testament to America's anxieties as they relate to terrorism, nuclear proliferation, and the intersection of the two, that is, a nuclear terrorist attack on the United States. Three real-world terrorist bombings brought these urgencies to the forefront of American consciousness: the first World Trade Center bombing in 1993, the Oklahoma City bombing in 1995, and the Khobar Towers bombing in 1996. Of the three, the first two transpired on American soil and the last one on a housing structure for American Air Force personnel in Saudi Arabia. The first and third happened at the hands of Muslims, whereas non-Muslim Americans were responsible for the bombing of the Federal Building in Oklahoma City.

The Peacemaker visualized those American concerns about terrorism. In the era of nuclear proliferation, that fear also intertwined with nuclear weaponry. Consequently, the 1997 film focuses on the Russian and American nuclear arms reduction borne of the Strategic Arms Reduction Treaty (START I) that went into effect in 1994. A rogue Russian general, however, intercepts and steals ten nuclear bombs on their way to being decommissioned. In order to mask the robbery as terrorism, one is detonated at the site of the heist in the Ural Mountains. The general planned to sell the bombs on the black market for a reported sum of $200 million each. Assisted by a band of Serbian nationalists angry with the West over the Balkan Wars, the general siphons off one bomb to his allies, who are determined to detonate a plutonium-packed primary as a "backpack nuke" in New York during a meeting of the United Nations General Assembly to finalize Yugoslavia's disintegration.

The film follows haughty U.S. Army Special Forces lieutenant colonel Thomas Devoe (George Clooney) and a nuclear security expert, Dr. Julia Kelly (Nicole Kidman), as they first try to retrieve the bombs and then, when they learn of the Serbian plot, try to stop the attack. The movie ends with the suicide of the terrorist and Kelly and Devoe's last-second destruction of the bomb, thereby preventing the nuclear detonation.

More to the point, the film shows a nuclear explosion not in the United States, but in Russia's Ural Mountains. The scene of the blast was over in a manner of seconds with a flash of light and a blast wave that quickly scorched the earth and an elderly couple in the countryside—without any visual of a mushroom cloud. The film's final explosion transpired in a New York church that remained standing since the detonation was nonnuclear. Furthermore, there was no connection to Islamic terrorism other than the fact that the Russian general who was intercepted transported the eight bombs en route to Iran, and a Pakistani astrophysicist, "Amir Taraki," modified the tenth bomb into a "backpack nuke."

Admittedly, America's anxieties over Islamic terrorism and an Islamist nuclear explosion on U.S. soil were in their infancy at that point.[6] Nonetheless, the film includes transient moments that touched on those emerging anxieties. For example, Devoe is introduced to audiences when he is explaining his overseas expenditures: "Dimitri and I went into this bar to try and buy some nerve gas off this ex K.G.B. guy that we had heard was selling black market surplus munitions to Iraq . . . Colonel Vertikoff identified the K.G.B. guy, and we were able to stop the nerve gas from getting to Iraq."[7] Iraq was mentioned only in the context of preventing it from acquiring chemical weapons. This line coincides with the United States enforcing a real-world UN-mandated sanctions regime that largely dismantled Iraq's post–Gulf War chemical weapons stockpiles and prevented Iraq from acquiring dual-use technologies for re-creating such "weapons of mass destruction."

As a corollary, there is an assumption touched upon by the references to Iran, Iraq, and Pakistan that underscores a sentiment in the United States that Muslims are unable to appreciate properly the strategic consequences of having a nuclear arsenal. According to the narrative accompanying the doctrine of deterrence, the United States and the USSR during the Cold War were nuclear-armed states that preserved a nuclear peace because both were rational actors. The use of one nuclear weapon by one belligerent would necessarily provoke a nuclear counterattack that would result in mutual as-sured destruction (MAD). By contrast, Muslims are presented as irrational actors unable to make similar calculations. Iranians are especially projected as trapped in a "martyrdom complex" rooted in Shi'ite Islam and keen on deploying nuclear weapons even if it results in the devastation of their en-tire population.[8] Thus, as Iranians are infantile in their inability to calcu-late like other states, they cannot be trusted with nuclear technology, let alone nuclear weapons. Such discourse has its antecedents in the Cold War when Prime Minister Mohammad Mossadeq nationalized Iran's oil industry, thereby garnering the reaction of the Western press that painted him as a "dizzy old wizard" with a "fanatical state of mind" and the "weeping, faint-ing leader of a helpless country."[9] In sum, as the U.S.-backed coup toppling Mossadeq's government in 1953 revealed, Iran's natural resources, vital to the reconstruction and rearmament of Western Europe as it faced down Soviet encroachment, were too important to be trusted to this "appalling caricature of a statesman."[10] If oil was too strategic to be trusted to the Iranians, accord-ing to the prevailing logic, then nuclear technology is likewise too dangerous for these "mad and suicidal . . . lemmings."[11]

In that vein, *The Peacemaker* was about America's real-time fears of nu-clear terrorism and its self-affirming quest to safeguard the homeland (see Varadarajan, this volume) and protect the life of its citizens, or in the words of the film's director, Mimi Leder: "we are a vulnerable world and we need to protect ourselves. This is the message I hope gets across with the film."[12] An early conversation between Kidman and Clooney's characters reflects Leder's words. In explaining to Dr. Kelly, a nuclear security expert without any military experience, Devoe pontificates: "In the field, this is how it works. The good guys, that's us, we chase the bad guys, and they don't wear black hats. They are, however, all alike. They demand power and respect, and they're willing to pay top dollar to get it. And that is our highly motivated buyer."[13] In saying so, he speaks to America's self-image as a country that wields power as a means, not an end, to defend the values of "good"—presumably order, justice, life, and, above all, liberty—by fighting the lawless men who seek power as an end goal. Dr. Kelly's response attests to America's other concern over those who do not seek power but aspire to suicidal mass murder as the end goal: "There are people out there who don't care about money and don't give a damn about respect, people who believe the killing of innocent men and women is justified. For them it is about rage, frustration, hatred. They feel pain, and they're determined to share it with the world."[14] In a quote that links to the contrasting movie, she underscores her point with an effective tagline: "I'm not afraid of the man who wants ten nuclear weapons, Colonel. I'm terrified of the man who only wants one."[15]

The Sum of All Fears (2002)

Four years after the release of *The Peacemaker*, America's cinematic anxieties about inhabiting "a vulnerable world" seemed to manifest in the real world. The two planes that hit the WTC on the morning of September 11, 2001, were caught on film in real time, as was the subsequent dramatic collapse of both towers. Networks broadcast footage of the impact and collapse of the towers on a loop in the United States and around the world for days. Outrage, shock, and, most palpable of all, trauma were globally shared emotions.

Unlike the terrorism of the 1993 WTC bombing or the 1995 Oklahoma City bombing, 9/11 was interpreted as constituting acts of war akin to Imperial Japan's attack on Pearl Harbor in 1941. There were many points, however, that made the 2001 attacks unique. It was not orchestrated by the conventional military of a nation-state, but a transnational radical Islamist network. It was also the first act of war in the modern period that transpired on the continental United States since 1916 (the attack on Pearl Harbor occurred in Hawaii). No longer confined to Europe or the Hawaiian archipelago, the Korean Peninsula, Vietnam, the Middle East, or other peripheries of empire, the war came home in an unprecedented way. Despite the country's vast military superiority, 9/11 showed that America's nuclear arsenal, fleet of aircraft carriers, military bases around the world, bloated budget, and radar systems were ineffective when it came to nineteen extremists' commitment to attacking America's political, military, and economic symbols of global power. As such, the trauma of 9/11 also translated into a general sense of vulnerability among Americans. A slew of films and television shows released in the post-9/11 United States exemplified that real-world feeling of vulnerability as well as offering potential direction about how best to retrieve that lost security.

Like 1997's *The Peacemaker*, 2002's *The Sum of All Fears* visualized America's anxiety over nuclear terrorism. This time, however, the post-9/11 climate changed how this anxiety was imagined. The movie stars Ben Affleck as CIA analyst Jack Ryan, an expert on Russia, and Morgan Freeman, who plays CIA director William Cabot. The story begins in the Golan Heights when a Syrian finds the wreckage of an Israeli plane shot down during the 1973 Yom Kippur War. The plane was carrying a nuclear warhead unbeknownst to the Syrian, who sold it for a paltry sum to an arms trafficker. The buyer then sold it to a secretive neo-Nazi group determined to right Adolf Hitler's catastrophic and strategic wrong of fighting the United States and the USSR simultaneously. Instead, the group sought to instigate a nuclear war between America and the successor to the USSR, Russia, ensuring their mutual destruction. Integral to their plan was detonating the purchased nuclear bomb on American soil and leaving a trail of blame that led to Russia. The rest of the film follows Ryan's quest to uncover the plot and the true culprits.

Interestingly, a discussion between Morgan Freeman's character and the American president echoes in very similar language the anxieties over nuclear terrorism expressed in *The Peacemaker*. When debating America's true enemy, the president alludes to Russia by asking a rhetorical question: "Who else has 27,000 nukes for us to worry?" to which Freeman's character responds using Dr. Kelly's slightly modified line from the preceding film: "It's the guy with one I'm worried about."[16] In other words, both films underscore the real-life American fear about zealots or groups committed to detonating a nuclear bomb inside the United States.

In *The Sum of All Fears*, the antagonists succeeded where they failed in *The Peacemaker*, successfully exploding a nuclear bomb in Baltimore near the nation's capital. Unlike the nuclear explosion in *The Peacemaker*, which was in Russia's Ural Mountains and not shown thoroughly, the detonation in the latter film was complete with a white light, destructive shockwave that dramatically tore through a hospital, flipped the car carrying the president, brought down the helicopter on which the film's protagonist was riding, and, most importantly, included a prolonged shot of a terrifying mushroom cloud on American soil. The real-world fear of nuclear terrorism striking the United States was now depicted on the big screen for American audiences and constituted an integral part of a tapestry of "countless popular culture images about dread and suffering."[17] Whereas before 9/11, the American protagonists were able to ward off the terror plot, after 9/11, Americans' sense of vulnerability was affirmed in Ryan's inability to prevent the calamity. The terrorist attack using a nuclear weapon indeed amounted to "the sum of all fears."

That *The Sum of All Fears* fared much better in the domestic box office over *The Peacemaker*, which was a better edited, scripted, paced, and acted film, demonstrates how much the former resonated with audiences in the context of the post-9/11 climate. *The Sum of All Fears* grossed roughly $119 million and was the twenty-second-highest-grossing film of 2002, whereas *The Peacemaker* grossed just over $41 million and was the fifty-fifth highest grossing film of 1997.[18]

In addition to the two films' plots, the movies also demonstrate the solution to these security threats: the U.S. government—the quintessential rational actor. As in *The Peacemaker*, Ryan prevented the neo-Nazi plan of pitting the United States and Russian against in each other by uncovering the true perpetrators of the attack and diffusing tensions between the nuclear powers. Ryan and his counterparts Lieutenant Colonel Devoe and Dr. Kelly are all government personnel deploying America's awesome might—always in a measured way—in the service of good, protecting innocent American lives. In sum, both films celebrate and, according to Matthew Alford, "make light of the enormous covert powers of a globally operating U.S. national security state and its allies—endorsing its methods, dismissing its victims."[19]

These characters embody the American government, thereby fostering trust in audiences by demonstrating that the state is the ultimate guarantor of American security. It should not come as a surprise, then, that films affirming a pro-government aesthetic are supported, altered, and occasionally informally censored by the Department of Defense (DOD). According to Tom Secker and Matthew Alford, films that require military hardware are subject to DOD screenplay editing and rewrites.[20] If the producers object, then the DOD withdraws support. Given the nature of some movies, such withdrawal amounts to the film's cancelation.[21] Thus, movies such as "*Top Gun, Transformers* and *Act of Valor* are so dependent on military cooperation that they couldn't have been made without submitting to this process."[22] Other movies like *Countermeasures* were never made for included references to the Iran-Contra Affair—a scandal that the government prefers to erase from public memory.[23] Even films that have little do with the government, such as *Meet the Parents*, were edited. The original scene in which Ben Stiller's character stumbles into a secret room that includes CIA memorabilia was initially scripted to include torture manuals.[24] In sum, Secker and Alford's research shows the U.S. government has "worked behind the scenes on over 800 major movies and more than 1,000 TV titles."[25]

Insecurity and the Case for War in Iraq

The case for war in Iraq was made at a time when Americans were still in a state of shock from the attacks of 9/11—a trauma that was affirmed by the government. On July 16, 2002, less than a year after the attacks, the Bush administration unveiled a color-coded threat level system in which red alerted viewers that the nation faced a "severe risk of terrorist attacks," and green meant "low risk of terrorist attacks." There were three colors in between those points: blue meant "guarded risk," yellow signified a "significant threat," and orange amounted to "high" level of danger. According to one critic, the color system was highly flawed because "they don't tell people what they can do—they just make people afraid."[26] More than anything, the color system and its effects on the population "was a relic of our panic after 9/11."[27] In February 2003, this panic even resulted in a rush to hardware stores to buy duct tape after the U.S. fire administrator described it as part of a list of useful items that "can be helpful after a biological, chemical, or radiological attack."[28] Duct tape, many believed, would be the difference between life and death in case of such an attack when it could be used to seal windows and doors with plastic sheeting. Acquiring these items became a dire necessity in the context of "concerns growing about al-Qaeda's interest in acquiring weapons of mass destruction."[29]

The U.S. government argued, and the mainstream media parroted, that al-Qaeda harbored a suicidal hate of America for its culture and freedoms. Such an explanation was a convenient way to affirm stereotypes of "martyrdom-seeking" Muslims while also side-stepping the legitimate grievances that underscored the attacks, such as the stationing of U.S. troops in the land of Islam's two holiest sites (Mecca and Medina on the Arabian Peninsula), America's support for Israel, the sanctions-induced death of 1.5 million Iraqis throughout the 1990s, U.S. intervention in the region, and military, financial, and diplomatic support for autocrats. Moreover, unlike the Soviet Union, which was rational and subscribed to the doctrine of mutual assured destruction, al-Qaeda could not be reasoned with. However false the perception that al-Qaeda was irrational, 9/11 prompted a heightened fear among Americans about the terror group's ability to carry out further attacks.[30]

Fear and obedience often affirm one another. When overwhelmed with real or imagined fears, such sentiment "encourages political actors . . . to frame messages about fear in order to get the most public attention and gain support that they are looking out for the public's interest and well-being."[31] One critic remembered his Cold War days in a powerfully relevant way: "As a child, I learned to get under my desk at school whenever we heard an air-raid siren. This was to protect us from a nuclear attack from the 'Russians' and the 'communists,' but the real political purpose was to indoctrinate young children as well as our parents that we were threatened by a major enemy and that we had to rely on the U.S. government to protect us."[32] In the post-9/11 climate, the color-coded system and the duct tape likewise affirmed the population's vulnerability while also presenting the government as the one that can restore the lost security. The USA PATRIOT Act (2002) attests to the latter point when the populace consented to the curtailment of its civil liberties on the grounds that it enabled the state to better secure the homeland's breaches. More to the point, the government tapped into these fears to make its case for war with Iraq, which commenced ten months after the release of *The Sum of All Fears* and roughly a month after the panic to buy duct tape.

The Bush administration's case for war rested on several premises: that Iraq evaded United Nations inspectors after they were sent in to confirm that Iraq was not building weapons of mass destruction (WMDs); that Iraq was indeed building chemical, biological, and nuclear WMDs; that the country's government was working intimately with al-Qaeda, the perpetrators of 9/11; and that Iraq would supply al-Qaeda with the WMDs to attack the United States.

All of these premises were proven false months after the war commenced, especially when inspectors did not find any evidence of a WMD program. It is important to note that at the time, many, including Hans Blix, the leader of the UN inspection team, did not find any evidence of an active program, nor did the absence of evidence mean the Iraqis were guilty of concealment.[33] Furthermore, Middle East experts also argued in real time that not only did Saddam Hussein's regime not have ties to al-Qaeda, but his secular government also constituted a repressive bulwark against radical Islamist groups. These assertions, however, fell on proverbial deaf ears as Bush administration officials tapped into the American anxieties in a manner that resonated on a popular level.

Mushroom Cloud as the Smoking Gun

The Iraq War was based on evidence that was either compromised after coming from unreliable Iraqi defectors, selective framing of the data—such as the case with the aluminum tubes—or orchestrated like the Judith Miller and Michael Gordon *New York Times* cover page story from September 8, 2002, titled: "U.S. Says Hussein Intensifies Quest for A-Bomb Parts."[34] Some of the article's "facts" were based on unscrupulous Iraqi defectors in the service of their own pro-war agendas; others were fed by the Bush administration, officials of which then turned around and invoked the *Times* article to legitimize their case for the war (see Barnard, this volume).

The article also introduced an imaginative visual that resonated with readers in a deeply traumatic way: the authors posited that unnamed administration officials feared that "the first sign of a 'smoking gun' might be a mushroom cloud." According to Michael Isikoff and David Corn in *Hubris: The Inside Story of Spin, Scandal, and the Selling of the Iraq War*, this tagline was not "a spontaneous remark; it was the public debut of a carefully constructed piece of rhetoric. The smoking gun/mushroom cloud sound bite had been conceived by chief speechwriter Michael Gerson and discussed at a WHIG [White House Iraq Group] meeting just three days earlier. For the White House, Gerson's vivid metaphor, an administration official later said, perfectly captured the larger point about the need to deal with threats in the post–September 11 world." Indeed, in a well-timed and choreographed remark, National Security Advisor Condoleezza Rice went on CNN that same day to say:

> No one can give you an exact time line as to when he [Hussein] is going to have this or that weapon, but given what we have experienced in history and given what we have experienced on September 11, I don't think anyone wants to wait for the 100 percent surety that he has a weapon of mass destruction that can reach the United States, because the only time we may be 100 percent sure is when something lands on our territory. We can't afford to wait that way . . . The problem here is that there will always be some uncertainty about how quickly he can acquire nuclear weapons. But we don't want the smoking gun to be a mushroom cloud.[35]

The visual of the mushroom cloud and its long genealogy, which was affirmed and updated through its depiction in *The Sum of All Fears,* when the sheer horror of nuclear terrorism unfolded near the nation's capital, was now repeatedly harnessed in the run-up to the war to instill in the population the fear and fantasy of cataclysmic violence at their door. By the time of the war's commencement on March 19, 2003, the population was so accustomed to the phrase that the president did not even have to spell it out in his televised address to the nation. It was sufficient merely to invoke the metaphor: "The people of the United States and our friends and allies will not live at the mercy of an outlaw regime that threatens the peace with weapons of mass murder. We will meet that threat now with our army, air force, navy, coast guard, and marines so that we do not have to meet it later with armies of firefighters and police and doctors on the streets of our cities."[36]

According to Peggy Rosenthal, "The mushroom cloud is a 'menace,' icon of evil, but it stands also for the will to exorcise the evil, expel it from the earth."[37] Thus, Americans were compelled to support the rush to war with Iraq and prevent grave danger; nearly six in ten Americans supported the invasion, believing that time was running out and waiting to obtain UN support had "taken too much time."[38] Traumatized by September 11, when the violence on the periphery of empire spilled onto the continental United States, the mushroom cloud imagery convinced an already primed citizenry reeling from a distinct sense of vulnerability that only trusting the government with its case for war on Iraq could prevent the violence of "over there" coming home, but this time in a more catastrophic way.

In Freudian terms, if a mushroom cloud represented a phallic symbol that could penetrate and violate America, then the best way to avert such a violation would be to become the predator and exact that very violence onto the would-be offender. As such, the fear of apocalyptic terrorism gave way to a U.S.-led war on Iraq to prevent the mushroom cloud from exploding on U.S. soil by exploding thousands of smaller mushroom clouds via supposed precision guided missiles that not only led to mass destruction in Iraq, but also the gradual unraveling of much of the region.

Smokescreen and Destabilization

The mushroom cloud has a long history in the United States; it is part of America's visual heritage. Of all the meanings that this image contains at once, the dread that it invokes became paramount after 9/11—underscoring America's vulnerability after that horrific day. At the same time, it portended even worse horrors ahead if urgent preventative action was not taken. In that vein, the Bush administration integrated the terror of the mushroom cloud into its discourse and symbolism of what would happen if the government did not take immediate action to ward off the evil of mass murder.

"Mushroom cloud," "nuclear terrorism," "al-Qaeda," and "9/11" had been rendered synonymous with "Iraq."

In the end, however, the mushroom cloud became part of a web of deceit that the administration spun in its ill-fated war of choice in a country that had nothing to do with the traumatic events of September 11, 2001. No peril was at hand, except for all the destruction that the war caused as the world's most powerful military was unleashed on a largely defenseless nation that had already experienced two preceding wars and twelve years of debilitating sanctions. The reverberations of this war, which Iraqis saw in apocalyptic terms as the earth trembled from beneath them, continue to this very day. Whereas before the invasion of Iraq, there was virtually no terrorist threat emanating from the country, afterward the Iraq War became a cause célèbre as thousands of jihadis from around the world answered the call to arms and came to fight the United States—a destabilization and radicalization that devolved into the emergence of countless terrorist groups. This cataclysmic violence gave birth to the Islamic State terror group, which al-Qaeda, the perpetrator of the attacks of 9/11, denounced as too radical.

Such tactics used to legitimate the rush to war were not unique to America on the eve of the 2003 invasion. They happened before and will happen again—unless citizens are able to decipher for themselves the uses and abuses of such powerful symbols of fear.

Catherine Tedford, *Invaders*.
Reprinted with permission of the artist.

CHAPTER 3

Ecoterrorism

On September 11, 2001, Representative Don Young (R-Alaska) wasted no time linking radical environmentalists to the collapse of the Twin Towers: "I'm not sure they're that dedicated, but eco-terrorists . . . there's a strong possibility that could be one of the groups" behind the attacks.[1] The timing of Young's statement is significant because it demonstrates how the language of ecoterrorism was already circulating before the war on terror began and reveals the eagerness of some elected officials to use this tragedy as an opportunity to draw attention to radical environmentalists even though it quickly became clear they played no role in the 9/11 attacks.

In this chapter, I trace how acts of sabotage committed to protect ecosystems (eco-sabotage) became redefined as acts of ecoterrorism and how this redefinition affects the U.S. government's handling of these acts, especially in the context of the post-9/11 war on terror. I argue the concept of ecoterrorism is an illuminating example of collateral language because it challenges the assumption that the Federal Bureau of Investigation (FBI) and Department of Homeland Security (DHS) prioritize the prevention of threats that are most likely to result in deaths and injuries. Rather, successful lobbying by industries whose businesses have been targets of eco-sabotage has pressured counterterrorism agencies to devote their time and energy to investigating actions that caused significant economic damage but have not resulted in any deaths or injuries. The broad definitions of ecoterrorism put forward by industry groups and their allies in government depart significantly from legal precedent and are part of a political project that involves mobilizing state resources to protect a particular notion of American interests—namely, the preservation of property to the point that this interest is prioritized over protecting the lives of members of marginalized communities targeted by perpetrators of right-wing violence.

From Eco-sabotage to Ecoterrorism

Edward Abbey's 1975 novel *The Monkey Wrench Gang* captured the imagination of environmentalists who felt the legislative victories of the late 1960s and early 1970s weren't sufficient for protecting the remaining wilderness in the United States from development.[2] It chronicles the adventures of four people who commit acts of eco-sabotage, or monkey-wrenching, including setting fire to billboards, toppling power lines, and destroying logging and mining equipment. A few years later the novel inspired several environmental activists to make life imitate art by forming organizations that would engage in and advocate for eco-sabotage to protect threatened species and their habitats from devastation. After being expelled from Greenpeace in 1977 for refusing to rule out the use of property destruction as a tactic, Paul Watson founded the Sea Shepherd Conservation Society, an organization with a history of sinking whaling ships that are running afoul of international law. In 1980 Earth First! was formed to promote more confrontational approaches to wilderness protection through civil disobedience campaigns as well as the endorsement of monkey-wrenching.

Abbey's fictional portrayal of eco-saboteurs was first criticized as an endorsement of terrorism by an environmental ethicist sympathetic to the cause of wilderness preservation. Questioning the merits of eco-sabotage on both moral and political grounds, Eugene Hargrove noted how the protection of private property is a deeply held value in the United States and will motivate a fierce backlash against acts of eco-sabotage.[3] In response to Hargrove's objections, Abbey draws the following distinction between sabotage and terrorism: "terrorism means deadly violence—for a political and/or economic purpose—carried out against people and other living things. . . . Sabotage, on the other hand, means the application of force against inanimate property, such as machinery. . . . [S]abotage—for whatever purpose—has never meant and has never implied the use of violence against living creatures in order to defend a land they [the saboteurs] love against industrial terrorism."[4] One need not agree with Abbey's insistence that ecological devastation should be understood as terrorism to appreciate the difference between sabotage directed at artifacts and terrorism that seeks to cause serious bodily injury and death. While Hargrove did not challenge Abbey's distinction between sabotage and terrorism, his prediction regarding a backlash against eco-sabotage in defense of private property proved true.

In the early 1980s, as the Reagan administration sought to roll back the environmental movement's legislative victories, acts of eco-sabotage proliferated in the Pacific Northwest. Ron Arnold of the Center for the Defense of Free Enterprise takes credit for coining the term "ecoterrorism" in response to these acts. In 1983 he argued that what appeared to be "isolated incidents . . . are actually related acts of 'ecotage' or eco-terrorism—deliberate destruction of the artifacts of industrial civilization in the name of environmental

40

protection."[5] This definition is notable because it collapses the distinction between sabotage and terrorism drawn by Abbey, a distinction that Arnold later dismissed as "naïve." According to Arnold, "Federal law does not agree with Ed Abbey. . . . Property has always been protected by law on the presumption that damage to a person's belongings, especially one's home or means of livelihood, is damage to the person."[6] Arnold correctly notes that the FBI's definition of terrorism includes property destruction, but a cursory review of federal law reveals how the distinction between sabotage and terrorism isn't as naive as he suggests. Title 18 of the U.S. Code, which covers crimes and criminal procedures, devotes separate chapters to sabotage and terrorism, and did not contain a definition of (international) terrorism until the passage of the Antiterrorism Act of 1990. This definition applies only to *"violent acts or acts dangerous to human life* that are a violation of the criminal laws of the United States."[7] If property destruction does not endanger human life, then it does not qualify as terrorism according to this definition.

Despite the lack of a legal justification for collapsing the distinction between sabotage and terrorism, Arnold later expanded his definition of ecoterrorism simply to "a crime committed to save nature."[8] As Arnold makes clear in his 1998 testimony to the House Judiciary Committee, according to this definition *any* crime committed to save nature, even nonviolent civil disobedience, counts as ecoterrorism: "These crimes generally take the form of equipment vandalism, but may include package bombs, blockades using physical force to obstruct workers from going where they have a right to go and invasions of private or government offices to commit the crime of civil disobedience. . . . [T]he range of ecoterror crimes ranges from the most violent felonies of attempted murder to misdemeanor offenses such as criminal trespass." For Arnold, the essential component of terrorism is the presence of a political ideology motivating the unlawful action; whether action involves direct physical harm to people, solely involves the destruction of property, or simply involves trespassing is irrelevant. Nonetheless, Arnold portrays his account of ecoterrorism as nuanced insofar as it "make[s] very, very strict distinctions between noncriminal acts that we just might not like—pressures on lobbying, lawsuits, other things of that nature—and not bunch those in with ecoterrorism. . . . We don't want to corrupt the meaning of the word, so we are talking only about things that have arrests, convictions, prison sentences and such things as that."[9] One could argue, however, that by labeling *all* crimes committed to save nature, regardless of whether they pose a threat to human life, Arnold's definition of ecoterrorism is ultimately corrupt, especially when contrasted to the definitions of terrorism enshrined in federal law at the time. This criticism, however, misunderstands Arnold's aim: not satisfied with merely interpreting terrorism laws, his point was to change them.

The Federal Government's Initial Response to Ecoterrorism

Although acts of eco-sabotage took place throughout the early 1980s, it was not until the 1988 edition of its *Terrorism in the United States* report that the FBI first documented two "terrorist incidents" related to environmental demands, both of which were actions performed in Arizona by a group with ties to Earth First! who called themselves the Evan Mecham Eco-Terrorist Conspiracy (EMETIC).[10] While the specific reasons for choosing this name are not clear, it seems as though the group was willing to risk increased scrutiny from the FBI by including the word "terrorist" in their name for the sake of a clever acronym. The FBI categorized one of these incidents as "sabotage" (the cutting of power line poles near uranium mines on the rim of the Grand Canyon) while it categorized the other as the "malicious destruction of property" (the cutting of a pole holding up an unoccupied chair lift at a ski resort). This was also the first time the FBI included these categories of terrorist incidents in its annual report.

While Earth First! cofounder Dave Foreman did not participate in the EMETIC actions, he was nonetheless a target of the FBI, due to his role as coeditor of a monkey-wrenching handbook and his alleged financial support of EMETIC. Embarrassingly, an undercover FBI agent inadvertently recorded himself admitting that Foreman "isn't really the guy we need to pop . . . in terms of the actual perpetrator. . . . This is the guy we need to pop to send a message, and that's all we're really doing. . . . If we don't nail this guy . . . we're not sending a message."[11] This admission highlights one of the troubling consequences of ecoterrorism discourse: it can be used to stifle the civil liberties of radical environmentalists who do not themselves engage in criminal acts of eco-sabotage.

Several of the earliest proponents of eco-sabotage, including Foreman and Watson, denounce the use of arson to damage property even when measures are taken to ensure that no living beings will be harmed, due to the difficulty in controlling fires and thus the increased likelihood of unintentional harm to living beings.[12] These risks, however, did not deter a new wave of more militant activists from committing acts of arson to maximize the economic damage inflicted upon their targets. In the late 1980s and early 1990s, the Animal Liberation Front (ALF) took responsibility for several animal releases and arsons at research facilities, including an incident at Michigan State University in 1992 that served as the catalyst for the passage of the Animal Enterprise Protection Act (AEPA).

The AEPA includes a section entitled "animal enterprise terrorism" that outlines punishments for anyone who "intentionally causes physical disruption to the functioning of an animal enterprise by intentionally stealing, damaging, or causing the loss of, any property . . . used by the animal enterprise," even if doing so does not result in any "serious bodily injury."[13] The AEPA also called on the Department of Justice and the Department of Agriculture to research the impact of terrorism on animal enterprises. The report was published in 1993, but because the FBI had only categorized three ALF actions as incidents of domestic terrorism, the authors took the liberty of expanding the scope of the study to cover the broader phenomenon of "animal rights extremism," which "includes all acts of destruction or disruption perpetrated against animal enterprises or their employees."[14] Arnold sees this decision as validating his particular conception of ecoterrorism when he celebrates how "even the government has to sidestep the FBI's narrow definition of terrorism so it can use a little common sense."[15] The report concluded that more than half of the instances of animal rights extremism were minor acts of vandalism, which raises the question of whether it's common sense to categorize graffiti writing, window breaking, and lock gluing as terrorist acts.

As the federal government paid closer attention to ALF actions, Earth First! distanced itself from its history of endorsing eco-sabotage in favor of civil disobedience campaigns inspired by the civil rights movement. The Earth Liberation Front (ELF) formed in 1992 to fill this niche by adopting the tactics of the ALF, including arson. After the Oklahoma City bombing in 1995 and the 1996 Olympics bombing in Atlanta by right-wing extremists, the then FBI director Louis Freeh could state with confidence that ALF and ELF actions were not a major concern.[16] His opinion changed, however, in October 1998 when the ELF claimed responsibility for an arson at Vail ski resort that caused approximately $26 million in damages. The federal government was determined to pursue eco-saboteurs as ecoterrorists, but it would take the war on terror to develop the tools to do so effectively.

Ecoterrorism after 9/11

Congress hastily prepared a legislative response to the 9/11 attacks in the form of the USA PATRIOT Act, which is significant for the discourse of ecoterrorism because it added a definition of domestic terrorism to federal law

for the first time. This definition was narrower than the FBI's definition insofar as it focused solely on "acts dangerous to human life that are a violation
of . . . criminal laws"[17] and did not encompass acts of property destruction
that do not endanger human life. The act also made it easier for the FBI to
monitor the communications of and gather information about suspected
domestic terrorists. Congress wasted little time in calling for the FBI to use
these newfound powers to combat ecoterrorism.

In February 2002, the House Committee on Resources held a hearing
on ecoterrorism, and some participants seized the opportunity to associate
the actions of the ALF and ELF with those of al-Qaeda, despite the former
groups' commitment to not harming living beings and their effectiveness
in upholding this commitment. Representative Greg Walden (R-Oreg.),
for example, equated the ELF's firebombing of the unoccupied company
headquarters of U.S. Forest Industries to the 9/11 attacks in his plea that all
terrorism matters: "It is only a matter of time before an innocent life is lost
in a future ELF or ALF attack. That is why it is imperative to treat all acts of
terrorism equally. The terrorists behind the attacks of September 11, 2001
and December 27, 1998, both used terror and destruction to further their
cause. Terrorism is terrorism whether it is international, domestic, economic,
religious, social or environmental."[18] Representative Walden would be deeply
disappointed if he discovered that the FBI does not treat all acts of terrorism
equally, as it appears to categorize a wider range of acts perpetrated by the
ALF and ELF as terrorist incidents than it does in the case of other domestic
terrorists, including white supremacists.

In his statement to the committee, the then FBI Domestic Terrorism section chief James Jarboe notes how radical environmentalists and animal liberationists "have turned increasingly toward vandalism and terrorist activity in
attempts to further their causes."[19] While Jarboe treats vandalism separately
from terrorist activity in this statement, the FBI's own chronology of terrorist
incidents from 1980 to 2005 includes three incidents attributed to the ALF
and ELF involving only vandalism and seven incidents in which ALF and ELF
vandalism is accompanied by another crime. There are no other vandalism
incidents listed in this entire chronology, which gives the impression that, for
the FBI, the ALF and ELF have a monopoly on the use of terrorist vandalism.
Another section of this same report, however, tells a different story when it
describes how the arrest of white supremacist Sean Michael Gillespie for his
2004 firebombing of a synagogue in Oklahoma City not only thwarted his
plans to attack another synagogue in Las Vegas but also led Gillespie to admit "to having previously committed random acts of vandalism and violence

against minorities."[20] For whatever reason, the FBI chose not to amend its statistics from previous years to include these acts, even though they meet the FBI's own definition of domestic terrorism. This raises the question of how many other instances of white supremacist vandalism and violence were not categorized as terrorist incidents, and whether their omission enabled the FBI misleadingly to conclude that nearly "all of the domestic terrorist incidents were committed by special interest extremists active in the animal rights and environmental movements."[21]

45

Additional remarks by Jarboe during the question and answer portion of the 2002 hearing also suggest the FBI was focusing on "ecoterrorism" at the expense of white supremacist threats of violence. He reassured the committee that "the No. 1 priority in the Domestic Terrorism Program . . . is ALF/ELF. Actually, the only thing that has slowed us down and put us behind schedule is the unfortunate attack on September 11, and then the anthrax issue in October that affected Congress so badly. That has put us behind because all of our resources have been put into those investigations. We're now getting those resources back . . . and we intend again to have ALF/ELF at the top of our list of terrorist groups that we're going after." Jarboe implies that the 9/11 attacks were unfortunate not only because of the thousands of lives lost but also because it has distracted the FBI from its *real* domestic counterterrorism priority of breaking up two groups who have not physically harmed anyone but have caused millions of dollars of damage through acts of arson, property destruction, and vandalism. One would think the FBI's most wanted domestic terrorists were those who were most likely to kill and hurt people. However, Jarboe sends mixed messages in this regard. At one point he suggests that the ALF/ELF pose a greater "danger to the public at large" than any other domestic terrorist group but then backtracks by admitting that "the white supremacists . . . [are] more dangerous because they purposely go out to harm individuals or kill them. ALF/ELF says they don't do that, but if you take the totality of it, a one-time event versus the whole structure, then ALF/ELF by and large is the most active, most prolific group we're now looking at."[22] In other words, the frequency of ALF and ELF actions, even though they have not caused any deaths or injuries, makes these groups a more significant threat in the eyes of the FBI than the actions of white supremacists that are intended to and often do result in deaths and injuries.

Other divisions within the Department of the Justice raised the concern that the FBI's focus on ecoterrorism was distracting it from more serious threats. A 2003 audit by the Office of the Inspector General, for example, recommended that the FBI investigate eco-sabotage as a crime as opposed to a terrorist act unless a "group or individual uses or seeks to use explosives or weapons of mass destruction to cause mass casualties." The FBI disagreed with this recommendation, citing the definition of terrorism established with the PATRIOT Act. Their primary justification for rejecting this recommendation, however, is due to the "considerable damage to the U.S. economy" caused by the ALF and ELF, which does not fulfill the PATRIOT Act's criteria for domestic terrorism so long as human lives are not endangered. In response, the Office of the Inspector General reiterated its belief "that the FBI's priority mission to prevent high-consequence terrorist acts would be enhanced if the Counterterrorism Division did not have to spend time and resources on lower-threat activities by social protestors or on crimes committed by environmental, animal rights, and other domestic radical groups."[23]

Similarly, a 2005 Senate hearing on ecoterrorism revealed how the federal government's focus on ecoterrorism also comes at the cost of adequately addressing threats of domestic right-wing violence. In his opening statement, Senator James Inhofe (R-Okla.) claimed that "the widespread use of arson . . . makes ELF and ALF the No. 1 domestic terror concern over the likes of white supremacists, militias, and anti-abortion groups."[24] Senator Jim Jeffords (D-Vt.), however, drew attention to a recent report authored by a member of the House Homeland Security Committee that suggests that the DHS's counterterrorism priorities are misguided. According to the *New York Times*, the DHS's 2005 Integrated Planning Guidance Report, for example, "identifies animal rights activists and radical environmentalists as possible backers of plots. But it does not mention any domestic extremist groups, like World Church of the Creator, Aryan Nations or anti-abortion activists, which have previously been identified by federal officials as domestic terrorist threats."[25] The then senator Barack Obama's (D-Ill.) statement pressed John E. Lewis, then the deputy assistant director of FBI, on the bureau's handling of hate crimes, over 7,400 of which were committed in 2004. Lewis responded by explaining how hate crimes are not "generally committed with a political or philosophical motivation in an attempt to effect political or societal change," which is an essential feature of domestic terrorism.[26] A cynical interpretation of Lewis's answer is that hate crimes often have the effect of *preserving* structural forms of oppression rather than *changing* them; therefore, they do not fulfill the criteria for domestic terrorism.

As Congress devoted its energy to holding hearings on ecoterrorism and the FBI refused to follow recommendations that eco-saboteurs be investigated as criminals rather than as terrorists, industry-backed organizations lobbied for laws at the state level that would establish new crimes and punishments

in response to ALF and ELF actions. In 2003 the American Legislative Exchange Council (ALEC), which drafts model bills for state legislatures that
reflect the interest of its corporate members, issued a report that included a
sample piece of legislation, versions of which had already been introduced
to legislatures in six states earlier that year. The model Animal and Ecologi-   47
cal Terrorism Act defines an "animal or ecological terrorist organization" as
"supporting any . . . activity through intimidation, coercion, force, or fear
that is intended to obstruct, impede or deter any person from participating
in a lawful animal activity, animal facility, research facility, or the lawful activity of construction, mining, foresting, harvesting, gathering or processing
natural resources." This definition is so broad that a group advocating the
economic boycott of a resource-extracting company could arguably count
as an ecological terrorist organization. The model legislation then goes on to
specify prohibited acts, but even these enumerated crimes stretch the meaning of "terrorism" to the point of absurdity. The prohibition on "entering
an animal or research facility to take pictures by photograph, video camera,
or other means with the intent to commit criminal activities or defame the
facility or its owner," when combined with the prohibition on "publiciz[ing]
or "promot[ing] . . . an act of animal or ecological terrorism" appears to be
an effort to criminalize the publication of footage that exposes animal cruelty
taking place behind the closed doors of some animal enterprise facilities.

While the report acknowledges the ALF's and ELF's principled commitment to not harming any living beings in its actions, it also justifies the need
to implement the proposed ALEC legislation by claiming that "this principle
seems to be largely ignored by the highly extreme wings of the organization" and by emphasizing the potential for future harm implied through the
increasingly militant rhetoric adopted by some people affiliated with these
groups. This justification, however, is in tension with another reason provided in the report for adopting ALEC's model legislation: the supposed in-
adequacies of the PATRIOT Act. While most critics of the act express concern
that its scope is so broad that it results in the infringement of civil liberties,
ALEC contends that the act's definition of domestic terrorism is not broad
enough: "within the realm of eco-terrorism, the act can rarely be used, because the federal definition of terrorism requires the death of or harm to people, an element not characteristic of eco-terrorists."[27] The deep irony of this
criticism of the PATRIOT Act, as Will Potter notes, is that ALEC is forced to
concede that the ALF and ELF actions have not resulted in any physical harm
to people after attempting to portray radical environmentalists as violent
terrorists by making tenuous connections between them and both al-Qaeda

and the Unabomber. In other words, the ALF and ELF are supposedly so violent that new antiterrorism laws must be written to stop them, *and* existing laws aren't up to the task because many ALF and ELF actions *aren't violent enough* to qualify as domestic terrorism.

48 ALEC succeeded in having modified versions of its Animal and Ecological Terrorism Act passed in several states, and in 2006, Congress amended the section of the U.S. Code created by the 1992 Animal Enterprise Protection Act with the passage of the Animal Enterprise Terrorism Act. Confusingly, despite its name, the act removed the language of terrorism from the title of the section. Originally called "animal enterprise terrorism," it was renamed to "force, violence, and threats involving animal enterprises."[28] That said, the act broadened the focus of the section from the "physical disruption" of animal enterprises to the "damaging or interfering with the operations of an animal enterprise," which means that affected animal enterprises can claim restitution for profit loss as well as damaged property associated with unlawful economic disruption. It also established more severe punishments for those found guilty of illegally interfering with animal enterprises.

The federal government's legislative and investigative efforts culminated in the FBI's Operation Backfire, which resulted in seventeen indictments and fifteen guilty pleas of ELF members responsible for forty criminal acts from 1995 to 2001.[29] Federal Judge Ann Aiken of the Oregon District Court applied terrorism sentencing enhancements to the defendants who plead guilty to crimes that involved governmental targets. In addition, one of the ELF defendants, Daniel McGowan, was assigned to a Communication Management Unit where prisoners have severe restrictions on phone calls and visits, supposedly as a security measure to prevent convicted domestic terrorists from continuing to operate behind bars. Yet around the same time Eric Rudolph, who killed three people and injured over one hundred others in his bombing campaign that not only targeted the Olympics but also two abortion clinics and a queer nightclub, was allowed to publish writings in which he ridiculed the victims of his attacks.[30] Once again, this suggests a double standard in the way the federal government handles eco-saboteurs and violent right-wing extremists.

Ecoterrorism in the Trump Era

ALF and ELF activity declined significantly as a result of Operation Backfire, but the discourse of ecoterrorism made a comeback with the election of Donald Trump in 2016. In response to the Trump administration's plans to reverse the Obama administration's decision to halt the construction of the major oil pipelines by expediting the completion of these projects, some radical environmentalists resorted to monkey-wrenching by setting fire to heavy machinery and using torches to cut holes in empty sections of the Dakota Access Pipeline (DAPL). In response to these actions and the civil disobedience campaign led by indigenous water protectors to prevent the pipeline from being built under Lake Oahe, the freshwater source for the Standing Rock Sioux Reservation, elected officials and corporate executives attempted to tar environmental activists with the ecoterrorist brush so that oil could flow from the Alberta tar sands and the oil fields of the Dakotas. In October 2017, eighty-four members of Congress cosigned a letter to the then attorney general Jeff Sessions calling on the Justice Department to investigate the sabotage that occurred along the DAPL. While they refrained from using the language of ecoterrorism, they asked the attorney general to consider whether the definition of domestic terrorism established by the PATRIOT Act applies to these incidents. Similarly, Energy Transfer, the company building the DAPL, announced a strategic lawsuit against public participation in an effort to remove activists from the site. The lawsuit accuses Greenpeace and Earth First! of having "incited, funded, and facilitated crimes and acts of terrorism to further these objectives."[31] A federal court rejected the lawsuit, but that did not stop the company from using counterterrorism measures in response to pipeline opposition at Standing Rock. It hired the private security firm TigerSwan, "which originated as a U.S. military and State Department contractor helping to execute the global war on terror" and likened the civil disobedience campaign to a "jihadist insurgency."[32]

The California wildfires of 2018 are another context in which the language of ecoterrorism reemerged. Rather than treat the fires as an occasion to highlight the harms associated with climate change, the then secretary of the interior Ryan Zinke chose to blame environmentalists for the severity of the blazes. According to Zinke, the American people "have been held hostage by these environmental terrorist groups that have not allowed public access, that refuse to allow the harvest of timber." When pressed for specifics, Zinke highlighted "frivolous lawsuits" pursued by "radical environmentalists" who also sometimes "close off roads" to prevent logging from taking place.[33]

The attempt to delegitimize environmental activists by labeling them ecoterrorists is troubling, as is the use of enhanced surveillance techniques and enhanced terrorism sentencing to investigate and punish radical environmentalists and animal liberationists who have been accused of committing acts of property destruction but have not endangered any lives. These disproportionate punishments seem particularly unjust when contrasted to the federal government's relative lack of attention to threats associated with right-wing violence and lenience when punishing those found guilty of hate crimes. This discrepancy can be explained in part by the pressure that industry groups placed on Congress and the FBI to treat eco-sabotage as ecoterrorism. As former DHS domestic terrorism analyst Daryl Johnson argues, "You don't have a bunch of companies coming forward saying I wish you'd do something about these right-wing extremists. . . . If enough people lobbied congresspeople about white nationalists and how it's affecting their business activity, then I'm sure you'll get legislation."[34] This differential treatment of eco-sabotage and hate crimes has resulted in excessive attention to the former while allowing the latter to proliferate.

The Trump administration's response to the March 2019 white supremacist attack on two mosques in New Zealand, however, signaled a particularly pernicious turn in the discourse of ecoterrorism. Previously the problem was the government's misaligned priorities that downplayed the threat of right-wing violence by exaggerating the threat of violence posed by the ALF and ELF. Now the federal government was using the specter of ecoterrorism to actively divert attention away from white supremacist violence. When confronted about the New Zealand shooter's endorsement of President Trump as a symbol of white nationalism, White House spokesperson Kellyanne Conway dismissed this part of the shooter's manifesto by claiming it was an inaccurate portrayal of the president, and she chastised the media for not focusing on other aspects of the shooter's political ideology by suggesting it "sounds like he's an eco-terrorist."[35] White House chief of staff Mick Mulvaney deployed a similar rhetorical strategy when asked about the shooter's manifesto: "I don't think it is fair to cast this person as a supporter of Donald Trump, any more than it is to look at his 'eco-terrorist' passages in that manifesto and align him with Nancy Pelosi or Ms. Ocasio-Cortez."[36] Setting aside the facts that the shooter's manifesto expresses support for Trump "as a symbol of renewed white identity" (but not "as a policy maker and leader"), and never mentions Pelosi or Ocasio-Cortez (cosponsor of the Green New Deal resolution), the shooter describes himself as an eco-fascist as opposed to an ecoterrorist. Either Conway and Mulvaney coincidentally made the exact same slip of the tongue, or they shared talking points with the intention of establishing a connection between eco-saboteurs and a mass murderer who targeted a minority community to shift the public conversation away from the rise of violent white supremacists emboldened by the election of Donald Trump.

"Ecoterrorism" is collateral language that in turn inflicts its own collateral damage. It targets not only eco-saboteurs who engage in property destruction but also environmental activists who engage in civil disobedience by trespassing onto private property. In the aftermath of the 9/11 attacks, one might have expected U.S. counterterrorism agencies to focus exclusively on groups that seek to physically harm and kill civilians. Yet groups such as the ELF and ALF continued to be the main enemies on the domestic front of America's war on terror, despite the persistent threat of violent white supremacists. Rejecting the language of ecoterrorism is imperative not only for the sake of environmentalists who are accused of being terrorists, but also for the sake of the communities targeted by white supremacist violence, for the political project associated with this language privileges the protection of private property over the protection of these communities.

Women

"You have read Saba Mahmood, right?" an interlocutor asked me during a conversation about feminism in Palestine. I knew the late anthropologist and feminist thinker Saba Mahmood's work very well; for an anthropologist working on gender in the Middle East, her work is a must-read. So I was not surprised that in 2011 Mahmood's work had been taken on board by feminists in Palestine, where there is a well-established feminist movement, closely interwoven with the anticolonial struggle for Palestinian statehood.[1] Nonetheless, even with this anecdote demonstrating the global interconnectedness of feminist circuits, how does my Palestinian interlocutor's question to me, a Danish anthropologist, about a Pakistani feminist thinker relate to collateral language twenty years on from 9/11?

As John Collins and Ross Glover argued in the first volume of *Collateral Language* (2002), it is fair to think of 9/11 as a critical moment when the narratives of the "war on terror" swiftly became a central orientating force in our social and political lives. Two decades later, this volume takes stock of the ways in which America's war on terror has now dispersed across the globe and found resonance in political projects, discourses, and civil society interventions that often have little to do with terrorism. The urge to "save" Muslim women in the Middle East and among Middle Eastern diasporas in Europe is one such political project. In the emergence of this project, we see how processes of war making blend with the anti-immigration sentiments in the Global North.

In this chapter, I therefore demonstrate how discourse surrounding themes such as "patriarchy," "fundamentalism," and "Islam/Islamism" has been received, confronted, and acted upon in particularly social science discourse on Muslim women in the Middle East and in the Middle Eastern diaspora dispersed globally. The 9/11 attacks, I argue, provided the ideal occasion for the solidification of the West's cultural hegemony and, with it, the perception of Muslim women as fundamentally unfree. But while this political project adopts the discourses of Orientalism as detailed by Edward Said,[2] in this chapter I also explore the possibility of circumventing this discourse through close attention to the concepts we use to analyze the world around us in social science. To this end, I discuss the work of feminist scholars such as the late Saba Mahmood. In her groundbreaking article "Feminist Theory, Embodiment and the Docile Agent," Mahmood encourages us to break with the (politically determined) "conventional wisdom" that considers the lives of Muslim women to be entirely determined by their religiosity. Instead, she insists, Muslim women have agency in the particular form of piety that they cultivate.[3] Similarly, Lila Abu-Lughod argues that studying women and victimhood, domestic violence, or female-only mosques in the Middle East and among diasporic populations is not a politically neutral endeavor. Rather, such approaches to studying the women of the region are deeply informed by the politics of the field of study as well as the funding behind it.[4]

What this means is that scholarly works, rather than being free of judgment, might occupy a space of either, or both, complicity and opposition to an effort to formulate an unnuanced, stereotypical characterization of women's lives in the Middle East. Such a characterization, as Abu-Lughod has taught us, can have a direct and damaging effect on public discourse regarding not only women in the region but also Muslim women globally. In this way, feminist scholars challenge the underlying politics of the project to "save" Muslim women. By coupling women and agency in their analyses of women's lives, they may also inadvertently provide a retort to the Bush administration's notion of the Middle East as part of an "axis of evil," a part in which women were the prime victims. This attention to concepts in social science is in this sense less about academic disputes irrelevant beyond the ivory tower than it is about offering an alternative conception of women that is not determined by the collateral language of America's war on terror.

In what follows, I investigate how Muslim women became a hostage of collateral language in public discourse as well as social science literature. In doing so, I draw on insights from my own research in Palestine on the families of martyrs and Palestinian political prisoners as well as an instance of how the practice of veiling among Muslim women was made into a "problem" by right-wing politicians in Denmark. I conclude by offering some thoughts on the ethical responsibility of doing social science research in a time when the collateral language of 9/11 leaves neither people's lives nor the concepts we use as social scientists immune to its destructive power.

Political Tragedy and the "Will of God"

Palestinian mothers who have lost their sons, martyred in the ongoing Palestinian national struggle, often say, "The death of my son is the will of God."

My fieldwork in Palestine on the meaning of loss in a context of enduring political violence showed me the omnipresence not only of loss caused by violence but also of the political meaning ascribed to such losses by those left behind. As a thirtysomething Dane who has lived comfortably in the Global North, however, I soon realized that getting my head around the idea of how losing a child could ever be meaningful demanded both a deep ethnographic engagement and a study of the history and culture of Palestine through the different stages of Israel's occupation.

For audiences who have been conditioned to view Islam and the Middle East through narrow, ethnocentric lenses, a statement such as "The death of my son is the will of God" would evoke a post-9/11 narrative where any expression of religious belief, especially by Muslim women, would conjure a powerful cultural image of their oppression by patriarchal structures. Yet as anthropologist Talal Asad argues in *On Suicide Bombing*, while martyrdom in Palestine might make use of religious terminology, the meaning invested in these words is more political than religious.[5] Moreover, to say that the death of a son is the will of God is not as much a reflection of the mother's religious beliefs as it is a way for her to situate her son's death as part of the wider struggle for Palestinian freedom. This act of framing an event like a death of a child in nationalist language rather than as a deeply personal experience took me a long time to understand. But why?

The West's cultural hegemony lays its claims to freedom, individualism, choice, and free will.[6] In comparison, the only categories the Orient is allowed to personify are the opposite concepts of unfreedom, collectivity, and domination.[7] The war on terror not only intensified these divisive lines between the West and the rest but also gave rise to considerable scholarly production. There has also been a proliferation of scholarship that unintentionally describes the patriarchal dominance over women in the Middle East, the lack of women's rights, and the oppressive role of Islam and religion more generally in opposition to the secular, liberal West where gender and ethnic equality were seen to be societal pillars.

In this new political climate, such works take on a life of their own and were seen to provide the allegedly "scientific" grounds on which Western nongovernmental organizations (NGOS) operating in the Middle East could run programs on "women's empowerment" in the name of liberal feminism. While a full exploration of such programs is beyond the scope of this essay, I bring them up here to underline how the concepts we have available for describing and understanding the social world around us are part of that very social life.[8] As such, the collateral language of Western feminism serves as a vessel for ostracizing gendered ways of living in the Middle East as well as other Muslim-majority countries and Muslim diasporas.[9]

Woven into such representations is the portrayal of the role of Islam in these "unfree" Muslim women's lives. In much of the literature on the way in which women's freedom is constrained, unfreedom for women was seen to be rooted in Islam and the failure of Muslim-majority states to become modern and secular and hence able to secure gender equality. Further, these understandings assumed that as long as women adhered to Islam, they would be forced to align with patriarchal systems and hence live what to Western feminism seemed like unfree lives.

"Unveiling" Oppression

Following 9/11 it was the practice of veiling—either in the form of the *hijab* (a headscarf covering only a woman's hair), the *niqab* (a covering that allows only a woman's eyes to be visible), or the *burqa* (a dress that allows gendered bodily expressions to evade the public eye)—that became the most significant symbol of Muslim women's oppression. Without ever pausing to take in, or even take seriously, how and under which circumstances Muslim women themselves might choose to wear the Islamic veil, many outside observers saw the hijab as synonymous with women's lack of agency.

In Denmark, a close ally to the Bush administration's war on terror, what became known unofficially as the "Burqa Ban" came under consideration following heated public debate on whether a women whose face was covered should be allowed to work as a pedagogue at a publicly funded childcare institution or serve in a governmental role.[10] These discussions were led by the Danish People's Party (Dansk Folkeparti). Representatives of this populist right-wing party argued that veiling—in particular its most covering form, the burqa—was not acceptable for anyone undertaking a job where meeting or caring for others were part of the task. They further declared the need to find out how many women were actually wearing burqas in Denmark so as to get an idea of how widespread "the Burqa problem" was. A group of scholars of the sociology of religion took on the task and produced a "Burqa study" that revealed that in Denmark, a country of 5.5 million citizens, some 100–200 women wore the burqa at the time. Dismantling what in public discourse had become a "problem," the researchers henceforth concluded that speaking about the burqa as a widespread issue of Muslim men's power over Muslim women in Denmark might have been grossly exaggerated.[11] Another finding of this study that upset the attempt of right-wing political parties to cast Muslim women on the wrong side of the oppressed/free divide in Denmark was that veiling was, largely, the women's own choice even in the face of kin members who did not support it. Thus, the report deeply challenged the political discourse on the practice of veiling as a materialization of "Islamist oppression of women." Deflating such orientalizing public discourse, the study's findings thereby confirm El Said, Meari, and Pratt's assertion that we need a more nuanced understanding of women's agency that upsets the secular/fundamentalist binary.[12] As scholars, we have the responsibility to pause before falling into an all-too-easy understanding of veiling as oppressive and a speech act such as "The death of my son is the will of God" as an expression of fundamentalist belief in God's will or the belief that the mother in question simply reflects stereotypical characteristics of (Muslim) women in the Middle East.

Here again we see how the collateral language of "women," when specifically referencing Muslim women, is connected with the broader process of cultivating public support for the political project of the war on terror.

Agency beyond "Free Will"

Is it possible for us to escape from the effects of this collateral language? Saba Mahmood's work on the piety movement in Cairo offers an alternative path that hinges upon the need to complicate the dominant discourse of "women" by bringing it into dialogue with a critical understanding of another term: "agency." El Said, Meari, and Pratt argue that Mahmood presents a form of religious agency as an alternative to liberal individualism; I propose that Mahmood's understanding of agency achieved more than that. In her landmark formulation "that we take agency not as a synonym for resistance to relations of domination but as a capacity for action that historically specific relations of subordination enable and create," Mahmood encourages us to stop divorcing religion from a wider societal context in which oppression, expression, and desires are interwoven in ways that hardly lend themselves to a comfortable either/or analysis.[13] Instead, her detailed investigation of women's submission to forms of religious dominance provoked both scholars and secular feminist movements, because she poses a fundamental question: What forms of agency can be found in women submitting to religious devotion and its implicit structures of patriarchy? Here we see the forms of pressure that ethnography poses on our concepts—in this case a Western, liberal understanding of a self-determined individual. In her encounters with her interlocutors, Mahmood fundamentally unsettled the concept of agency as we know it. An important element of this reconceptualization is her insistence that agency is not only action but also not acting, including endurance, giving in to the circumstances in which one's life is folded, without giving up. This complex notion of agency lends itself well to the culturally salient idea of *sumoud* (steadfastness) in Palestine. As anthropologist Lena Meari argues, *sumoud* entails a similar idiom of resistance as Palestinians resist not just by willfully engaging in narrowly understood forms of political action such as demonstrations or violent resistance, but also by simply staying put, standing tall in the face of continuous adversity.[14] As such, *sumoud* holds promise as a Palestinian ethnographic theory of resistance, perhaps even agency.

Anthropologist Ilana Feldman, however, urges us to be cautious regarding the value of *sumoud* due to its simultaneous life as a powerful, political ideology with its own dynamics of inclusion and exclusion.[15] Insofar as our concepts are parts of our forms of life,[16] a concept such as *sumoud* is therefore not immune to the ideologies with which it is attached. Thus *sumoud* poses a similar problem as the women's mosque movement in Mahmood's study: How do we treat our interlocutors' own verbalizations of agency in the face of what we as researchers might read as permeating oppression, be it political or religious? What do we do as scholars when denoting such actions as agency? And how can we make sure that our work does not unintentionally contribute to the operation of collateral language that positions "women" as two-dimensional characters in need of "saving"?

Listening deeply to what women are saying can be one of the most powerful ways of pushing back against this sort of collateral language. During another period of fieldwork in the West Bank in 2011 among families in which both parents had been politically active during both the first (1987–1993) and the second (2000–2005) Palestinian Intifadas (uprisings), I spoke with couples about the meaning of imprisonment and activism in their individual and shared lives. Some of my interlocutors were people I had known since the days of my graduate fieldwork in 2007 and 2008. Others I knew both through these former interlocutors of mine and political activists in the broader landscape of NGOs working to alleviate the potential trauma of imprisonment. During this latter study, I worked with a research assistant who helped me set up my appointments. She, too, was a former activist who had turned to further education after her children came of age. Working in the NGO and university sector, all of the families in this second study belonged to an upper-class, urban, Palestinian elite. Hence, returning to the opening quotation by an interlocutor of mine, naturally Saba Mahmood's understanding of feminist agency was part of her vocabulary to respond to my questions about self, kinship, and political struggle in Palestine after the Intifada.

My interlocutors, being educated activists, seemed to fit Mahmood's notion of agency as an intentional, cultivated mode of subjectivity. For them, not being committed to the anti-colonial struggle was considered unthinkable, and politics shaped their desires down to the particular men with whom the women fell in love. Rather than engaging in the preferred form of marriage in Palestine—namely, lateral cross-cousin marriage—the women who came of age during the first Intifada married the political activists with the most impressive political CVs. As such, these women were different from the women who were front and center of my graduate fieldwork. The latter were less educated and lived in rural areas understood locally as more traditional. Importantly, these women had not committed themselves to the fight for political statehood, aside from practicing *sumoud* in the face of their absent, haunted, imprisoned, or administratively detained husbands.

Thus, in different ways, both the urban and the rural women I studied seemed to fit the bill for a conceptualization of women's agency shaped by the historical traditions in which they were living. In the Palestinian context, I would argue, this tradition is determined by Israel's military occupation rather than by Islam. Yet Mahmood's understanding of agency is apt in a further way, too: the idioms of expression in which the women reflected about their lives seemed to gel particularly well with a nationalist rhetoric of resistance, *sumoud*, and Palestinian statehood. The elasticity of *sumoud* fits well with an understanding of agency where submitting to the condition into which one is thrown is part of agency itself. More importantly, it is relevant in cases where people were not engaged in any political action at all apart from simply going about their everyday lives and trying to sustain their families.[17] Thus we can understand the vital importance of the national struggle for Palestinian statehood in the lives of Palestinians who occupy the center stage of political activism as well as those who practice *sumoud* simply by staying put.

In 2020, the long-term effects of the Israeli occupation on livelihoods, employment, mental health, and political/territorial separation in the Palestinian community seem to have become permanent threads in the ordinary lives of Palestinians. Following Abu-Lughod's insistence that we need to exercise caution in terms of romanticizing resistance, there seems to have been a tendency on the part of scholars across the humanities and social sciences during the last two decades to gesture at women or marginalized groups in the Middle East or Muslim communities more broadly and proclaim "this is agency." The political background of this gesture is evidently centuries of brutal colonialism with ensuing victimization of indigenous communities. Simultaneously, this gesture also involves the different scholarly responses to colonialism, in the form of postcolonial critique as well as more recent attempts to decolonize scholarship.[18]

A key point across these efforts is to underline that victimization does not necessarily equal a lack of agency. Hence, many social science studies document the surprising avenues of agency in circumstances that are indeed, and on a permanent basis, compromised. Albeit with some caution, the attention to agency seems to hold the promise of not dehumanizing people living in adverse conditions by simply documenting their victimhood. Pointing to their agency "in spite of" becomes a way of showing the human capacity of creativity and innovation across different forms of life at the same time as it also represents a political act of acknowledging that agency does not only belong to Western, so-called liberal democracies in which its political connotations of freedom and individuality are praised. Rather, agency, like modernity, relatedness, and other vital concepts in the social scientific archive, can unfold in multiple and unforeseeable ways. The task for us as researchers is to be able to recognize them when we witness them.

Withholding the need to conceptualize as agency what we learn from the ethnographic sites is, however, not a call for renewed empiricism nor an atheoretical social science. Rather, the power of social science at its best is through rigorous conceptual analysis that may help us unsettle die-hard notions of, for instance, oppressed Muslim women in need of saving.

Scholarship and Responsibility

By way of conclusion, I wish to revisit a question, once posed by Abu-Lughod: "Do Muslim women really need saving?" Here, Abu-Lughod argues "that rather than seeking to 'save' others (with the superiority it implies and the violences it would entail) we might better think in terms of (1) working with them in situations that we recognize as always subject to historical transformation and (2) considering our own larger responsibilities to address the forms of global injustice that are powerful shapers of the worlds in which they find themselves."[19] What does that mean in the context of doing research in the Middle East and with Middle Eastern researchers in and outside the region? For any researcher, ethics and responsibility are constantly in the process of being achieved, not only in the field but also through careful attention to the concepts that are used to open up our research to students, peers, and others who are interested in our fields of study. Because of such collaterals of cooperation, social science research can take on a social life with great consequences for the people it claims to study. These are not just scholarly obligations for scholars and students to evaluate critically the way in which they study the Middle East. Further, the contentious politics of collateral language of a world in which 9/11 happened also makes it a responsibility to be taken seriously not only when planning or doing a study but also in writing and speaking about it. Because, after all, language creates our social worlds.

Insurgency

It is July 2010, and Oakland, California, is bracing for another riot. Since January 2009, the city had been rocked by a series of angry rebellions in response to the shooting death of Oscar Grant at the hands of transit cop Johannes Mehserle. On January 7, we were tear-gassed and shot at with rubber bullets. On January 14, we were chased through the streets by armored personnel carriers. On January 30, I nearly lost a limb when a flash-bang grenade missed me by a matter of inches.[1] Now in July of the next year, as the city tensely awaited the Mehserle verdict, word arrived that the Oakland Police Department (OPD) had acquired yet another weapon of war: a $675,000 crowd-control sound cannon known as a Long-Range Acoustic Device (LRAD). Activists and lawyers scrambled to file an injunction against the LRAD's use. In the words of local attorney Michael Siegel, "OPD should not use such a dangerous and little-understood device on Oakland civilians. This device appears unfit for any use at all, much less against local residents exercising their First Amendment rights of expression and association."[2] While the police ultimately backed down under pressure, the crucial question remained: Were we civilian protesters, as Siegel insisted, or were we dangerous insurgents to be met with weapons of war? As the brutal deployment of military force against protesters in Ferguson, Missouri, in 2014 and Standing Rock in 2016 reminds us, this question remains as pressing as ever.

The Colonial Rupture

Political concepts are the fraught products of a fraught world, subject to the same tensions and pressed into motion by the same contradictions. While appearing as universal reflections of an idea, in reality they are momentary crystallizations, temporary truces in a permanent tug-of-war over which meaning will prevail. In a world as divided along colonial and racial lines as ours, we should not be surprised when our concepts also reflect this division. And these tensions are especially powerful when it comes to concepts that describe division, rupture, and opposition—ideas that are simultaneously vehicles and reflections of dialectical motion. "Insurgency" is one such concept. Insurgency denotes a relationship between two radically unequal actors; not of outright war between equals but something more and something less at the same time. But crucially, to name a movement an insurgency also does ideological work for those in power. To call something an insurgency is to minimize the conflict in question and legitimize the existing order by marking one party as official and legitimate and the other as a usurping upstart.

The etymology and history of the term "insurgency" is the history of the strategic deployment of these literally warring meanings. If we take Google's Ngram search engine as a starting point (see figure 1), we might think that insurgency is a relatively new term whose usage only becomes generalized in the mid-twentieth century. This makes sense, given the eruption of Third World anti-colonial insurgencies and revolutions at that time. We do in fact see that the spike in the popularity of the term "insurgency" corresponds to similar upticks in "decolonization" and its own brutal opposite, "counterinsurgency" (coined in 1960 by the Rand Corporation in response to decolonization struggles). It is noteworthy that this cluster of terms only diverges in the context of the Second Iraq War, where colonialism lives on without the name—further proof that the "postcolonial" is pure ideology.

However, this recent history of the term "insurgency" is misleading in two ways. First, if "insurgency" is a relatively new term, the noun form "insurgent" was older and more widespread, peaking in the mid- and again in the late nineteenth century, and of course again in our (counter)insurgent present. But here, too, the history is longer still: "insurgency" is anchored etymologically in "insurrection," which dates back further to the Age of Revolutions unleashed in the mid-eighteenth century and debates around the legitimacy of rebellion against unjust tyranny.[3] This longer history reveals that insurgency's (de)colonial content is older as well. Insurgents were occasionally the poor, but most often to be an insurgent was to belong to a less-than-human population: Black slaves, Indian rebels West and East, and other colonized peoples, including those borderline humans like the Irish and Scots.[4] The populations in question corresponded, moreover, to a specific form of action that insurgency was meant to denote: irrational revolt by innately irrational peoples against the existing rational order of things. The coloniality of insurgency was not unique, either, but extended to other concepts. As Étienne Balibar puts it, "In the dominated colonial peripheries, there were no 'revolutions' but only 'resistances,' 'guerillas,' 'uprisings' and 'rebellions.'"[5]

But this strictly colonial concept of insurgency could not hold in a moment marked by new justifications for resistance and of insurgent *revolutions* in the United States and France that were considered by many, amid the crisis of the ancien régime, to be legitimate. These triumphant bourgeois

Figure 1. Google Ngram search data related to the term "insurgency."

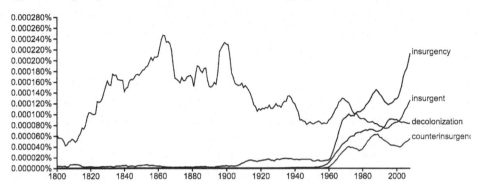

revolutions needed, paradoxically, to both celebrate and contain their in-surgent origins, while also stemming the contagion of insurgency to those they dominated, enslaved, and dispossessed. A colonial rupture thus opened up *within* the idea of insurgency, between legitimate insurgencies against unjust, despotic rule (by rational European subjects) and chaotic, irrational revolts (by inhuman, colonized subjects), with the first gaining a peculiarly positive content as not simply revolts *against* the status quo, but revolution-ary movements *for* a new state of affairs.[6]

William Dupré's *Lexicographia-neologica Gallica*, a lexicon of neologisms added to the French language after 1789, exemplified this shifting tension within insurgency.[7] Insurgency was one such neologism, but this meant ad-justing the negative valence the term had held up to that point. To be an in-surgent means to rise up, but no longer "as a lawless body." Instead, the term "is now applied to the rising of an entire people in opposition to their rulers on the grounds of oppression." Insurgencies are not mere revolts or "acts of rebellion against the established laws," but instead bespeak a new and supe-rior law grounded in the people acting as a whole, marking not only resis-tance *against* but also a movement *for* some positive content. But even Dupré could not fully exorcise the tension within insurgency, which persisted in the question of the day, namely, the slippery slope of the right to rebellion. As one example he cited asks: "the Jacobins, by preaching *insurrection* to the people against the national convention, the body representing the people . . . would they not thereby instigate the people to *insurrection* against them-selves"?[8] From this point on, insurgency would be deployed to denote both grassroots and anti-colonial resistance as well as more "legitimate" struggles against tyranny, blurring the lines of affirmation and denigration in both cases depending on the source.

This newly centered positive content would not hold, however, especially after the consummation of the bourgeois revolutions, and particularly what Gerald Horne calls "the counterrevolution of 1776," made further celebration of insurgency unnecessary, and as fresh insurgency against the French Revolution in the Vendée in 1793 served as a sharp reminder that insurgency can very easily cut both ways.[9] And this tension would remain, bordering on schizophrenia amid the uptick of global insurgency against colonial domination in the mid-twentieth century and producing an especially sharp cognitive dissonance among Americans, who retained at least a vestigial identification with anti-colonial insurgency. According to the RAND Corporation, which played a key role in popularizing the term "counterinsurgency," Americans tend to "oscillate between sympathy and identification with an insurgency on the one hand and impassioned and self-righteous hostility on the other" in part because "we are, or conceive ourselves to be, an insurgent people originating in a tradition of rebellion against inequitable, onerous, and illegitimate authority."[10] But this ambivalence would ebb in the context of direct U.S. involvement in the Vietnam War and arguably would disintegrate entirely in the postpolitical, post–Cold War, "end of history" context framing the Second Iraq War, untethering "insurgency" from "decolonization" in the process.

Counterinsurgency Today

It would seem only logical that counterinsurgency (COIN) would stalk insurgency like a cruel shadow, and while we will see that this is not inevitably the case, it is nevertheless true that COIN doctrine bears all of the colonial content of its sparring partner:

> The Carlisle Barracks (site of the U.S. Army War College) was constructed in central Pennsylvania in the mid 1700s "for the purpose of instructing British and Provincial troops in counterinsurgency, which back then meant fighting Indians." Much later, counterinsurgency became a label for a type of warfare that had existed for centuries. It has gone by a range of names including "imperial policing," "counter-guerrilla" or "counter-revolutionary" operations, "small wars," and (beginning in the 1970s) "low-intensity" conflict. In general, the goal of counterinsurgents, imperial police, counter-guerrillas, counter-revolutionaries, and those engaging in "small wars" was (and is) the suppression or annihilation of revolutionary movements in occupied territories.[11]

The transhistorical continuities of colonial counterinsurgency were often utterly seamless: "Many American troops involved in the 'Philippine

Insurrection' (1898–1902) had experience in fighting the Indian Wars. In letters and diaries they described their opponents as uncivilized savages."[12] More than a century later, famed "American Sniper" Chris Kyle said the same of Iraqi insurgents: "I hated the damn savages."[13] Recent decades have seen parallel shifts in domestic and international counterinsurgency strategy, but in neither sphere has COIN proven effective in disarming global insurgencies or shaking off this deeply racial-colonial content.

In the midst of the Iraqi quagmire more than a decade ago, General David Petraeus spearheaded a long-belated revision of the army's *Counterinsurgency Field Manual* (*Field Manual FM 3–24*)—belated because the prevailing model had failed so catastrophically against insurgent forces in Vietnam, but rather than confronting this failure, U.S. military commanders had instead repressed this painful memory.[14] Enter Petraeus, who not only reintroduced COIN to army doctrine in general, but who did so by emphasizing the political over strictly military force. The goal was to win hearts and minds by guaranteeing security and development, and thereby—inverting Mao's famous metaphor—to deprive insurgent fish of the water they need to survive. In this vein, the revised *FM 3–24* advocates "a balance between the discriminate targeting of irreconcilable insurgents and the persuasion of less committed enemies to give up the fight with the political, economic, and informational elements of power."[15]

This revision of COIN doctrine would seem to entail a softening—if not the total dissolution—of the colonial divide so central to both the theory and practice of insurgency. For the anti-colonial revolutionary Frantz Fanon, the distinction between colonial core and colonized periphery was one between hegemony, ideology, and the winning of European hearts and minds on the one hand and "rifle butts and napalm . . . a language of pure violence" on the other.[16] While Petraeus certainly sought to bring the question of hearts and minds across the colonial divide, we should not lose sight of the fact that what appears to be a kinder, gentler counterinsurgency is instead simply a more *targeted* counterinsurgency: for those identified as "irreconcilable insurgents," Fanon's "pure violence" remains the order of the day.

So too for domestic policing, which has converged dramatically with counterinsurgency in recent years. While the post-9/11 era has witnessed a dramatic militarization of local and state law enforcement, this was more about strategy than military hardware. In brief, whereas protests in the 1960s were subject to "mass and unprovoked arrests and the overwhelming and indiscriminate use of force," the public scrutiny that such tactics generated was untenable, giving rise in the 1980s to a strategy of "negotiated management" characterized by close collaboration between police and protest leaders.[17]

But when negotiation failed—most spectacularly in 1999 protests against the World Trade Organization—police turned to a strategy of "strategic incapacitation" that "emphasizes the application of selectivity whereby police distinguish between two categories of protesters—contained and transgressive—in order to target those most likely to engage in disruptive activities."[18] In other words, separating bad protesters from good—insurgent fish from the water—negotiated free speech for the former, force for the latter. Just as the exporting of a concern for hearts and minds did not completely erase the colonial distinction between insurgents and civilians, the simultaneous importation of weapons and strategies of war by U.S. police did not mean that these were deployed indiscriminately or evenly. The gap persisted in the distinction, often racially determined, between good and bad protesters.

This persistence is nowhere as clear as it was in Ferguson in 2014 and at Standing Rock in 2016, where both Black struggles against police murder and indigenous-led struggles against dispossession and environmental catastrophe were met in the same way, with the kind of military violence reserved for "irreconcilable insurgents." From the moment that police left Mike Brown's lifeless body lying in the street for more than four hours after he was killed by police officer Darren Wilson, it was clear that we were witnessing a colonial relationship. In the words of one resident, "they left his body in the street to let you all know this could be you."[19] This colonial relationship, moreover, had been evident for some time in the scandalous way that the white-controlled city deployed police force to extract resources from the population, which even the *Washington Post* deemed "plundering."[20] When protesters took to the streets furious at Brown's murder, they were therefore coded as insurgents, and mine-resistant armored personnel carriers were soon rolling through the streets. As Jamelle Bouie put it at the time, "they're treating demonstrators—and Ferguson residents writ large—as a population to occupy, not citizens to protect."[21]

In other words, the use of military force in Ferguson does not contradict, but instead confirms, the persistent coloniality of insurgency, because while the theater may have been domestic, this was an internal colony whose residents were insurgents-in-waiting.[22] And, if anything, it is precisely in the colonial core that the distinction between good protester and bad is most likely to be racially determined. From the beginning, Ferguson was by definition an insurgent city for which no force was excessive. This is nothing new for Black Americans. From the annihilation of slave resistance, to former Commissioner of Public Safety Bull Connor's deployment of police dogs and a homemade tank against protesters in Birmingham, to the targeted assassination of Black Panthers and the 1985 MOVE bombing in Philadelphia—there has been hardly a moment in U.S. history when Black protesters have *not* been subject to the unrestrained force often reserved for colonized populations.[23] Furthermore, as was revealed at the time, police in Ferguson had been trained in settler-colonial Israel.[24]

It should be of little surprise, then, that the unified resistance of the Oceti Sakowin—the "Great Sioux Nation"—and allies to the Dakota Access Pipeline at Standing Rock in 2016 would be given the same treatment as the Ferguson insurgents. Not only were the historical continuities with prior indigenous struggles clear—in the words of Nick Estes, "What happened at Standing Rock was the most recent iteration of an Indian War that never ends"[25]—but the tentacles of this global counterinsurgency were national and global as well. The governor of North Dakota invoked the Emergency Management Assistance Compact (EMAC), as had the governor of Maryland when faced with the popular rebellion that followed the police killing of Freddie Gray a year before. EMAC specifies applicability to "community disorder, insurgency, or enemy attack."[26] Private security contractors TigerSwan even labeled Standing Rock protesters "an ideologically driven insurgency with a strong religious component" and outlined a strategy to "defeat pipeline insurgencies."[27] It is no coincidence that TigerSwan had been engaged in counterinsurgency warfare in Iraq and Afghanistan before turning its sights on Standing Rock. As Estes commented, "The connections were clear: local law enforcement and private security imagined themselves participating in a global counterinsurgency against civilian populations that extended from Palestine to Baltimore, Ferguson, the U.S.-Mexico border, and now Standing Rock. The war was against Black life, Palestinian life, migrant life, and Native life."[28]

The same has been true in Latin America where counterinsurgency has not narrowed its scope—as *FM 3–24* would advocate—but has instead expanded it to the breaking point. For example, in Venezuela the targeted counterinsurgency of the 1960s and 1970s gave way—in the context of the growing economic crisis of the 1980s—to the targeting of first unarmed student militants and later the insurgent poor as a whole.[29] Similarly in Mexico, Dawn Paley has described the mass narco-violence of recent decades as an "expanded counterinsurgency," a counterinsurgency without an insurgency where, in the absence of fish, the entire water becomes the target of unrestrained brutality.[30] And then, of course, there is Iraq, which proves that the conceptual delinking of insurgency from decolonization does not mean that colonialism has disappeared, but simply that it has been more effectively concealed. With half a million left dead by the brutal dialectic of a paradoxically named 2007 troop "surge" alongside Petraeus's so-called countersurge, one thing is clear: "A kinder, gentler counterinsurgency is a myth and a fantasy."[31]

We, Insurgents

From insurgency to counterinsurgency, we now spiral back to reclaim the radical kernel of insurgency and to ask: what would an insurgent politics look like today? For some, such as Susan Buck-Morss, insurgency is simply not a risk worth taking, as its possibilities and perils are enclosed within what she calls the "dilemma of the insurgent." A strange mirror image of *FM 3–24's* "paradoxes of counterinsurgency," Buck-Morss's dilemma is one in which "violent resistance, apparently justified by moral sentiment, sets the stage for new brutalities that are repugnant to that sentiment, because against the enemy of humanity, every barbarism is allowed."[32] All insurgency is apparently reduced to the same: "At this crossroad Osama bin Laden meets [Haitian revolutionary] Jean-Jacques Dessalines, and Vladimir Lenin meets George W. Bush . . . the recurring cycle of victim and avenger."[33]

Such defeatism is unsurprising in a moment in which insurgency has become detached from decolonization, becoming instead a free-floating, postpolitical signifier synonymous not with justice but brutality. It erases all distinctions *among* Iraqi "insurgents" and the legitimacy—indeed the inevitability—of resistance to occupation. It upholds the coloniality of insurgency by concealing the violence of conventional forces, and it obscures the fact that certain populations are deemed intrinsically insurgent. And if what Buck-Morss calls "insurgency" is indeed trapped within a "recurring cycle of victim and avenger," then needless to say this has little in common with the history of the term, the contradictions it seeks to contain, and the movements from Ferguson to Standing Rock and beyond that have been given the name of insurgencies. In other words, the question of the insurgent marks "Buck-Morss' liberal limit," and it is not despite this but precisely because of it that an insurgent politics bears such promise.[34]

Beyond this liberal limit lay the radical possibilities opened up by an insurgent turn in political theory, but only if we preserve the term's original tension and anti-colonial content. For example, Antonio Negri binds insurgency directly to constituent power in a manner faithful to the term's origins: the coming together against the existing order (constituted power) and toward a new political horizon.[35] But if we focus so singularly on the (formal) axis of constituent power, we run the risk of losing sight of insurgency's (substantive) anti-colonial content—as rebellion not only against the institutional order, but resistance by the wretched of the earth against the conditions of their condemnation. In this vein and from the Brazilian context, James Holston speaks of an "insurgent citizenship" on the global peripheries, which, while valuable in underscoring insurgency's *expansive* orientation toward ever greater inclusion of the poor and racialized, says less of the radically anti- and trans-institutional potential of an insurgent politics beyond strict citizenship.[36] More ambitious still is Massimiliano Tomba's "insurgent universality," which breaches not only the bounds of citizenship but broader institutional structures as well.[37]

Pressing further, the late Venezuelan guerrilla Kléber Ramírez Rojas proposed a permanent process of insurgency against state institutions themselves. Theorizing what he called an "insurgent republic," or more provocatively "a government of popular insurgency," Ramírez sought to bind together these two apparent opposites—government and insurgency—into a confederated network of grassroots assemblies, providing a vision of a nonstate form of government that would become real in Venezuela's communes today. But crucially, Ramírez's anti-state insurgency was also an anti-colonial one that sought to dismantle the bloated, extractive colonial state and that drew inspiration directly from the "armed resistance to the colonial invader" by indigenous peoples and rebellious slaves.[38]

Insurgency means coming together to rise up against. And while this may seem to say precious little, it actually says a great deal. It says that insurgency is a collective phenomenon, that it comes from below, that it challenges the existing order, and that it does so through the vision wrought in the process of insurgence. On the one hand, this means that we can exclude from insurgency those top-down rebel organizations not grounded in local resistance (al-Qaeda, Islamic State, and right-wing paramilitaries, for example). But more importantly, even in borderline cases such as the American insurgency against the British, an insurgent politics refuses to stop with the liberation of a new ruling class and instead empowers those—the poor, slaves, indigenous people—who continue to come together, rise up, and press forward to radically transform or overthrow those exclusionary orders left in the wake of prior insurgencies.

This means fusing together the two tensions present in the history of the concept of insurgency: the constituent power of the grassroots against the constituted power of the state on the one hand, and the colonial divide between the West and the rest on the other. It means embracing the radical grassroots, indeed binding the grassroots to permanent political resistance. It means centering this coming together over individual acts of revolt, collective resistance *for* over mere rebellion *against*. It means grasping that a truly insurgent politics takes aim at colonialism and the coloniality of a concept that would disavow the capacity for the colonized to engage in a positive program for revolutionary change. It means recognizing, in sum, that the truest insurgency is that undertaken by those with nothing to lose but their literal chains, the wretched of the earth struggling the ontological apartheid of our still-colonial world. And this insurgency is as endless as it is boundless.

Catherine Tedford, *Homeland Security*.
Reprinted with permission of the artist.

Democracy

> This seems very strange at first sight; but . . . democracy is
> also a state and . . . consequently, democracy will also
> disappear when the state disappears.
>
> —Lenin, *State and Revolution*

Democracy is disappearing before our eyes. The Trump administration carried out a wrecking operation against its basic norms and
institutions on a daily basis. More than the ever-shifting coterie of
officials, advisers, and generals around him, Trump himself played an
increasingly personal and incendiary role in this process, which, as of
this writing, threatens to find a fitting and potentially explosive finale
in the form of his unprecedented refusal to concede the election. Ex-
ercising immense executive power recklessly and capriciously, intim-
idating enemies and allies alike, brazenly disregarding procedure and
precedent, threatening to obliterate entire populations abroad, fo-
menting virulent nationalism and racism at home, making repeated
references "in jest" to extending his rule beyond constitutional limits—in short, behaving in the manner of an ignorant and infantile
aspiring dictator—Donald Trump presided over not just the world's
leading democracy but its ongoing demise.

Trump, however, was not a sudden and malignant aberration in an
otherwise healthy system. His ascent to power represents a significant
inflection point in a deep-seated process of democratic erosion that
began long before him and is now assuming a cascading character.

First, the disappearance of democracy is not confined to the
United States but is a global phenomenon. The opening of the
seventy-fourth session of the United Nations General Assembly debate in 2019 paints an instructive picture in this regard. In addition
to Trump, the opening speeches were given by Jair Bolsonaro, who
once described twenty-one years of military dictatorship in Brazil as
a "glorious" period and lamented, incorrectly, that while that regime
tortured, alas "it did not kill"; the Egyptian military dictator Abdel
Fattah el-Sisi, a key figure in the strangling of a popular revolution;
and Turkey's Recep Tayyip Erdogan, who in his fifteen years in power
has behaved more and more brazenly as a strongman. This is a very
partial list of the ongoing rising tide of authoritarianism and, worse,

includes, to mention only three major European countries, the rise of far-right parties with deep connections to the police and military apparatus in Germany; the state of emergency in France, inaugurated in 2015 and then reformulated by draconian "anti-terrorism" and "anti-riot" laws; and violent attacks and plots against politicians and journalists in England in the midst of an unprecedented constitutional breakdown. Rather than the blooming of democracy in the advanced as well as developing countries, it is now becoming increasingly difficult to ignore malodorous fumes resembling that which spread across the world in the 1930s.

Moreover, far from appearing suddenly, the ugly present for which Donald Trump served as a convenient shorthand is the culmination of a protracted history of reaction that was carried out with varying degrees of consciousness and complicity by the entire political establishment. Trump's warm embrace of the thoroughly illiberal and unconstitutional doctrine of the "unitary executive" is only the latest stage in the steady growth of the "imperial presidency," which saw his immediate predecessor claim, among other things, the power to assassinate American citizens after "due process" consisting of careful deliberations in his own head. In fact, the forty-fourth was the only two-term president to spend every single day of his eight years in power with the country at war, while deporting more people than any commander-in-chief before him. And if Trump's economic policies, along with his own biography, expressed the boundless greed and parasitism of the financial aristocracy, one would do well to remember how Obama began his presidency by extending an utterly unpopular financial bailout, "saved" the auto industry by insisting on slashing entry-level pay for workers by half, and generally oversaw a staggering redistribution of wealth from the bottom to the top of society, himself comfortably landing in the latter category as a multimillionaire.

This process stretches further back still, certainly to the eight years of George W. Bush's presidency. His election, decided by a Supreme Court and a sitting justice who helpfully reminded the American people that they have no constitutional right to elect a president, signaled a decisive shift in the attitude toward democracy in ruling circles. Bush's "war on terror," as readers of the first edition of *Collateral Language* well understand, announced a perpetual assault not against Islamic fundamentalism, which proved useful once more later on in Libya and Syria, but against all international and domestic opposition to the voracious appetites of American imperialism. Before that, the Clinton years, a period of political stupidity and reaction if there ever was one, ironically inaugurated by "End of History" triumphalism; the collapse of the post–World War II regime and the onset of neoliberalism, beginning with Carter and continuing with Reagan. One could go on.

The disappearance of democracy takes as its immediate form the fact that the vast majority of people are essentially excluded from political life except every so often, when they are ritualistically summoned into the sad and cramped space called the voting booth to decide, borrowing a phrase from Marx, which member of the ruling class will misrepresent them during that particular period. Their social interests, their basic needs and aspirations, find no expression in the political establishment, as certified by almost half a century of continuous and bipartisan austerity, a quarter century of uninterrupted and bipartisan wars, and a perpetual cycle of great expectations stimulated by candidates promising some permutation of hope and change, followed by political demoralization and disorientation. Militarism and war, the attack on constitutional rights and protections, unprecedented levels of social inequality, and more, all quite intimately bound up with democracy, currently serve as pallbearers to its funeral.

The impulse behind the publication of this chapter is not to wail or to mourn. Neither is it advisable, however, to simply fling oneself against all of this, rushing to the defense of democracy in a spontaneous and impulsive manner. This is particularly true if the disappearance of democracy is actually a desirable and historically necessary outcome, albeit in a totally different manner than the way it is current unfolding. Its ongoing demise is the product of an entire historical process that has to be understood in all its complexities and contradictions in order to be able to find, in this vast and terrible world, the fundamental political form and social subject that can redeem democracy. What follows is an attempt to identify certain essential aspects of this history, in a necessarily abridged and incomplete form. The central issue that will serve as a guiding thread for these reflections is the changing and generally poorly understood relation between capitalism and democracy, that is to say, the latter's social and historical roots.

Democracy before Capitalism

As the story goes, capitalism is directly responsible for the rise of democracy. Breaking through the stifling mist of traditional society, finally unlocking the power of self-interest, capitalism didn't just succeed in lifting humanity from its ancestral poverty but also brought into this world political equality, in the form of parliaments, elections, and all the other basic trappings associated with democracy.

Like all successful false narratives, this one contains elements of truth. It is certainly the case that, in a broad historical sense, the rise of modern democracy is the product of capitalism. It is also true that the capitalist class, through its political and literary representatives, was responsible for developing the foundational ideas necessary for modern forms of political equality. Finally, the capitalist class did at one point play a revolutionary and progressive role in this history. However, once the more specific dynamics involved in the relationship between capitalism and democracy are put into focus, one is led to political conclusions quite opposite from the ones the prevailing narrative is meant to encourage. Before doing this, it is necessary to say a few words about democracy's prehistory.

There are two principal historical antecedents to the modern capitalist, parliamentary forms of democracy: "primitive" and ancient Greek democracy. The first characterized the vast majority of our existence as a species in the form of small, universal, and universally fragmented hunting and gathering communities, while the second, lasting less than two centuries over a fairly restricted territory, nonetheless constituted an enormously significant and influential experiment in self-government. Although little of substance can be said here, these two forms are important insofar as they mark out some of the fundamental limitations of modern democracy, even at its ideal or historical best.

Primitive democracy featured no state, that is, no apparatus of rule and representation separate and apart from society. These small communities were far from peaceful in their relations with others and were condemned by their inability to produce food to live right at the edge of existence. However, their "chiefs" did not possess any sort of independent political power over others, as decisions were made on the basis of consensus.

Similarly, Ancient Greek democracy was effectively the exploitative dictatorship of a minority of society against the majority, which included slaves, women, and "metic" foreigners. Political relations within this numerically significant minority, however, replicated in a much larger and in many ways astonishing form primitive democracy's absence of a separation between state and society. Most of the important government and legal positions, from a military general to the president of the assembly, from a juror in a legal case to the treasurer of public finances, were either elected positions or were selected by lot on a rotation principle. There were no professional members of a separate caste of state officers. Considered from the standpoint of the significant minority of citizens, generally estimated to be 30 percent of the total population, the state was little other than the people, assembled or armed.

When important matters were being decided, precapitalist democracy did not defer them to dubious delegates, who effectively control political power with varying degrees of tenuous or outright fictional legitimacy. On the life-or-death question of whether or not to wage a war, both the ancient Athenian and modern American democracy have decided in the affirmative a great number of times over the course of their tumultuous history. In the former case, this was the outcome of a majority vote on the part of assembled citizens that was cast directly on the question, generally after extensive, open, and public deliberation among them. The Athenians can thus meaningfully be said to have assumed political responsibility for this decision, which they themselves had to turn into action as armed members of a citizen army led by an elected and revocable military leadership. None of this can be said in the case of the United States, where the decision to wage war has routinely been made not *by*, but *for* and *in the name of* the people who had in fact no say in it, except in the sense of having chosen at some point prior this as opposed to the other candidate with their all-too-familiar, pleasant-sounding banalities, their often identical corporate backers, and their invariably similar results.

Unlike previous forms, then, modern democracy is characterized by a permanent and unbridgeable separation between state and society. This means, concretely, that it can never deliver what it promises, and that in its daily operations and strategic planning alike it must necessarily summon a host of ideological deceptions, some more sophisticated and effective than others. By means of another comparison with earlier forms we must consider an even more fundamental limitation of modern democracy that is bound up with its social foundation.

Primitive democracy was not an arbitrary construct. The absence of a separate state and the existence of substantial and cooperative freedom for all its members was a function of a more fundamental characteristic: the absence of class divisions in society. Operating at an abysmally low level of development of productive forces, they were not capable of producing a surplus that could in turn be appropriated individually. No layer of society could thus live off the labor of another, every one of its members had the same relation to the scarce means of production, and out of this primitive communism arose the norms and practices of primitive democracy. The rise of the state as an apparatus of rule and representation separate from society is associated with the later transition from food collection to food production, the possibility and then the reality of surplus production and its exploitative appropriation by a distinct social layer.

The impressive democratic institutions of Ancient Greece developed in teetering fashion on a social foundation riven by class divisions. The exploitation of slaves, who were completely excluded from political life, was the crucial economic factor in the functioning of those societies. But the vast majority of free citizens—farmers and artisans of various types—also had very tenuous hold on the economic independence that was the basis of their political status. Ancient democracy was not an ingenious invention agreed upon by generic and undifferentiated "people," but the product of a violent political revolution carried out by the lower classes in Athens. The first appearance of democracy onto the world scene signaled exactly the unprecedented political victory of the laboring poor over the wealthy and the powerful. And the question was not settled in one fell swoop. The tumultuous history of democracy in Athens and in the rest of the Greek world where it spread is little more than the permanent (now hidden, now open) struggle between the "many," seeking to protect it, and the "few," plotting to overthrow it. It is no accident that the great property-owning intellectuals who bequeathed us a rather tendentious literary account of Greek democracy were either viciously hostile to it (Plato) or at best manifested grudging tolerance for its less radical versions (Thucydides and Aristotle).

Liberalism without Democracy

We can now consider modern democracy from the standpoint of its historical origins and social foundations. The central issue to be examined is "liberal democracy," two distinct words that are typically pronounced in such a breathlessly compressed manner as if to emphasize their indissoluble unity. This unity is an ideological construct concealing the fact that the two, in reality, are not the same, did not arise simultaneously, and are not the product of the same social interests. Unpacking this construct will provide the historical signposts necessary to understand the ongoing disappearance of democracy.

It was the capitalist class, through its literary and political representatives, that introduced revolutionary conceptions of political equality in the seventeenth and eighteenth centuries. Having emerged within the framework of the old feudal system, this new social force began to recognize and assert more and more openly its distinct social interests, while at the same time persuasively presenting them in the universal language of the "people" and their natural and inalienable rights, to be protected by a suitably representative government. In the seventeenth century, the English Parliament began to fight the Crown on the basis of these revolutionary ideas. In the eighteenth century, the North American colonists reenacted and re-elaborated the same struggle in an anti-colonial vein, seeking genuine popular representation against the dictates of a distant king. In France, on the eve of its great revolution, the third estate proclaimed itself to be "everything" while denouncing priests and aristocrats, along with the arbitrary and absolutist ruler they propped up, as a parasitic excrescence to be removed.

In the course of these struggles, broad popular layers were indeed mobilized, initially finding the banner raised by the capitalist class inspiring, and ultimately playing a decisive role in their victory. However, in spite of the universal language through which these ideals were expressed, and even in spite of the conscious intentions of many of those who elaborated them, there were definite limitations to the kind of political equality the aspiring ruling class was prepared to put in place. Far from being an ephemeral political bias, these limitations were determined by the objective conditions through which the capitalist class accrued and expanded its social power and in turn by the political institutions necessary for its functioning and protection. It was one thing to proclaim equality at birth against the archaic and multitiered layers of feudal estates and privileges. It was quite a different matter to suffer, under pressure from the lower classes, more concrete and dangerous forms of political and social equality. These limitations could already be detected between the lines of the founding texts of liberalism. They were revealed more decisively in the course of the actual revolutionary struggles through which the ancien régime in its various forms was overthrown. It was exactly the alarming and unexpected bursts of independent action by the lower classes in these revolutions, threatening to spill over the capitalist conception of political equality, that clarified this question for the new ruling class in a way that ultimately defined a whole epoch: centuries of liberalism without democracy.

The victory of liberalism meant the institutionalization of certain principles such as the rule of law, representative government, individual rights, and the tangible presence of a constitutional framework, of parliaments and elections. This was a revolutionary and progressive victory over the old organization of state and society. In addition to constituting a valuable political inheritance that is presently being dismantled, liberalism can also be thought of as the necessary historical precondition for modern democracy. But it was not modern democracy, understood as universal suffrage, one person, one vote. Democracy did appear on the agenda in the great revolutions of the seventeenth and eighteenth centuries. But it was placed there, impertinently and unexpectedly, by the popular masses, only to be forcibly removed by the new ruling class.

England, as the birthplace of both capitalism and liberalism, is a particularly instructive case. In the struggle waged by Parliament against the Crown, the Levellers eventually emerged as the militant left wing of the revolution, based on the popular urban classes and on the rank and file of the New Model Army. Working out theoretically as well as practically the deeper implications of political equality, they raised a demand not just for liberalism, of which they were the most consistent and principled defenders, but for democracy as well, albeit in the incomplete form of male universal suffrage. They did so in 1647, by means of a proposed democratic constitution called the Agreement of the People and in a series of interventions at the debates held by the general council of the army at Putney. Giving voice to mounting frustrations directed no longer just against the monarchy and lords, but now also against a House of Commons elected and staffed only by men of property, and having already secured a significant democratic representation within the general council—Levellers participated as elected representatives of various military units and as invited civilian delegates—they powerfully articulated the case for a genuinely representative democratic government: "the poorest he that is in England hath a life to live, as the greatest he; . . . every man that is to live under a government ought first by his own consent to put himself under that government; . . . the poorest man in England is not at all bound . . . to that government that he hath not had a voice to put himself under."[1] There was more than a hint of a threat to this argument, and it was a credible one since the Levellers were not pious reformers but a politically organized faction of the revolutionary army. The response by Cromwell's Independents and the army grandees revealed the social interests they were determined to defend. Democracy had to be rejected because it constituted an existential threat to private property, and it was essential to preserve existing property qualifications restricting the right to vote to men of property.

This was not just an individual or episodic response. It expressed the attitude of the capitalist class toward democracy for an entire epoch across centuries and continents. Having won the debate, the Levellers were politically outmaneuvered and eventually crushed by Cromwell. His short-lived "Commonwealth" co-opted many of the radical liberal proposals advanced by the Levellers—abolition of the monarchy and of the House of Lords—but had no democratic content or control whatsoever. After Cromwell, the new ruling class restored the monarchy under the primacy of a manifestly bourgeois

Parliament. Thereafter came almost three centuries of liberalism without democracy. When universal suffrage finally came to England in 1928, it was the result of centuries of protracted struggles to expand the franchise by gradually loosening property as well as other kinds of qualifications. It was the working class, particularly organized in the Chartist movement, that played a leading role in this struggle. Their manifold and impressive initiatives to expand the franchise during the nineteenth century consistently crashed against the same arguments and interests that were raised by propertied men at Putney in the seventeenth century.

The essential features of this history were repeated during and following the great revolutions of the eighteenth century. The American Revolution also included independent and threatening outbursts by the lower classes. The specter of Shay's Rebellion haunted the Federalists, their liberal and antidemocratic "Papers," as well as their efforts to secure a strong government by means of a constitution. The subsequent disappearance of property qualifications in all the states of the new union in relatively quick succession went hand in hand with a disastrous racial bargain for which the Democratic Party served as political vehicle. Only white workers were granted the vote in an attempt to secure their allegiance in defense of slave and capitalist property. New restrictions on voting for blacks but also white workers after the failure of Reconstruction inaugurated another long phase in the struggle for democracy that was only ultimately successful in 1965. In this case, too, bracketing the issue of the massive distortion of the former through slavery and Jim Crow, as well as of the latter, for example, with the Electoral College, liberalism existed for centuries without democracy.

In France, the same pattern can be recognized, although compared to England it was punctuated there by more dramatic advances and reversals. On one side were the Jacobin short-lived enactment of male universal suffrage in 1793, in that case not coincidentally paired with the abolition of slavery in all the colonies, the revolutionary "social republic" of 1848, and the Paris Commune of 1871, which were the expression first of the political pressure and then of the more conscious and direct political initiative of the working class. On the other side were Thermidor, the Directory, Napoleon's first Empire, the Restoration, and Louis Napoleon Bonaparte's coup.

In sum, a sober examination of the origins and development of democracy should lead to a conclusion quite different from that of the dominant narrative. Capitalism is historically responsible for modern democracy, but only in the paradoxical sense that its most important and revolutionary product—the modern working class—successfully fought for it against the intransigent and often violent opposition of the capitalists and the state they controlled. Moreover, although the men of property at Putney and thereafter really did fear the coming of democracy as the antechamber to communism, their fears turned out to have been somewhat exaggerated. While the advent of democracy was undoubtedly a landmark achievement for the working class, it did not and could not offset the fact that the immense economic and social power of the capitalists would inevitably find ways to assert itself politically. Formal political equality, so long as the legal and economic bastion of private property remained in place, was destined at best to remain a defensive instrument for the working majority and at worst to turn into a demoralizing exercise in deception and futility. Modern democracy remained capitalist—the peculiar, contradictory, often unwanted and always unstable form taken by the political dictatorship of capital over those who are exploited by it. Capitalism, however, did not remain unchanged.

Imperialism against Democracy

Beginning with the last quarter of the nineteenth century, capitalism underwent a qualitative and epochal transformation. In its initial manufacturing stage, capitalism was generally characterized by free competition among small independent producers. Though as ideal types they stood as polar opposites, in the real movement of history monopoly grew organically and relentlessly out of competition. Monopoly, moreover, did not abolish competition once and for all but displaced it onto the higher plane of world economy and world politics, reactivating it in more explosive forms. The tendency toward monopoly is also connected to the rise of unprecedented levels of social inequality, as concentration, far from remaining insulated in the realm of production, also found a significant expression in the distribution of wealth and income. Although significantly curtailed in the period between World War II and the end of the 1970s due to an exceptional historical conjuncture, the growth of social inequality has since then been relentless, leading to a series of now well-known facts such as the three richest individuals in the United States reportedly owning more wealth than the poorest half of the population. These and many other staggering figures are the most significant culmination of a series of epochal economic changes, to which one could add the domination by finance capital and, related, brazen and socially destructive forms of parasitism.

It is not difficult to see how the economic changes associated with the rise of imperialism would have profound political repercussions. In the mid-nineteenth century, Marx famously registered the capitalist class's accomplished political dominance by describing the modern state as a committee for managing the common affairs of the whole bourgeoisie. This pronouncement, which no doubt cuts a series of important political and ideological mediations, is often regarded as an exaggeration. Yet the actual composition of the state today, even when it is nominally democratic, validates it. In the case of the American government, ordinary citizens are by now accustomed to the reality that many politicians and government officials come into office with or subsequently get to amass considerable personal fortunes. The link between the ruling class and the state is of course more than a mere matter of tax returns. It is an organic relationship that draws together financial as well as professional, political, and ideological threads. Government officers regularly come into such posts because of these manifold links and develop them further while in office. There are, at any rate, myriad subtle and not-so-subtle devices by which the capitalist class "owns" the state without necessarily having to staff it themselves. From the well-documented "revolving door" between the public and private sectors, to campaign finance laws, to the corporate control and immense concentration of the media, economic power systematically finds a political expression. It is this thoroughly capitalist state, not the mythical construction presented as the mere executor of the people's democratic will, that ruthlessly protects its own national bourgeoisie at home and projects its interests abroad, leading to one imperialist crime after another.

The long-term incompatibility of imperialism and democracy was diagnosed long ago. Writing of the eve of World War II in an international landscape rife with totalitarian states, Leon Trotsky explained: "Competition had to have certain liberties, a liberal atmosphere, a regime of democracy, of commercial cosmopolitanism. Monopoly needs as authoritative a government as possible, tariff walls, "its own" sources of raw materials and arenas of marketing. . . . The last word in the disintegration of monopolistic capital is fascism."[2] These words echo all the major, sinister developments of the present, allowing us to return to the ongoing disappearance of democracy.

Democracy beyond Democracy

Democracy only began to come about after centuries of liberalism and against the determined opposition of the capitalist class. Even in its accomplished form it necessarily remained bourgeois—a state of formal political equality resting unsteadily upon a social foundation of systematic inequality.

But just as the working class began to win the battle for democracy, the objective transformation of capitalism along imperialist lines began to make even formal political equality and capitalist representative democracy less and less tenable. Caught between these two long historical waves, modern democracy never really came about in a finished and stable form. Its present state of decay is thus not arbitrary or conjunctural and cannot be altered by well-meaning politicians or alchemic reforms. It flows out of objective and long-brewing conditions such as unprecedented levels of social inequality that are simply incompatible with political democracy and the domination of economic and political life by a narrow and parasitic social layer.

Democracy is disappearing and in a certain historical sense deserves its fate. But should democracy definitively expire in the manner that is now underway, by the actions of criminals and arsonists occupying the highest reaches of power, it will undoubtedly drag humanity down with it. The history sketched out above shows that there is a powerful constituency for its defense, in spite of being routinely excluded from the prevailing narrative of modern democracy, as well as scorned as a social and political subject in academia: the working class. But for the working class and anyone else wishing to continue the fight for democracy, it is too late to defend it by merely trying to preserve the little that is left of it in its capitalist form. Entirely new forms of rule and representation are necessary, precisely as was the case for the capitalist class in its initial struggle to secure political power. Through these new forms, democracy can be massively expanded to the point of altogether transcending its historical limitations and indeed its character as a kind of political rule over people. To conclude by returning to the epigraph at the beginning of this chapter, there is another, entirely progressive way in which democracy could disappear. As a specific state form, certifying and enforcing the division of society into antagonistic classes, democracy can find its worthy place in the museum of political antiquities, being finally reabsorbed into an at last genuinely free and equal society that will reproduce its prehistoric traits at the highest level of development of our productive forces.

Fake News

On the morning of September 11, 2001, I learned about the attacks on the World Trade Center while walking across a college campus on the way to journalism class. When I arrived, we spent the period crowded around a big screen TV watching cycles of cable news footage of burning buildings and the second plane crash. In the weeks and months that followed, I spent hours glued to cable news programming of night-vision bombings from cameras on the rooftops of U.S. military strongholds, with few analyses of the impact those bombings were having on the people on the ground. I learned that coverage from the most prominent U.S. news networks and newspapers was serving to continue the spectacle that had begun with the imagery of fire, destruction, and suffering—in other words, terror. Many critics refer to such coverage as "disaster porn."

Rather than offer thorough examinations of the historical context behind what happened on 9/11 and what diplomatic options U.S. officials might consider in responding to the events, most coverage by establishment media helped beat the drum for war by uncritically repeating the Bush administration's claims. In doing so, many reporters suspended or disregarded the rulebook on professional journalism, which typically requires a higher standard of evidence than unsubstantiated claims by official sources to report something as fact. The most infamous and blatant example of this error was the claim that Iraq possessed "weapons of mass destruction" (WMDs), a claim initially reported by the *New York Times* (*NYT*). Rather than independently verifying the claim, as the rules of journalism require, many other media outlets repeated the misinformation as if it were fact.[1]

Nevertheless, thanks to some reporters and officials who remained willing to offer a reality check, the American public would later learn that this fear of Iraqi WMDs was entirely unfounded.[2] Instead of being grounded in fact, the claims were part of a propaganda strategy by the Bush administration, which sought to use the agenda-setting power of establishment media to generate widespread support for war against Iraq. Notwithstanding the endless array of "collateral damage," the strategy worked. On March 20, 2003, the United States began what it called "Operation Iraqi Freedom," a phrase that was widely parroted across television news.[3]

Less than two months later, on May 1, 2003, President George W. Bush gave a televised speech from a U.S. aircraft carrier. Standing in front of a banner that read "MISSION ACCOMPLISHED," Bush opened his speech by stating that "Major combat operations in Iraq have ended."[4] This statement flew in the face of the facts: the vast majority of people killed in the war died after the speech, and as I write this essay, the war still rages on.

Nearly twelve years after publishing the false assertion about WMDs in Iraq, the *NYT* was once again complicit in a disinformation campaign built upon questionable research conducted by investigative journalist and Breitbart editor Peter Schweizer.[5] The source of the *NYT*'s error was similar to the one it made in the lead-up to the Iraq War, although this time it bolstered Donald Trump's bid for the White House. It failed to uncover the inaccuracies in Schweizer's reporting, which promoted a conspiracy theory connecting Hillary Clinton to a uranium mining company owned by the Russian state. Instead, the *NYT* repeated Schweizer's claims in bold, sensational headlines while concealing contradictory details later in the story where readers were less likely to venture. Other "liberal" establishment media outlets such as the *Washington Post*, as well as the centrist organizations such as the Associated Press, followed similar patterns.[6]

It may be that these outlets were tricked into spreading propaganda. But their own habits and biases also made them vulnerable. Of course, this is hardly news, since establishment media have long played a central role in the transference of propaganda to the masses. In fact, Edward Herman and Noam Chomsky's propaganda model "suggests that the 'societal purpose' of the media is to inculcate and defend the economic, social, and political agenda of privileged groups that dominate the domestic society and the state." Rather than asserting that publishers do this explicitly and intentionally, Herman and Chomsky describe how it occurs via the "selection of topics, distribution of concerns, framing of issues, filtering of information, emphasis and tone, and by keeping debate within the bounds of acceptable premises."[7]

By today's standards, each of the above examples might rightly be labeled "fake news." Yet, the term is so overused that its meaning seems to have gone the way of the American public—filled with affect, outrage, and perhaps irrevocably fractured. Nevertheless, the term plays an important and necessarily contested role in the contemporary lexicon. This chapter offers a critical assessment of the discourse of fake news—its history and the political contexts in which it is used. It concludes with a warning about the shortcomings of many prevalent responses and a call for a more critical approach to news media writ large.

The Many Meanings of "Fake News"

Shortly after the start of the Iraq War, Google began providing information about which terms users entered into the search engine. There was relatively little interest in the term "fake news" back in 2004. And searches for the phrase remained marginal for over a decade until November 2016, when Donald Trump was elected president of the United States. Thereafter, interest in the term skyrocketed, eventually climaxing in early 2017 following Trump's inauguration and anti-press rhetoric and again in early 2018 following a surge of activity in Southeast Asia. Although searches for the phrase peaked in October 2018, just in time for the Brazilian presidential election, they remain significant today (see figure 2).[8]

FIGURE 2. Google Trends data on searches for "fake news" worldwide.

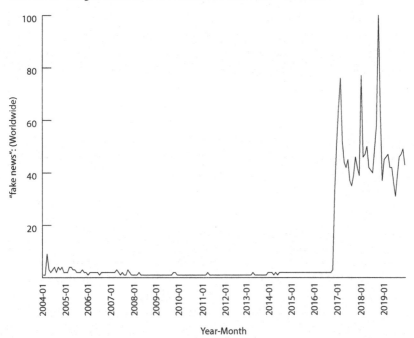

Trump most certainly did not invent fake news—neither the phrase nor the phenomenon. But perhaps he did reinvent it. Between his inauguration on January 20, 2017, and the time of this writing, Trump has written "fake news" over 760 times on Twitter alone.[9] Considering this alongside Trump's countless references in other public (media) appearances, not to mention the recent proliferation of false or highly misleading reports made to look like news, it is no surprise that interest in the phrase has spiked. *Collins Dictionary*, which defines "fake news" as "false, often sensational, information disseminated under the guise of news reporting," declared "fake news" to be their 2017 word of the year due to its "ubiquitous presence."[10]

But what practical meaning does the phrase carry? Predictably, it depends on whom you ask. Donald Trump and his disciples employ "fake news" as a way to discredit fact-based news that clashes with their worldview. This is in stark contrast to the many meanings ascribed to the phrase since it first appeared in the academic and journalistic literature over a century ago. These have included news satire, news parody, news fabrication, photo manipulation, advertising and public relations (pr), and propaganda.[11] While in the contemporary lexicon it is commonly used to describe fabricated information circulating through social media, there is reason to question the term's utility given its shrouded and increasingly nefarious meaning.

I would be remiss not to call attention to the deep irony underlying this rift. Whereas Trump has made a habit of levying charges of "fake news" against reporters and organizations that draw conclusions he dislikes, he himself has been the foremost generator of it. According to an April 2020 estimate from the *Washington Post*, Trump made at least eighteen thousand false or misleading claims since the start of his presidency.[12] And, in a strange twist, Trump has even suggested that he invented the phrase.[13] It is this sort of absurdity that has led some to caution against using the phrase because it has become "a mechanism by which the powerful can clamp down upon, restrict, undermine and circumvent the free press"—both in the United States and across the globe.[14]

"Fake News" Goes Global

While the discourse of fake news may be inextricably tied to the forty-fifth president of the United States, the phrase also carries broad significance outside the country. According to Google Trends data, the three countries with an even greater public interest in the phenomenon are the Philippines, Singapore, and Brazil.

There is good reason for Filipinos to be concerned about fake news. Theirs is a highly connected society that is rife with Internet trolls spouting disinformation—that is, intentionally false or misleading information meant to sow confusion. Such threats to the legitimacy of democratic discourse come not only from outside amateurs but also from political insiders and communications professionals. As in many other countries, in the Philippines it is common for PR professionals to bolster support for political candidates, celebrities, and corporations using thousands of fake accounts on Facebook and Twitter. Many share positive messages about their clients in an attempt to sway public opinion. This strategy has become increasingly common in recent years and was even used to help elect Filipino president Rodrigo Duterte. Armed with proof of concept, one PR firm has expressed interest in taking their operations to other nations, such as Singapore.[15]

Both the Philippines and Singapore passed legislation aimed at curbing the spread of fake news. But critics have insisted that the policies may be used to crack down on free speech.[16] While it may be unlikely that elected officials will use their newly established powers to put a stop to practices that helped them get elected in the first place, it is within their purview to demand the revision or removal of legitimate reporting, as well as other content shared on social media, regardless of its origin—foreign or domestic. The irony is that these policies do little to address the threats posed by government-run propaganda campaigns. Instead, they are used as justification to further the reaches of authoritarianism in the name of protecting democracy.

Social media platforms have undoubtedly made strides, however narrow, in their efforts to limit the spread of propaganda, fake news, and other forms of problematic information in various national contexts. At the same time, they continue to allow, encourage, and profit from such campaigns. For example, Twitter played an active role in helping Chinese government officials spread disinformation.[17] The company later identified and removed such content while enforcing their policies barring state-run media from promoting content on its platform. Yet Twitter and Facebook—another preferred outlet for Chinese propaganda campaigns—continue to allow U.S. state-funded media organizations such as Voice of America and Radio Free Europe to advertise on their platforms.[18]

A cloud of fake news also hangs over Brazil after right-wing populist Jair Bolsonaro was elected president in 2018 amid a flurry of problematic information. Prior to the election, Bolsonaro supporters, including many business leaders, paid marketing firms "to spread tens of thousands of attack ads" using encrypted messaging services such as the Facebook-owned WhatsApp.[19]

Given the app's reach—WhatsApp is reportedly used by two-thirds of Brazilian voters—and the lack of transparency in how mass messages are spread, the strategy proved effective in making efforts backed by private interests look like grassroots actions. Pro-Bolsonaro activists also relied on YouTube—another widely popular social media platform that reaches more viewers than "all but one TV channel" in the country—to spread his message.[20] Beyond providing a platform for creators of original content, YouTube's algorithms helped amplify and promote their false, misleading, and otherwise sensational content, ultimately playing a key role in the radicalization of Brazil's public sphere.[21]

In the American context, where government officials' power to regulate published speech is limited, charges of "fake news" are more often debated in the court of public opinion and in the private board rooms of Silicon Valley. Nevertheless, if social media companies' operating definition of what constitutes fake or harmful content remains opaque and subjective and continues to carve out exceptions for powerful violators, then their enforcement will likely reify many of the biases built into the twentieth-century media system. That is, they would continue to disproportionately amplify influential voices while doing little to address professional media's proclivity for propaganda.[22]

Consequences of "Fake News"

There is little doubt that the rise of fake news matters. Nevertheless, questions about its effects, like the phenomena themselves, are inevitably complicated. Even if one rarely comes into contact with the most extreme forms of false or misleading information, its sheer existence in today's information ecosystem is bound to sow confusion among the public. Such threats increase when there are powerful entities actively working to erode the public's trust in (the possibility of) a discernable reality.

In 2002, nearly a year before the U.S. invasion of Iraq, and years before the birth of social media, Karl Rove—the same Bush administration official who orchestrated the "Mission Accomplished" moment—spoke to a reporter about the difference between those who act irrespective of what is true and those who belong to "the reality-based community."[23] In response to the reporter's insistence in the importance of decision-making based on empirical facts, Rove maintained: "That's not the way the world really works anymore. . . . We're an empire now, and when we act, we create our own reality. And while you're studying that reality—judiciously, as you will—we'll act again, creating other new realities, which you can study too, and that's how things will sort out. We're history's actors . . . and you, all of you, will be left to just study what we do."[24] If one looks back on this moment in history, some two decades ago, it is hard to deny its prescience. It was a necessary precursor to Trump administration spokespeople claiming that they have their own "alternative facts," or that "truth isn't truth."[25] Together, these moments in history offer a sobering reminder that the era of fake news has been decades in the making and is inevitably rooted in a degeneration of the democratic process.

To be clear, those practicing post-truth politics are still in the minority. But establishment media have amplified their reach. According to Lexis Nexis, 6,647 English-language news stories used the phrase "alternative facts" in the month following its initial utterance. Even if a majority were casting a negative light on the assertion, the proliferation of such claims, like the discourse of fake news itself, disturbs the potential for a common belief in facts and further disarms the public of the tools necessary to do the work of democracy.

This raises a fundamental question about the broader consequences surrounding the discourse of fake news. On the one hand, increased public attention to the issue may appear to foster greater media literacy. On the other hand, given that "fake news" has been used interchangeably to describe many different kinds of information—from demonstrably false, to misleading, to factually correct but undesirable—the concept may also foster narrow understandings of media manipulation or further encourage some to continue practicing relatively uncritical approaches to news consumption. That is, the discourse of fake news places unnecessary emphasis on extraordinary types of misleading information while obscuring the more mundane limitations of everyday news. Furthermore, given the additional meaning ascribed to it by Trump and his contemporaries, use of the phrase runs the risk of perpetuating the narrative of the press as the "enemy of the people" while reaffirming the public's allegiance to particular thought communities.[26]

Even if news media remain committed to fact-based reporting, many establishment outlets inevitably feed their audiences heavy doses of classic propaganda that uses emotion and a range of more or less truthful claims to shape perceptions and promote political ideals. One glaring example can be found in the bulk of news coverage from establishment media in the wake of 9/11. As critical news analyses have shown, news reporters were—and still are—far too reliant on government officials to produce independent journalism.[27] In other words, by subtly excluding and at times actively discrediting outside perspectives, even nonpartisan news media participate in the construction of a national echo chamber. More troublingly, explicitly partisan news media also work with other political actors to *undermine* some of the foundational principles of deliberative discourse.[28] For example, similar to Fox News' infamous motto, "fair and balanced," politicians' levying charges of "fake news" to stave off criticism erodes public trust in the discourse of truth, as well as in the mainstream institutions that uphold it.

At the risk of sounding overly clichéd or alarmist, this is precisely the effect of "newspeak" and "doublethink," made famous in George Orwell's *1984*. As Orwell said: "To know and not to know, to be conscious of complete truthfulness while telling carefully constructed lies, to hold simultaneously two opinions which cancelled out, knowing them to be contradictory and believing in both of them, to use logic against logic, to repudiate morality while laying claim to it, to believe that democracy was impossible and that the Party was the guardian of democracy. . . . Even to understand the word 'doublethink' involved the use of doublethink."[29] It would not be difficult to imagine a similar description of "fake news." For starters, the phrase is the epitome of contradiction. If "news" is defined as "information about a recently changed situation or a recent event," and "information" consists of "facts," then there is, by all normative standards, no such thing as fake news.[30] Its very conception requires a post-truth mindset. By this standard, Trump's frequent use of the phrase as an affront to factual reporting may be seen as peak (or rather, nadir) doublethink.

It is tempting to consider the potential implications of this as a battle having been won or lost by either side (i.e., democracy versus authoritarianism). But the reality is that having such a bitter fight over what constitutes truth already spells a loss for democracy. Yet such challenges, like claims to truth themselves, are rarely as straightforward as they may seem. Although the current moment has many extreme characteristics, history is full of examples where leaders disregarded truths that were inconvenient. The real question, then, is whether such rhetoric has lasting, damning effects on public discourse, or whether the public can reorient itself around a shared set of standards, if not values.

While the discourse of "fake news" indeed may have ushered in a new kind of crisis for democracies around the world, the moment has been many years in the making. From the days of newspapers printing "yellow journalism" to those of broadcasters from elite institutions (whether state or corporate) spewing propaganda, publics have long had reason to question what they see in the news. And indeed, they have. According to Gallup, while Americans' trust in mass media peaked at nearly 70 percent following the triumphs of investigative reporting in the Watergate era, it has trended downward since. After reaching its lowest point at 32 percent in 2016, trust grew to 41 percent by 2019.[31] Trust in the news has also waned across the globe, down to 42 percent across thirty-eight countries.[32] Although perhaps not disastrous, when seen alongside the decline of trust in most other public institutions, the trend spells trouble for the future of anything resembling self-governance. Democratic societies rely not only on the news to provide the public with the information necessary to guide their decisions, but also on a faith in other institutions central to individuals' participation in public life. Given the power of news media to construct reality, significant losses for one could well mean the loss of all.

"Fake News" in the Trump Era (and Beyond?)

If news media are powerful because of their ability to tell people what to think about, then one of their greatest failures may be their complicity in the former president's attempts to set the public agenda. Indeed, while many called on media professionals to "suspend normal relations" with the Trump administration due to their history of deceit and combativeness,[33] most establishment news providers continued to allow him to play the role of agenda-setter-in-chief.

There may be no better example than Trump's use of Twitter. Given that the medium is open to the public, and given how entrenched professional journalists are on it, it has proven to be a convenient platform for opinion leaders to shape public conversation and, therefore, consciousness. One particularly egregious instance of Trump's use of social media to direct the attention of media and the public was his April 12, 2019, tweet of a propaganda video splicing together a clip from a speech by Representative Ilhan Omar with video footage of the terrorist attacks on 9/11.[34] Whether reporting on the sensational post itself, or the numerous responses to it, media outlets from across the world played into Trump's hands by increasing the attention given to one of his favorite wedge issues: immigration and race politics.

Consider, also, Trump's visits to El Paso, Texas, and Dayton, Ohio, in the aftermath of the August 2019 mass shootings. Rather than face more public scrutiny over his role in stoking fear of immigrants, or for capitalizing on the moment to further his political goals, Trump administration officials blocked reporters from attending the president's visits with victims and their families. As a result, reporting on the event was a vague, incomplete narrative that sheltered him from the truth about the power of his words.[35] Indeed, a report by ABC News "identified at least 54 criminal cases where Trump was invoked in direct connection with violent acts, threats of violence or allegations of assault."[36] While the report was run by a prominent network news outlet, the story, let alone the broader issues it raises regarding the consequences of Trump's rhetoric, received scant attention on their (or other networks') national broadcasts.

92   The day after Trump's private visit with victims, I found myself in New York City, where I paid a visit to the National September 11 Memorial and the Statue of Liberty. Less than a week later, Ken Cuccinelli, the acting director of U.S. Citizenship and Immigration Services under the Trump administration, gave an interview with National Public Radio (NPR) where he announced a new policy restricting access to citizenship for legal immigrants in need of public assistance. In doing so, he suggested the inscription on the Statue of Liberty be revised accordingly: "Give me your tired and your poor who can stand on their own two feet and who will not become a public charge."[37]

Each of these examples illustrates how white supremacists and other extremists systematically manipulate media in order to steer coverage in a particular direction and to broadcast their rhetoric to mass audiences. Thus, the real threat of fake news is less about foreign amateurs than about domestic professionals seeking to distract or mislead us for personal gain. While we should reject the premise that fact-based news can be considered fake if it does not align with one's own beliefs, we cannot ignore the troubling reality with which we all must live (at least for now): there is great power in deciding what is seen as legitimate news, establishment institutions have lost much of that power, and public discourse is unquestionably, albeit often imperceptibly, skewed because of it.

However untenable this situation may be, news media providers might take it as an opportunity to address the criticisms of their role as purveyors of propaganda and also to increase transparency regarding their professional practices and values. Such openness will not only help repair trust but may also encourage self-reflexivity regarding the limits of contemporary approaches to news making and the potential for greater effectiveness in their work as arbiters of democracy. For their part, the public would be better served by resisting the temptation to direct our attention toward the newest and most extreme forms of problematic information and to focus instead on the promises and perils of the news media writ large, however mundane they may be. A failure to do so will inevitably reinforce the zeitgeist of oversimplified understandings of media and political bias, further insulate many from the "reality-based community," and leave us even more vulnerable to manipulation from within establishment institutions and beyond.

Life

President Trump has been the most pro-life president in modern history.
—Penny Nance, Concerned Women for America

The year I started high school, which was also the year Title IX became law, and the Equal Rights Amendment (ERA), which would
have guaranteed all Americans equal legal rights regardless of sex,
passed the Senate and was sent to the states for ratification, and the
Supreme Court ruled that it was unconstitutional to prohibit the sale
of contraceptives to single persons, and *Ms.* magazine was launched;
which was the same year Bob Woodward and Carl Bernstein reported
a financial link between the Watergate break-in and CREEP (Committee for the Re-election of the President), and the Justice Department secretly agreed not to break up International Telephone and
Telegraph Corporation (ITT Inc.) in a pending antitrust suit when
the latter donated $400,000 to the GOP's reelection coffers, and the
antiwar Democrat George McGovern lost the presidential election in
a landslide to Richard Nixon; and the rail workers and coal miners in
the United Kingdom went on strike; and severe droughts desiccated
Chinese and Soviet grain, and a tropical storm named for a woman
forced thousands of people in my neighboring states to flee their
homes; and "American Pie" was the song we heard most often as we
filed into the school cafeteria while the Dow Jones Industrial Average
closed above the one thousand mark for the first time in history, and
my fellow Americans, who represented 6 percent of the world's population, consumed a third of the world's energy output; and a human
skull was found in Kenya, casting doubt on the age and geographic
origins of humankind; and a California legal scholar trying to deter-
mine why reports of rape were rising pondered whether "hostility to
women's increasing acquisition of freedom ha[d] led to an increase in
forcible rape"[1]—which all happened in the same year that my mother
was able to secure enough clerical work to afford a basement studio in
a low-income apartment complex called the Stewart House (a huge
step forward for us after a crippling series of nervous breakdowns
had forced her to move us back into her parents' home, where our
grandfather had, more than once, tried to touch our breasts when he
tucked us in at night, as he had likely done to her), which happened

also to be the year *Seventeen* magazine ran a cover story with the question "Would a Woman President Really Make a Difference?," and I got straight As and auditioned for the school play and dieted so strenuously that my period had yet to start—in this watershed year of progressive legislation and antiwar marches and end runs around democracy and epic droughts and storms and floods and my feverish self-improvement schemes—my best friend Ellie got pregnant.[2]

It would take me several years to see how these seemingly disparate events were connected, and how just as feminism was finally challenging white patriarchy with laws that could give women and girls some sovereignty over their own lives, a corrupt political party revealed its playbook, signaling the kind of moves it would make again and again and again to stay in power.

Ellie was fourteen years old.

From the moment we'd met in junior high I'd loved and revered her fiercely, crediting even her most offhand remarks as wisdom and prophesy. Tall, slender, worldly, fearless, what a figure she cut as she roamed the halls of our giant factory of a school in her tailored tweed bellbottoms, all cheekbones and elbows and swinging honey brown hair, her intelligent blue-gray eyes staring down all forces large and small that deigned to diminish her. I never guessed that she was lonely and scared: that in her hour of need she believed no one would come to her aid, not even me.

The idea of getting pregnant at fourteen was, for me—and here only one word will do—inconceivable. My whole life I'd been on a mission to break free of my oppressive family and become a writer, which could only happen if I kept my grades up and got a scholarship to a good college in a distant state. I doubted I'd even marry or have children. I was so terrified of getting stuck, trapped in Cleveland with my mentally ill, chain-smoking mother that I avoided any scenario that could derail me. Every day, it seemed, another girl was dropping out to have a kid—in fact, the class of '75 would shrink from a thousand to 789 by senior year—so I made a vow to wait until after I graduated to even think about having sex. By age fourteen, my sum total of sexual experience consisted of two closed-mouth kisses: the first in front of twenty other kids during a game of spin the bottle at someone's birthday party, the second by a cute boy who used to stand outside his house and talk to me when I walked past with the dog.

If Ellie had confided in me I would like to think I would have found a way to help her, but what would that have entailed? Abortion wasn't legal in

Ohio. The other options—keeping the child or putting it up for adoption—meant carrying the baby to term, which would mean dropping out with only a ninth-grade education, or dropping out and coming back later with a target on her back. And so I became an accomplice to her silence, willing myself not to look too closely at her body as it changed before my eyes.

Flash forward forty-five years.

The Women's March of 2017—inspired by our collective outrage that a misogynistic racist xenophobic con man ran a platform in which those traits were spun as strengths and managed to win (even while losing by nearly three million popular votes)—began at the intersection of Independence and 3rd in Washington, D.C.

As one who tends to read symbolism into everything, I reflected on how I never expected to still be fighting for *independence* at this age on this, my *third* march in the capital for women's rights (the first in 1989, when Bush Senior sided with Missouri's anti-abortion laws as they made their way to the Supreme Court, the second in 1992, when *Casey vs. Planned Parenthood* was pending in the Supreme Court). I had thought (naively, I suppose) that when fights got won, they stayed won.

And then there's that word, "intersection." The planning for the event got off to a rocky start when the women who launched it inadvertently appropriated the name for a landmark civil rights march and meanwhile managed to make the protest seem like a white lady thing. And so, under new multiracial, multigenerational leadership, the organizers adopted Kimberlé Crenshaw's word, "intersectionality," which speaks to the overlapping ways women experience marginalization and oppression.[3] This overarching concept means that we can't pluck each injustice out individually without taking into consideration how race and class and sexual orientation and gender identification and age and disability play their parts. It means that while all women get paid less than white men, and some of us earn even less because of our race or ethnicity. It means that while all of us have reason to fear sexual violence, some of us, such as LGBTQ and trans women, are disproportionally more likely to be assaulted or become the victim of a hate crime. And yet the guiding principle animating the march, "intersectionality," wasn't recognized as an actual word by Merriam-Webster until April 2017, perhaps the moment in history when mainstream America at long last understood that the broad, multiracial, economically diverse coalition we needed to build to fight Trumpism—that is, white supremacist xenophobic patriarchal capitalism—demanded of us that we seek common cause with people whose life stories may differ vastly from our own.[4]

Which brings me to the word "life," a word that fueled the religious Trump supporters who found him morally lacking but approved of his anti-choice rhetoric. For me, and, I imagine, the more than seven million people who marched on this day across the globe—in American cities and villages in the largest single-day protest in U.S. history, from Antarctica to Paris to Nairobi to Buenos Aires—this fight to have a say about how we conduct our lives—was and remains deeply personal.

As it was and is for Ellie, who was marching with me.

At first, I thought she was just gaining weight. I almost said something dozens of times. And then one day before gym class she watched me watch her snap herself into her onesie gym uniform. Her bone-thin arms, slender legs, and swollen belly. She saw my question hovering in the air between us and intercepted it with a question of her own. "Hey," she said casually. "Can I borrow a nickel for the Kotex machine?"

Then, reading the mix of relief and confusion that also must have spilled across my face, she went on to tell me how she was suffering from a liver infection that had caused her to "bloat," but she had a doctor's appointment and would get better soon.

For the rest of that school year I told that story loyally, defiantly, to anyone who dared to gossip about my friend to my face. "She has an infection!" I would insist, deeply aggrieved. "How dare you say that about my friend?"

I don't know if she really had an appointment lined up, but I do know that when she came back after Christmas break, she was no longer pregnant. Decades would pass before she told me the story. How she worked out like a maniac, running hard, jumping, pushing herself in gym class, trying to bring on her period. How she wore loose-fitting clothes and hid her pregnancy even from her own mother, who didn't confront Ellie until two weeks before she went into premature labor, when they made arrangements for her to give the baby up for adoption. How the hospital nurses pushed her down brusquely when she sat up and asked for water, treating her like she was some kind of criminal or rabid animal, a pariah unworthy of dignity, civility, or even the simplest of explanations as to what was happening to her body as she gave birth to a baby girl at thirty-two weeks, two weeks shy of her fifteenth birthday.

The baby died later that night. Ellie wasn't permitted to mourn her child's death or the death of her own childhood. Her mother never spoke of the incident again.

At the Women's March, which we couldn't really call a march at the beginning because all half a million of us seemed to be standing in place, elbow to elbow—college boys with pink pussy hats and signs saying "My sons will know the meaning of consent," women of every age with signs saying "This pussy grabs back" or "Vaginas brought you into this world, and vaginas will vote you out," extended multigenerational families, a mixed-race couple with ACLU pins, dads carrying baby girls and sandwich board signs reading "The future is still female," signs that said "I'm still with her" with arrows pointing in every direction, Black Lives Matter activists, women in hijabs, an elderly black man who told me he was marching for his five sisters, saying "Civil rights for all!"—Ellie carried a poster painted by her artist brother-in-law, James: Trump's orange head transfigured into a pile of crap with the caption, "Corruption Stinks." Many people stopped to compliment James on the sign he carried: Trump as a small dog with a collar on Putin's lap. I would use the lapdog and turd piles as guideposts whenever I got separated from my group.

An African American minister from New York told me she had come to the March to make friends. "This is a loving place to be," she said. I felt it too: the joy of finding common cause with so many different people, the one solace of this horrific historical moment. A metro worker had told me that the day before, by 1 p.m., 185,000 people had come through the turnstiles. Today, by 1 p.m., she had counted 485,000. (Later, when Trump's Whitehouse spokesperson Sean Spicer addressed the press, we expected to hear something bland and pro forma about what a "great" democracy we live in where we have this right to assemble en masse, but instead the gaslighting that was to be the trademark of that White House began at once with Spicer disputing the reported crowd size for Trump's inauguration and accusing the media of lying.)

As the crowd began to move again, we shouted, "We need a leader, not a creepy tweeter." We passed a delegation from Mexico on a raised stand with the banner: "We're not all rapists." It was unseasonably warm for January, and I took off my jacket; the green January grass was a reminder of what else is at stake.

When we were kids, Ellie wanted to become an organic farmer, but the only crop science classes at her college were geared toward industrial agriculture. Instead, she became an obstetrics nurse, the compassionate kind she should have had. She feeds her family with her backyard vegetables and has plans to plant a permaculture garden.

Not long after Ellie's crisis, our friend Eva got pregnant too. Her furious but pragmatic mother arranged for her to fly to New York, terminate the pregnancy, and fly home the same day. *Roe v. Wade* had just passed, but Ohio didn't have a clinic yet, whereas abortion had been legal in New York since 1970. At the last minute, a college-age friend of the family volunteered to accompany her so that at least she wouldn't have to go alone. Eva was scared, but by then the clinic was a well-oiled machine with its own airport shuttle. Eva doesn't remember much about the procedure itself except that afterward she decided to become a resource for others. A boy she knew said, "Aren't you worried you'll get a reputation for being too easy if you broadcast your story?" This had never occurred to Eva—that going through this harrowing thing should be a source of private shame for her and not a useful story that could help other people. To this day she credits Planned Parenthood, which provided the referral to the New York clinic, with saving her life, along with the lives of her children—the ones she eventually had when she got out of the terrible relationship she had with her high school boyfriend and met the man she has been married to ever since.

By the time our friend Maggie got pregnant, abortion was available in Ohio, but her devout Catholic mother sent her to St. Vincent de Paul's home for unwed mothers. In the convent, Maggie was made to scrub floors and toilets and do laundry in exchange for room and board. Contact with the outside world was forbidden except for a few minutes once a week, when the girls were permitted to use the lobby pay phone. On one of these phone calls she told her best male friend where she was; no one knew why she'd left school, and they were worried. He came for her in the middle of the night. Jailbreak: that's what they all called it. She had to scale a fence. Eventually Maggie's mom sent her to live with an aunt in a distant city, where she gave birth the same month Ellie and I graduated from high school. It was a closed adoption, and Maggie never saw her son. She had no say. It was all decided for her by her mother, who never forgave her for the shame she had caused the family and who, incidentally, had never explained sex to her daughter, or contraception, or the myriad of ways a girl's life could go off the rails.

Although by then Cleveland had a free clinic where girls could get birth control, it was way out on the East Side. To get there you needed a car. Boys could get condoms from older brothers, but most kids relied on the withdrawal method, as in, "he pulled out just in time." All my friends had the same problem—little or no access to contraception, and mothers who, victims of patriarchy themselves, made them feel lingering shame and self-hatred about what had happened to them. At a gathering last summer when Maggie shared her story with us for the first time, she wept as she told us how her mother refused to speak of these events ever again, not even as she lay dying decades later.

I never want a girl of any age to feel as alone as Ellie and Maggie did. Or, as Eva said when we spoke recently, to "be made to feel that because a sperm met one of her eggs she now has to give up herself, her present, her dreams, her health, for an imagined-but-not-alive thing. While the sperm providers legislate away more of her humanity."

We can't go back.

Eva's story ends differently because she never felt shame, only anger that girls and women even now are made to feel shame. She's still grateful that at age fifteen she had the power and support to make a choice.

As I was, when it happened to me.

My boyfriend and I had been together for a year and a half when a con-dom broke on the worst day possible, and I *knew*. I was twenty-three, the age my mother was when she had a back-alley abortion. In no way was I ready, emotionally or financially, to have a child. A recent college graduate, I was living in Seattle on unemployment benefits of $300 a month, having lost my job as a technical writer during Reagan's recession of 1981. I was lucky I could find an abortion provider nearby and that no right-to-life activists tried to stop me. Operation Rescue's sit-ins and blockades wouldn't begin for another five years, and the murders of doctors, receptionists, security guards, and clinic escorts—or, as Eva says, "violent deaths of living humans inflicted by terrorists who say they are 'pro-life'"—wouldn't start until the 1990s.

While blue Washington State has continued to promote reproductive health access to all its citizens (although a bill ensuring continued protection under Trump snagged when more conservative members of the state legisla-ture balked at providing free birth control to undocumented immigrants), purple Ohio has long been a battleground state for reproductive justice. My friend Lily, also from this same circle of friends, likes to tell the story of the time she got out of her car to chat with some pro-life demonstrators who had gathered to prevent women from entering an abortion clinic in Cleveland. "Hi there," she said. "I hear that you all like babies. Would you like to come with me? I'm going to Metro Hospital to hold some addicted little babies. Did you know that babies who are going through withdrawal symptoms need to be held by volunteers, and people who love babies sign up for shifts? Come with me. We need more people like you who love children to comfort them. Come on! Let's go! Let's hold some babies." The pro-life protesters, alarmed, began praying over the rosaries. She observed them wryly for a moment and then she said, "Wow. You kind of remind me of the Taliban."

In 2000, when an essay I wrote about my abortion was published, I found myself the subject of a right-wing chat room, maliciously mocked by people who hadn't read the piece, just a paragraph-long excerpt an antichoice reader had quoted.[5] These hundred or so people took evident pleasure in describing how I would be sodomized and branded as hell flames consumed my body. In hell, they said, I would join Hitler, my fellow architect of mass genocide. Their eroticized sadistic glee over what would happen to my naked body on fire made me ponder anew the meaning of that label, "pro-life."

Many researchers have pointed out that restricting access to abortion does not lower a nation's abortion rates—it simply makes women less equal, less able to fully participate in democracy, which is the point. As Jill Filipovic writes in *The Guardian*:

> A Supermajority/PerryUndem survey released in August of 2019 divides respondents by their position on abortion. On every question, anti-abortion voters were significantly more hostile to gender equity than pro-choice voters. Do men make better political leaders than women? More than half of anti-abortion voters agreed. Do you want there to be equal numbers of men and women in positions of power in America? Fewer than half of abortion opponents said yes—compared with 80% of pro-choicers, who said they want women to share in power equally. Anti-abortion voters don't like the #MeToo movement. They don't think the lack of women in positions of power impacts women's equality. They don't think access to birth control impacts women's equality.[6]

According to the Guttmacher Institute, "the abortion rate is 37 per 1,000 women in countries that prohibit abortion altogether or allow it only to save a woman's life, and 34 per 1,000 in countries that allow abortion without restriction as to reason."[7]

During the first thirty-one months of the Trump/Pence White House, emboldened antichoice state legislatures enacted thirty-seven new restrictions on abortion including a near-total ban in Alabama and a six-week ban (at which time most women don't even know they are pregnant) in Ohio, Kentucky, Mississippi, and Georgia (a state where race-based voter restriction brought the governor enacting this bill, Brian Kemp, into office). Missouri will likely become the first state in the nation without a single abortion clinic. In 2017, sixty-three new abortion restrictions were enacted; in 2018, twenty-three; in 2019, twenty-one, with more expected to come. Texas tried to pass a bill that would condemn to death women who get abortions. By the summer of 2019, nine states had passed highly restrictive abortion laws, in direct defiance of *Roe v. Wade*.[8] Radical bans and charges of manslaughter against the unborn are part of a deliberate strategy to elevate these cases to the Supreme Court, where abortion foes hope Trump's justices (Neil Gorsuch, Brett Kavanaugh, and Amy Coney Barrett) will overturn the landmark 1973 decision.

The year Donald Trump published *The Art of the Deal*, my sister and I went to Cleveland to see our mother. While we were cleaning the kitchen, we found a withered gray old hotdog under the counter. Our mother, in the bout of one of her psychotic paranoid delusions, told us that our home was being haunted by a "fossilized penis." When she said this, I laughed to keep from crying. Now I think she was onto something. The house of America is being terrorized by a fossilized penis.

What will history make of the grotesque, cartoonish masculinity of Trump and Pence, the id-and-superego tag team of white supremacist capitalist patriarchy? Who will play them in the movie? Who will best embody Trump's oozing misogyny? The puffy hair, swollen lips, and grabby hands? His Godzilla-like shadow looming over Hillary Clinton at the debates, enraged that she has deigned to speak, let alone occupy her own space, inspiring the battle cry at his rallies: "Lock her up!" Or churchgoing repressed Mike Pence like a stock character from *A Handmaid's Tale*, who calls his wife "mother" and refuses to conduct business or dine with nonchaperoned women? The man *USA Today* would name a "beacon of hope" for the pro-life movement, "the highest ranking official to appear in person at the annual March for Life demonstration."[9]

When I picture Trumpism writ large, I see six to eight dictators, all men, sitting around a table in a Trump resort carving up the world as in a game of Risk, trading guns and gigabytes and enslaved underage girls for fighter jets and wheat. For Trumpism to prosper unchecked, you need women to lose sovereignty over their bodies so that they can't escape their abusers or compete with your rage-filled supporters for jobs, let alone beat you in elections. You need unbridled access to the earth's resources, to plunder as you see fit, gutting all environmental protections so that the few of you at this table (and your corporate sponsors) can get even richer. And you need your citizens to fear the stranger at the border and the dark-skinned citizen on the street. That way everyone fights each other, in rallies or on Twitter, so they have no energy left to name and resist the super-rich who have robbed them of everything, including a democracy. Or, in the words of Ilhan Omar, the Somalian American elected into Congress in 2018 and attacked repeatedly by President Trump for her views on the Israeli occupation and her protest of the Muslim ban and the treatment of migrants at the border:

> Throughout our history, racist language has been used to turn American against American in order to benefit the wealthy elite. Every time Mr. Trump attacks refugees is a time that could be spent discussing the president's unwillingness to raise the federal minimum wage for up to 33 million Americans. Every racist attack on four members of Congress is a moment he doesn't have to address why his choice for labor secretary has spent his career defending Wall Street banks and Walmart at the expense of workers. When he is launching attacks on the free press, he isn't talking about why his Environmental Protection Agency just refused to ban a pesticide linked to brain damage in children.[10]

For Trumpism to do its worst, you also need members of the resistance to fight each other, because divide and conquer always wins. That's perhaps the most insidious part of why white supremacist patriarchal capitalism continues to prevail.

In *Good and Mad: The Revolutionary Power of Women's Anger*, Rebecca Traister recounts a story from the 1969 protest of Nixon's election win, when two female activists, Marilyn Salman Webb and Shulamith Firestone, fought to speak on "abortion, childcare, and how men on the left treated women." Enraged, the men in the crowd shouted them down, yelling "take her off the stage and fuck her!" and "fuck her down a dark alley."[11] Feminism apparently had no place in this movement for peace and equality. The story reminds me of how, nearly fifty years later, supporters of Hillary Clinton had to go to a secret Facebook site to praise her or share canvasing strategies, not just for fear of being harassed by Trump supporters but from Sanders supporters too. A particularly low point in this civil war was when Sanders followers pelted Clinton's motorcade with dollar bills. Critiquing her willingness to accept corporate donations was valid—decades of neglect by corporate Democrats have eroded the safety net and union rights, exasperating inequality—but that tableau of so-called progressives throwing money at the first woman to win the Democratic nomination was an ugly look for the left, as was the phenomenon of Sanders supporters filling Elizabeth Warren's twitter feed with snake emojis and misogynist insults when she said that he'd told her in a private conversation that a woman couldn't beat Trump.

A quote often attributed to Walter Benjamin reminds us that "behind every fascism, there is a failed revolution." If we don't view our fight for civil rights, reproductive justice, disability rights, trans rights, economic equality, and environmental justice as "all within a feminist framework," as Traister writes, we perpetuate the same flawed, failed hierarchies.

While I began work on this essay, services were taking place in El Paso to memorialize the dead who had been gunned down by a young white supremacist who was inspired by Trump to kill Mexican "migrants"; the ACLU (American Civil Liberties Union) counted more than 5,400 children who had been separated from their parents and detained in cage-like detentions at the border; ICE (Immigration and Customs Enforcement) raided Mississippi food-processing plants, leaving small children without their parents; the Trump Department of Justice's Office on Violence Against Women changed and narrowed the definitions of domestic violence and sexual assault to what they had been about fifty years ago, limiting it to cases where physical violence occurs; the lives of some women of color in Congress who have spoken out against some of these outrages were threatened by white men who used life-size posters of these women as target practice after Trump told the women to "go back where they came from"; hate crimes had increased 226 percent in the cities where Trump held rallies in 2016;[12] white gunmen shot up synagogues and music festivals and box stores, defaced cemeteries and homes with racial slurs, and burned people's homes to the ground; and the White House imposed a gag rule on Planned Parenthood, an essential healthcare provider for low-income women who rely on these clinics for regular health screening, HIV and sexually transmitted infection testing, contraception, and family planning advice, including information about abortion—a move that will likely lead to increased cancer deaths and deaths from self-induced abortions while also curbing free speech; and as this essay goes to press during the global pandemic of COVID-19, governors in red states such as Texas have used quarantine guidelines that they don't follow to nonetheless call abortions "non-essential" medical procedures and shut them down, decisions that directly violate constitutional protections that have nonetheless been upheld by Trump-appointed federal judges; and one out of five children in this country doesn't have enough to eat.

This, cumulatively, is what it means to be pro-life in America.

Sometimes I feel like we are back where we started in this essay—in 1972.

It's easy to lose heart, but when I do, I always return to this memory: Two-thirds of the way through the Women's March, I got separated from my friends and found myself alone in this surging sea of humanity, all those feet and hands clutching placards. I couldn't see Ellie's turd sign or James's Trump-as-lapdog-of-Putin sign, and I wasn't sure I could find our meeting point. My cell phone was dead. All I knew was where I was: in front of the Library of Congress. As I stood there, surveying hundreds of my contemporaries striding forward, I suddenly saw a cluster of people carrying giant signs of the heads of Americans who had fought for our collective emancipation: signs that towered over everything on the street except the library itself, so tall that fortifying them against the wind must have taken engineering chops. They looked heavy, and carrying them upright now took concentration, which I could see in the determined, fierce gaze of their bearers. These were the heads of the abolitionists and suffragettes who had carved out the trail of resistance that had brought us all here: Harriet Tubman, Frederick Douglass, Rosa Parks, Sojourner Truth, Abigail Addams, Elizabeth Cady Stanton. And just for a moment, I forgot about my own concerns, admiring instead the artistry and effort that had created this spectacle, so appropriately backlit by the glinting white marble columns and arches of the Library of Congress with the millions of books inside it. I was reminded of these words from Neal Gabler, posted widely on the Internet a day after the election. "Many years from now, future generations will need to know what happened to us and how it happened. . . . We are not living for ourselves anymore in this country. Now we are living for history."[13] Living and marching for others including, yes, the not-yet-born. That's the pro-life movement I am proud to take part in.

As Naomi Klein writes in *No Is Not Enough: Resisting Trump's Shock Politics and Winning the World We Need*, "With unleashed white supremacy and misogyny, with the world teetering on the edge of ecological collapse, with the very last vestiges of the public sphere set to be devoured by capital, it's clear that we need to do more than draw a line in the sand and say 'no more.'"[14] We need something to say yes to, together.

"Feminism without intersectionality is just white supremacy," I would read on another sign at another of the many marches to come. The era of the Trump presidency may have ended. However, it's on all of us to defeat Trumpism and whatever awful version of it comes next by reappropriating the word "life" to advance the rights of everyone: indigenous peoples, descendants of slaves and slaveholders and sharecroppers and abolitionists, immigrants and their great-great-grandchildren, people of all genders, religions, races, and all the nonhuman members of our biotic community on this gorgeous, imperiled planet. We need to say yes to all strands of this vast, tangled, tricky spider web of life and to believe that it is possible.

Invaders

Digital artist Douglas Edric Stanley raised significant controversy with an art installation in 2008 titled *Invaders*. Stanley's piece was intended to mark the thirtieth anniversary of the game Space Invaders at a show in Leipzig, Germany. His contribution featured a digital image of the Twin Towers within the rest of the familiar accoutrement of the original game. As in the original game, eventually the level of difficulty becomes overwhelming, and the invaders win. In the altered game, the players and observers are doomed to watch the low-resolution characters fall from the burning digital towers until the towers themselves finally fall. The original press release regarding the exhibit stated, "Like the original [game], this trial is ultimately unsuccessful, thus creating an articulated and critical commentary about the current war strategy."[1]

Whatever the artistic intentions behind the presentation, the outcry against this depiction of the events of 9/11 was sufficient for the owners of the video game property to insist that the installation be taken down and even suggest legal action against the artist.[2] The objections focused on what some perceived as the callous portrayal of the events of 9/11, baring feelings still raw after seven years. What is striking to me about the reactions to the display, however, is that they overlook the criticism of the war on terror behind the rendering. That the United States invaded Afghanistan and Iraq allegedly in pursuance of the war on terror did not register in the complaints. These invasions and subsequent occupations by the United States that put these populations in the nonvirtual position of watching their countries burn are obscured by Westerners' shocked response to the virtual destruction of the digital towers.

The trauma experienced by New Yorkers on September 11 was quickly mapped onto the entire Western world, even more than that experienced by those at the Pentagon or on Flight 93 (which crashed in Pennsylvania and was later memorialized in a Hollywood film). Yet in doing so, it overshadowed the experiences of those on the receiving end of the war on terror who live outside the boundaries of concern of most Westerners. This obfuscation of the suffering of others via a focus on Westerners' trauma is crucial to what I call "invaders discourse" since 9/11. This discourse emphasizes the precarity of the Western subject while minimizing the suffering and traumatic experiences of others who are constructed as threatening intruders posing an existential threat to the imagined Western way of life. So constructed, invaders become the targets of rhetorical, institutional, and extralegal forms of violence that are justified as self-defense, deemed necessary by the perpetrators to preserve European demographic majorities and their (Western) cultures in Western nations.

Invaders discourse, framed by anti-immigrant intellectuals and deployed by right-wing parties and politicians, is also applicable to the growing phenomenon of right-wing terrorism in the twenty-first century. But this has been neglected in part because the attackers in these cases are often described as lone gunmen with serious psychological problems rather than individual actors motivated by a common anti-immigrant and often white supremacist ideology. In this chapter, I briefly contextualize and explore this discourse and the violence it informs. I seek also to demonstrate the need for all of us to consider the implications of the political and social momentum that invaders discourse has gained in the twenty years after 9/11.

Context

On September 3, 2003, President George W. Bush stated, "We are fighting that enemy in Iraq and Afghanistan today so that we do not meet him again on our own streets, in our own cities."[3] In reality, those who see themselves as defending the American "homeland" (see Varadarajan, this volume) have perpetrated the majority of U.S. domestic terrorist incidents. After the 2018 attack on Tree of Life Synagogue in Pittsburgh, National Public Radio (NPR) referenced numbers from the Government Accounting Office and other sources to point out that between 9/11 and 2018 "deadly attacks in the U.S. by the far-right have outnumbered those by radicalized Muslims 70 to 26, a ratio of nearly 3-to-1." In that same report, Bill Braniff, director of the National Consortium for the Study of Terrorism and Responses to Terrorism (START) at the University of Maryland, stated that the number of such acts of domestic terrorism has increased since 2008. When asked about what motivates this particular violence, Braniff stated, "We find that believing in this collective sense of victimhood is a near necessary condition."[4]

Of course, anti-immigrant discourses framed as victimization by invaders are nothing new, and certainly not in the United States. In the famous

Thomas Nast cartoon published in *Harper's Weekly* in May 1875 titled "The American River Ganges," one can see the particularly vicious anti–Irish Catholic xenophobia then shared by many Anglo-Protestant Americans.[5] The cartoon depicts Irish Catholics destroying the institutions of the American Republic and Catholic bishops as ravenous crocodiles seeking to devour American schoolchildren who cringe behind a Protestant schoolteacher with a Bible tucked in his coat. The accompanying violence perpetrated by those acting on the belief that starving Irish immigrants were a threat to American democratic principles—everything from vigilante violence to the burning of Catholic orphanages—is well documented. The revived Ku Klux Klan of the 1920s also played on anti-immigrant tropes along with anti-Black racism and anticommunism to present themselves as the defenders of Americanism and Western civilization. They frequently justified their violence as self-defense against hordes of invaders as well as internal Marxist enemies.

This apocalyptic anti-immigrant sentiment persists. Although, more than the Klan, the tropes developed by European intellectuals in the late twentieth and early twenty-first centuries have come to influence post-9/11 anti-immigrant violence. In his rather infamous 1973 novel *The Camp of the Saints*, Jean Raspail, a hero to many anti-immigrant politicians and activists, describes an immigrant invasion originating in India. In a flotilla of ships, "the floating debauch" carting the mass of brown invaders, the "antiworld," sails onto the shores of the Western world.[6] Western leaders are powerless to stop the horde's advance, but not because of their lack of ability to do so. Rather, the invading mass of brown flesh successfully overcomes the West because Westerners lacked the will to destroy the flotilla and kill the invaders on sight. In the end, the West sinks beneath the wave of Third World migrants and the subversion of nonwhite immigrants already present, while the white population is left a mere minority. At the conclusion of the book, the narrator travels to Switzerland with a remnant of unassimilated whites, attempting to "hang on to something that [they] loved; a Western way of life, with our own kind of people."[7] However, even that hope was dashed as "Switzerland's foundations, too, had been sapped from within," Raspail writes. "The beast had undermined her, but slowly and surely, and it merely took her that much longer to crumble."[8]

Though Raspail rejected the characterization of the book and himself as racist, in 1982 he described his book as "an anti-epic, a crusade in reverse, a book charged with all the convoluted instincts and contradictions of the white man."[9] In his introduction to the 1985 French edition, Raspail doubled-down on the race talk by claiming, "Our world was shaped within an extraordinary variety of cultures and races, that could only have developed to their ultimate and singular perfection through a necessary segregation." However, Raspail describes European colonialism simply as a "consequence of our [Europeans'] appetite for conquest" rather than a moral failure or violation of that supposed "necessary segregation."[10] Taking his title from a passage in the Book of Revelation that refers to the period when the Devil and his followers had surrounded the last of God's people, Raspail clearly viewed this particular invasion differently than European colonial conquests.

The threat facing Europe and, in particular, France, Raspail argues, is that it has become too multicultural and therefore "no longer in solidarity with anything, or even cognizant of anything that would constitute the essential commonalities of a people."[11] This identity crisis coupled with the presence of an ever-growing population of immigrants, threatens, in his view, to overthrow the West, just as he imagined in his novel. "It seems we [Europeans] are facing a unique alternative," he writes, "either learn the resigned courage of being poor or find again the inflexible courage to be rich. In both cases, so-called Christian charity will prove itself powerless. The times will be cruel." Raspail's views seem only to have hardened since the 1980s. In a 2013 interview posted on the white nationalist website Counter-Currents, Raspail stated, "The people already know it all, intuitively: that France, as our ancestors fashioned it centuries ago, is disappearing."[12]

Among white nationalists, *The Camp of the Saints* and the statements made by its author years after its publication have confirmed their perception that the West is under attack by immigrants and that the white race is facing a genocide via demographic replacement. Raspail's book has more recently become important to the broader debate about immigration as well, especially for those associated with the policies of the Trump administration. For example, Steve Bannon, President Trump's former chief political strategist who ran the right-wing magazine *Breitbart*, has referenced the book on several occasions. On a podcast for *Breitbart* in January 2019, he stated, "The whole thing in Europe is all about immigration . . . this kind of global Camp of the Saints."[13] Later that same month on the podcast, Bannon claimed migration was "really an invasion," and stated, "I call it the Camp of the Saints."[14]

Other anti-immigrant intellectuals, too, have helped shape the perception that Europe is under invasion by non-Europeans. The Egyptian-born,

Swiss-Israeli dual citizen named Gisele Littman, known by her pen name Bat Ye'or, Hebrew for "daughter of the Nile," did not invent the term "Eurabia," but she has done more than anyone to popularize it. Though she has no real academic credentials and has never taught at any university, since 9/11 she has been able to gain attention from universities and governments and especially from the anti-Muslim right in Europe and the United States.[15] The core of her theory of Eurabia is that Europe, formerly a "Judeo-Christian civilization, with important post-Enlightenment secular elements," is now becoming a "post-Judeo-Christian civilization that is subservient to the ideology of jihad and the Islamic powers that propagate it."[16] Her general argument is that with the cooperation of submissive Western elites, Europe is becoming Eurabia and will thereby lose its sense of self and become subject to Muslim domination. Much like in *The Camp of The Saints*, Ye'or imagines a future when Europeans will lose their demographic majority and cultural identity. Most scholars have rejected her claims as conspiratorial and ahistorical. But her ideas, much like Raspail's, have had continued influence, most significantly on radicals such as Anders Behring Breivik, who put the full transcript of one of her speeches in his manifesto, using the term "Eurabia" more than 170 times before he carried out a massacre of more than seventy people in Norway in 2011.

Since the shootings in Christchurch, New Zealand, in 2019 in which Brenton Tarrant attacked two mosques, killing more than fifty worshippers, the work of another French writer has come to broader attention. Tarrant had taken much of the language in his manifesto, posted online before the murders, from Renauld Camus, a novelist turned political essayist. Camus codified his ideas in several essays, and, finally, in *Le Grande Remplacement*, he described the processes of European demographic replacement in European-majority lands with non-Europeans, especially Muslims.[17] He argues later in *You Will Not Replace Us!* that European societies have been subjected by cultural and political elites in the West to a "brutal change of population" in which "replacers, mostly from Africa, and very often Muslim," are replacing "the indigenous population, whose very existence has been denied, even in retrospect."[18] He goes on to argue that this "Great Replacement, ethnic substitution, the change of people and civilization, is by far the biggest and most urgent problem" facing Europeans. To this problem, he proposes removal of all replacers and "their return where they came from."[19]

For each of these writers, the West is under invasion leading to demographic and political marginalization in their own lands. Though they have each articulated their ideas in slightly different terms, they all agree the West is under invasion and that Western elites are partly to blame. They also agree that action is necessary. Something must be done, they say, to save the West from the *Camp of the Saints* scenario—deportation at the least, and murderous violence if necessary. Some of their admirers agree.

"In Self-Defense"

On July 22, 2011, Anders Breivik began his assault with a bombing outside the offices of the prime minister in Oslo. This bomb killed eight people and heavily damaged buildings in the immediate area. Breivik then traveled some twenty miles to Utøya, an island in the lake Tyrifjorden, which housed a youth camp for the Labour Youth Party, the youth wing of Norway's moderately socialist Labour Party. For over an hour, dressed as a police officer, Breivik moved across the island killing those whom he felt aided in the "Islamisation of Europe and Norway," killing sixty-nine people, mostly teenagers.[20] When police finally took Breivik into custody, seventy-seven people were dead in the deadliest day in Norway's history since World War II. When he made his defense before the court in Norway in April 2012, he claimed that he was the leader of "an 'anti-communist' resistance movement and an anti-Islam militant group he called the Knights Templar," and that he "acted in self-defense on behalf of [his] people, [his] city, [his] country."[21]

If there were any doubts about the motive for this attack, Breivik left behind a manifesto explaining his ideology, plans, and tactical preparedness before the attack. The 1,515-page manifesto, titled "2083: A European Declaration of Independence," was published under the nom de plume of Andrew Berwick in 2011. The title references both historical efforts to purge Christendom of Muslims and an imagined future civil war to complete this task by the date 2083. Berwick/Breivik writes, "By September 11th, 2083, the third wave of Jihad will have been repelled and the cultural Marxist/multiculturalist hegemony in Western Europe will be shattered and lying in ruin, exactly 400 years after we won the battle of Vienna on September 11th, 1683. Europe will once again be governed by patriots."[22]

Breivik chose targets that reflected this disdain of leftist governments and pro-immigrant European politicians and their supporters. While in the manifesto he decries the social welfare models of European governments, he is more critical of the ways in which they collaborate with the

European Union in the creation of "Eurabia" through "anti-Western hate ideology championed as an instrument for unilaterally dismantling European culture." He complains often in the manifesto about "the rise of cultural Marxism/multiculturalism and political correctness" since the end of World War II. Moreover, his attack was a part of a general plan for an eventual coup to overthrow liberal democracies in Europe. He wrote in his manifesto, "Waiting for the right time to strike or create an opportunity . . . can be accomplished by arranging incidents (assassinations or terror attacks on mosques during Id [*sic*] celebration etc) which would trigger major Muslim riots. If the riots are violent enough it can serve as a perfect occasion for the coup."

The goal of this particular attack was to shock the masses and to engage in the kind of warfare that is needed, in his view, to "take the appropriate measures to protect [the West's] own security and ensure our national survival." Breivik chose, however, not to attack the so-called invaders but rather those he felt were responsible for the invasion. They were, after all, aiding the forces of jihad to bring about Eurabia. Like Raspail, he admonishes his readers, "make excuses or express regret for you are acting in self-defence or in a preemptive manner. . . . For every free patriotic European, only one choice remains: Survive or perish."

Resisting Replacement

On March 15, 2019, Brenton Tarrant, a familiar figure in the Australian far-right scene, attacked two mosques in Christchurch, New Zealand. He killed fifty-one people, all Muslims, live streaming the attack on the Internet. He had planned the attacks for three weeks, and now viewers could observe, record, and share every kill captured from the point of view of the GoPro attached to the end of Tarrant's rifle. The stated motives for the attack were similar to those of Breivik, but, in this case, Tarrant targeted the invaders themselves. He stated in his online manifesto, titled "The Great Replacement: Towards a New Society We March Ever Forwards," that he wanted "revenge on the invaders" for the enslavement and death of Europeans at the hands of Muslim invaders through the centuries, as well as to affect policy concerning firearms in the United States and immigration policy more broadly. "Most of all," he wanted to "show the invaders that our lands will never be their lands, our homelands are our own and that, as long as a white man still lives, they will NEVER conquer our lands and they will never replace our people."[23]

Although Camus rejected the claim that his works inspired the attack, Tarrant referenced the language of his anti-replacement theory repeatedly in the manifesto and, of course, titled his manifesto after Camus's magnum opus. Rather, Camus insisted, "at the center of my work is the concept of innocence, which is to say non-aggravation, non-violence."[24] He went on to say that the Christchurch attacks resembled the terrorist attacks committed in France and that the true inspiration lies with those acts more than his ideas. The innocence of which he speaks is European innocence that stands in contrast to Muslim invaders' violence that he regards as the true inspiration for the attacks. The invaders are collectively the instigators. Camus seemed to miss the fact that Tarrant blamed the Muslims whom he murdered for attacks in Europe and sought revenge for Muslim crimes.

Camus's distancing himself from the attacks further misses a more crucial point. My claim is not that Camus instigated these attacks by some command to attack Muslims, but that there is a certain discourse about Muslims as "replacers" that operates within his work that Tarrant repeats in his manifesto to describe his motive. The tactics were thus inspired by Breivik's tactics, but Camus's ideas framed the rationale for the violence in the first place. Just as the conceptual framework of Eurabia shaped Breivik's rationale for his attacks, Camus's replacement theory shaped Tarrant's. In the end, Camus, Ye'or, and Raspail have constructed the motivating ideologies that not only justified these attacks for the attackers but also framed the reason for the attacks and their choice of targets.

Pittsburgh, Poway, and El Paso

Similar motives are stated by perpetrators of comparable attacks in the United States, though the targets of the violence were different. Whereas Breivik attacked political opponents whom he held responsible for Eurabia and Tarrant attacked those whom he regarded as invading Muslims, Robert Bowers and John Timothy Earnest attacked Jews, and Patrick Wood Crusius targeted Mexicans. What they shared in common with their European counterparts and each other was a deep sense of white European victimization at the hands of replacers and those internal enemies complicit in the invasion.

On October 27, 2018, Robert Bowers, a forty-six-year-old from Baldwin Borough in the Pittsburgh metro area, walked into Tree of Life Synagogue in Squirrel Hill, some eleven miles away, and opened fire on the congregants with handguns and an AR15 rifle. He killed eleven of them and injured others, including a responding police officer who wounded him in the exchange. When he was apprehended, he reportedly told police officers that "he wanted all Jews to die and also that they (Jews) were committing genocide to his people."[25] This is common discourse among white nationalists who allege the Jews are perpetrating a "white genocide." However, Bowers's social media activity offered more specific insight as to why he chose Tree of Life as his target.

On the social media outlet Gab, Bowers posted just prior to the attack, "HIAS likes to bring invaders in that kill our people. I can't sit by and watch my people get slaughtered. Screw your optics, I'm going in."[26] HIAS is the Hebrew Immigrant Aid Society, founded in the late nineteenth century to resettle Jewish refugees, primarily from Eastern Europe. Its mission has changed over the years. Now it has a more expanded mission "to resettle the most vulnerable refugees of all faiths and ethnicities from all over the world."[27] What HIAS and their partners saw as a humanitarian mission supported by their religious worldview to help the most desperate people in a growing population of refugees, Bowers saw as an insidious plan to replace the white race in America with invaders. This was, for him, reason enough to attack the worshippers at Tree of Life.

Bowers had long been active on social media, sharing and reposting content claiming the Jews were pushing the white race to extinction and that they were behind the presence of invaders in Europe and America. One post in particular, however, stood out in relation to the more common anti-Semitic content of his posts. Days before the attack he noted in another post on Gab, "I have noticed a change in people saying 'illegals' that now say 'invaders' I like this [sic]."[28] This, as I mention earlier, is an explicit reference to the momentum gained by the invaders discourse. Bowers did not specify here, but he could have been referring to the general discourse of his social community, or even the social media community to which he belonged. However, he may well have been referring to the shift in the broader discourse that one might find in the language of Trump rallies or even on major news networks. For example, Tucker Carlson on his show on Fox News stated in April 2019, while lamenting the aid the United States offers other countries, "What about our country? We're being invaded, no offense to the

Ethiopian Navy, but we could use American troops a lot closer to Tijuana than the Horn of Africa."[29] The question of illegals is a legal problem, but the question of invaders is a military problem. Once again, in this discourse, the only solution is violence.

On April 27, 2019, a young man named John Timothy Earnest drove to Chabad of Poway Synagogue in Poway, California, and while approaching the door opened fire with his "AR-15 style" weapon. In doing so he killed one woman and injured three others. He, too, had stated his reasons for this attack, this time on Mediafir.com and Pastebin.com.[30] In the rather blandly titled "The Manifesto," Earnest identifies himself and, after extolling the virtues of his European ancestry, claims, "Every Jew is responsible for the meticulously planned genocide of the white race." Among their crimes, in Earnest's view, was promoting feminism, cultural Marxism, killing Jesus, and "voting for and funding politicians and organizations who use mass migration to displace the European race."[31] In reading his manifesto, authorities discovered that in March of that year he also set fire to the Dar-ul-Arqam Mosque and Islamic Center in Escondido, California. His stated inspiration for that particular incident was the "sacrifice" that Brenton Tarrant made. Furthermore, he explicitly references both Tarrant and Robert Bowers as inspiration for the attack in Poway. "To my brothers in blood," he writes, "Make sure that my sacrifice was not in vain. Spread this letter, make memes, shitpost, FIGHT BACK, REMEMBER BOWERS, REMEMBER BRENTON TARRANT."

Patrick Wood Crusius, like Bowers and Earnest, felt that America was under an invasion. Like Tucker Carlson, Steve Bannon, and President Trump, he felt this invasion was coming through the border with Mexico. On August 3, 2019, Crusius drove from Allen in central Texas to 7101 Gateway West, the location of a Walmart in El Paso, Texas. There, after a drive of more than six hundred miles to the border town, he opened fire with an AK-47 assault rifle, as he told authorities, to kill "Mexicans."[32] He also left a manifesto, though one that was far shorter than Breivik's. In it he stated, "This attack is in response to the Hispanic invasion of Texas."[33] Crusius, like Breivik, claimed that the murders he committed were not murders at all. He was "simply defending [his] country from cultural and ethnic replacement brought on by an invasion."

The ring of Camus's great replacement thesis here is not incidental. Crusius claims in the manifesto that he was not motivated to attack the "Hispanic community" until he "read The Great Replacement." Crusius's manifesto was not merely imitating the invaders discourse in Camus's work, no more than Breivik was simply aping Bat Ye'or's Eurabia. They are all participating in a particular discourse that shapes motives and ideations on which people act. Some of them write books and treatises. Others run for office or are active in politics. Others still, inspired by the same ideas and sense of urgency, decide to kill those whom they perceive as invaders and their alleged allies.

"Only the Beginning"

In the months leading up to Crusius's attack targeting Mexicans at the U.S.-Mexico border, President Trump's reelection campaign posted ads on social media claiming that America is being invaded at the border. In one of the ads that circulated through social media, the president stated, "We have an INVASION!"[34] Ads similarly featuring the theme of invaders at the border have appeared more than two thousand times on Facebook alone between January 2019 and the time of the attack in El Paso. Republican candidates for lower offices also ran such campaign ads in the effort to position themselves opposite their incumbent or challenger opponents. Indeed, the dissemination of the idea that America is under an invasion became a key component of the campaign strategy for the 2020 elections and a talking point for political action committees and social media groups that support conservative candidates.

President Trump condemned the El Paso shooting, and in his manifesto, Crusius equally distanced himself from Trump, stating, "My opinions . . . predate Trump." I have no doubt they do. Trump did not invent invaders discourse any more than Breivik or Camus did. Again, the point is not to show that Trump caused the attack, but that Trump and Crusius share a relationship with a particular discursive formation and expressions of it. Trump, Crusius, Tarrant, Camus, et al.—all work within a particular discursive formation that frames their activity. In each case, the ideologue, politician, and mass murderer are animated by a conviction that the West is under imminent threat of invasion from predatory aliens, and that discursive regime demands one engage in self-defensive measures.

Invaders discourse is part of the very political fabric of the West. It redeploys the older narratives of colonial settlers who alleged self-protection to justify the slaughter of the indigenous peoples and echoes the rhetoric of regimes that perpetrated genocides in the twentieth century. It will persist in campaign language and proposed policies from far-right political parties. It will continue to permeate anti-immigrant intellectual production and animate violence directed at perceived invaders and their assumed enablers. Just as Breivik promised in his manifesto that his attacks were "only the beginning," so Crusius stated his attacks were "just the beginning of the fight for America and Europe." I think we should believe them.

Catherine Tedford, *Right to Life*.
Reprinted with permission of the artist.

Populism

When Donald Trump insulted women and Mexicans, he was called "sexist," "xenophobic," and "ill-mannered." When he insisted on building a wall on the border despite recent evidence that migrant flows into the United States have been decreasing, his critics accused him of "inventing a crisis." And when he repeatedly berated reporters, telling them they "ask a lot of stupid questions," he was caricatured as a "bully" and an "authoritarian." But such traits—chauvinism, scaremongering, despotism—are not unique to him; they are the very stuff of authoritarian forms of populism, and Trump shares them with several other current populist strongmen around the world, such as Brazil's Jair Bolsonaro, the Philippines' Rodrigo Duterte, and Russia's Vladimir Putin. The recent success of authoritarian populism, it seems, is closely connected to the populist leader's ability to capture popular attention by using coarse language, identifying enemies, and acting decisively, if not autocratically.

More broadly, populism can be seen as a style of politics—a rhetorical political strategy—that tends to divide society into two antagonistic groups: the "people" versus an "enemy" (elites, refugees, immigrants, terrorists, minorities, etc.). One thinks here of Trump's election slogan, "drain the swamp," portraying mainstream Washington politics as inept and corrupt, or Thailand's Thaksin Shinawatra, who championed "common folk" against the country's traditional elites. The political strategy is to mobilize and unite "the people" by identifying a common adversary. The latter is always portrayed in a negative light, precisely in order to be able to construct "the people" as pure and blameless. Thus, members of the anti-immigrant German protest movement, Pegida, often chant "We are the People" (*Wir sind das Volk*), implying that immigrants are not one of "us"; while Trump's inaugural address proclaimed: "We are transferring power from Washington, D.C., and giving it back to you, the American People."

Lately, this divisive style of politics appears to have met with much success. Indeed, the last decade has witnessed a wave of populism across the world, from street protests against neoliberalism and austerity in Venezuela, Greece, France, and Spain, to the rise of right-wing anti-elite and anti-minority populism in the United States, Turkey, Asia (India, Philippines, Thailand), and Europe (Poland, Hungary, France, the Netherlands, Austria, Britain, Denmark, Italy, Spain). In Europe, populist parties tripled their share of votes between 1998 and 2018, forming governments in several countries.[1] Even Putin, not usually associated with populism, appears to have jumped on the bandwagon to consolidate his power by drawing on populist rhetoric (e.g., vilifying Western imperialism, gay rights, and multiculturalism).

But lest we think populism is a new phenomenon, it is not; it has a long history, stretching back to at least the late Roman Republic, which saw the rise of a pro-people *Populares* movement, in opposition to a pro-aristocratic one. Modern populist movements span the world and include the likes of the 1860s Russian Norodniki movement, the 1890s U.S. People's Party, the 1890s French Boulangists, fascist and neofascist European movements (in Germany, Italy, France, and Spain) before and after the Second World War, Poujadism in postwar France, Latin American populism between the 1940s and 1960s (spearheaded by Juan Perón in Argentina and Getulio Vargas in Brazil), and Greek socialist populism during the 1980s.[2] What is notable here is that although populism has for the most part been associated with the Right, this is not necessarily the case, as the Left, too, has sometimes been successful in capturing public imagination with populist rhetoric (most recently in Venezuela under Hugo Chávez and Spain with the Podemos Party). This only points up the earlier idea that populism is a style of politics, which can be adapted to almost every political stripe.[3]

Causes

Yet, if populist politics has been around for a long while, how might one explain its recent reoccurrence across the globe? Let me suggest three main causes. The first is economic, having to do with our global capitalist system. While there have been unprecedented levels of growth in several parts of the world, especially since the 1990s, these have been accompanied by increasing inequality and crisis. Wealth, for example, has concentrated in the hands of the very few in the last twenty years, and the share of national income going to the richest one percent has increased rapidly across the world without exception, especially in the United States, China, India, Russia, and Brazil. In 2019, the richest one percent owned 44 percent of the world's wealth, with the world's twenty-six richest billionaires together owning $1.4 trillion, a sum greater than the total goods and services most countries produce every year.

While economic growth in such countries as China, India, South Africa, and Brazil has lifted many people out of extreme poverty, it is the richest one percent that has reaped the greatest share by far of these economic gains.[4]

Such growing inequality has happened along not just economic but also geographic lines, with unevenness between (and within) countries rising. For example, between 1960 and 2010, the GDP per capita gap between the richest and poorest countries increased by 252 percent. Between 1980 and 2016, economic growth in parts of Africa and Latin America declined relative to North America and Western Europe.[5] It is the resulting geographic disparity that has served as a pull factor for people seeking better economic and life prospects, leading in part to the recent growth in immigration and refugee flows from poorer to richer countries. Europe's ongoing "refugee crisis," for example, is the result of a combination of this geographic disparity and civil strife or war in North Africa and the Middle East, in which, ironically, several European countries played a key role.

But accompanying this rapidly growing global inequality and unevenness has been market instability. Since the turn of the twenty-first century, hardly a year has gone by without the outbreak of economic crises (notably the 2008 crisis in the United States and Europe), housing and mortgage crises (also in the United States and Europe), and financial and debt crises (in Uruguay, Venezuela, Greece, Portugal, Russia, Latvia, Turkey, Iceland, Ireland, Ukraine, Brazil, and India). In turn, these have translated into growing personal and government debt and, significantly, shrinking welfare safety nets. Neoliberal austerity and privatization measures have meant the reduction or loss of state-funded unemployment, health, and educational programs, particularly for the most socially disadvantaged.

The overall consequence of this growing inequality and crisis has been rising social anxiety. While taking on distinctive forms in different parts of the world, economic deprivation and disparity have fueled alienation, anger, and resentment. This is particularly true for the likes of slum dwellers, migrants, poor inner-city neighborhoods, racialized minorities, public housing residents, low-waged workers, unskilled or non-college-educated workers, the long-term unemployed, single mothers, the disabled, dispossessed farmers, and marginalized immigrants, all of whom have experienced acute forms of socioeconomic insecurity and shrinking welfare benefits. Their anxiety, disaffection, and rage have become fertile ground for populism.

A second major cause of populist resurgence (or neopopulism) is what can be called the crisis of democracy. Over the last two decades particularly, liberal democracies around the world have witnessed notable public dissatisfaction with democratic institutions and the state. The most obvious sign is lower voter turnout at elections, witnessed as much in the United States and Britain as in South Africa, India, and Argentina. The competitive party system appears to be failing, with political parties often indistinguishable and impervious. The same is true of the state, increasingly subjected to laissez-faire economic policymaking and the demands of the corporate sector, all the while growing its presence on questions of security, surveillance, and control. More and more, it seems, our political and economic institutions are beset with scandals (e.g., corruption, money laundering, surveillance overreach), with political leaders out of touch and economic elites untouchable.[6] The result is the increasing lack of accountability and responsiveness of our mainstream democratic institutions. Hence the draw of the political alternative represented by populist movements.

The final explanation is a cultural one, relating to what can be termed the "loss of meaning."[7] Our late capitalist times have given way to the loosening, if not unmooring, of mainstream value systems and traditions. The decline of the conventional family unit has seen parents working outside the home, often yielding more disjointed family relationships and weakening parental authority. Capitalist globalization, for its part, has uprooted local cultural institutions (language, religion, communal living, etc.), disorienting people across the world, causing them to adopt often alien and Westernized ways of life or to resist by reinventing old ones (hence the advent of religious resurgence or fundamentalism). Paralleling this has been the rise of Internet and media culture: while it may well have helped increase communication, it has also produced information overflow, making it difficult to sort out fact from fiction or reliable news from "fake news" (see Barnard, this volume).

The general consequence of such cultural deracination and flux is a search for more secure and stable meaning and authority, which populism appears to offer. Populist politics—particularly of the right-wing, conservative type—is in this sense a kind of backlash or doubling down against the cultural turbulence of our times, promising a return to traditional norms and authority.

Characteristics

The last decade has thus seen a ramped-up atmosphere of social and cultural alienation and turbulence in many places across the globe. People's anxiety and disaffection is rendered all the more intense in the face of the previously mentioned crisis of democracy and lack of meaningful political debate, making it difficult to find avenues to articulate political demands. The result has been a breakdown of political consensus, the rise of anti-establishment rage, mistrust of political and economic elites, and suspicion of the media (yielding to rumormongering and alternative and fake news). The time has therefore become ripe, as we have seen, for the emergence of demagogues and political opportunists—Chávez and Nicolas Maduro (Venezuela), Trump (the United States), Nigel Farage (Britain), Narendra Modi (India), Tayyip Erdoğan (Turkey), Duterte (Philippines), Marine Le Pen (France), Geert Wilders (the Netherlands), Golden Dawn (Greece), the Kaczynski brothers (Poland), Bolsonaro (Brazil), Putin (Russia), Viktor Orbán (Hungary), Vox (Spain), Thaksin (Thailand), and so forth. Each has successfully tapped into the generalized malaise, introducing political passion into an alienating and stale political establishment through paranoia, fear, xenophobia, racism, and misogyny.[8]

Indeed, a noteworthy feature of populism is its deployment of a politics of emotion. It tends to feed off and exploit people's anxiety, nostalgia, resentment, and anger. In appealing to the people, the populist leader is creating an emotional bond, rallying them against the enemy (e.g., politics as usual). When the leader summons "the people," he or she is conjuring a fantasy that promises a return to the good old days or the prospect of a bright future, pledging to heal their wounds (social anxiety, alienation, etc.). A political community, group, or nation is thus constituted emotionally as people identify with their leader's promise of social harmony—the expectation of greatness, strength, prosperity, autonomy, real change, unity, and so forth. The successful populist leader is able to link a slew of unsatisfied social demands into broader popular demands, thus effectively producing "the people." Often this is done with the help of slogans: Trump's "Make America Great Again," Farage's "Take Our Country Back," Modi's "Good Days Are Coming," Erdoğan's "Bring Strength to Turkey," Pablo Iglesias Turrion's "Yes, We Can," Duterte's "Change Is Coming," Chávez's "Fatherland, Socialism or Death." The slogans are emotionally charged, broad enough to encapsulate a spectrum of popular demands, and ambiguous enough for a range of people to identify with them and become passionately attached to them.

But as underlined earlier, in summoning a "good," "pure," and "virtuous" people, populism not only promises social harmony but also identifies obstacles blocking it. Populist discourse blames people's frustration and anxiety on an external enemy and intruder (Muslims, Jews, terrorists, European Union bureaucrats, refugees, immigrants, international bankers, American imperialists) or a social parasite (single mothers, gays, drug dealers, welfare bums, inner-city African Americans, federal bureaucrats). Often these adversaries are portrayed as preventing "us" from being happy: immigrants who take away our jobs, refugees who harass our women, single mothers who abuse our welfare system, bureaucrats who claw back our freedoms. Populist politics is therefore founded on stark us/them distinctions that glorify community pride and togetherness and revile betrayal and intrusion.

In attempting to create a unified people, populist leaders often prey on people's fears and paranoia, most frequently ceding to racism, homophobia, sexism, xenophobia, or aggressive nationalism. Here, the tendency is to rely on intolerance, invoking dangerous ideas (e.g., registries for Muslims, expulsion of refugees and immigrants), inventing or exaggerating claims ("alternative facts"), resorting to censorship (e.g., blocking social media), or threatening dissenting journalists and intellectuals. The character of debate thus frequently becomes one of increasing excess, vulgarity, and hostility. Think here of the strongman and authoritarian tactics mentioned earlier—"national boss rule" as they call it in the Philippines—or of Duterte's jokes about raping women and Trump's about grabbing women's genitals. Think also of the frequency with which Trump used provocative terms such as "disgraceful," "shameful," and "tremendous," as well as slogans aimed at vilifying his enemies ("Crooked Hilary," "Lyin' Ted," "Lock Her Up"). Social media, it must be noted, often enables such inflammatory discourse: its algorithmic model tends to promote soundbites and adversarial messages, favoring black-and-white opinions, polarizing tweets, and emotional excess.

A final notable feature of populism is its ability to hold together a number of contradictions and ambiguities. This is the case with its often-incongruous characterization of the enemy: refugees are lazy, but they steal our jobs; Asians are workaholics, but they drain the welfare state; terrorists are wily and calculating, but they are also brainwashed religious fanatics. This is also the case with frequently incompatible leadership traits: populists manage to convince people they are outsiders to the traditional system, yet they are often very much part of the broader establishment or elite—Trump as entrepreneur billionaire, Bolsonaro as congressman, Erdogan and Duterte as city mayors, and Modi as state chief minister. They get elected on the promise of making government more accountable, yet they most often resort not just to authoritarianism but also feudal or clientelist relationships (e.g., surrounding themselves with only trusted family members, loyal friends, and allies). These contradictions are once again evidence that emotions are very much at work here: it is the passionate appeal of the charismatic leader that ensures that people can relish the populist leadership and dream (of unity, social harmony, strength, greatness, and so forth), while ignoring their contradictions. Absent such gut-level emotions, the contradictions would more easily stand out, weakening the hold and credibility of populism.

Problems

So, let me end by illustrating the main failing of populism with a joke.[9] A man is looking for his cell phone under a streetlight. But when a passerby enquires where he dropped it, he admits that it was in the unlit section of the street. "So then why are you looking for it here?" asks the passerby. The man responds, "Because I can see much better under the light!" As in this joke, the problem with populism is that it looks for the causes to people's problems under the light where they appear to be more visible and easier to grasp, rather than in the dark corner where they are more hidden and complex to behold.

Indeed, the thing about populism is that it responds to real problems (social anxiety and alienation) but displaces them onto the wrong targets (the big bad bureaucrats, refugees, immigrants, terrorists, greedy bankers, biased judges, etc.). That is to say, symptoms and individuals are blamed rather than broader social and political structures (i.e., social inequality and dispossession, the rule of corporate and political elites, cultural turbulence). It captures well the popular anger and resentment of our times but mystifies the social causes, refusing to confront them directly. For the populist, the reason for our troubles is never really the system but an outsider or intruder who corrupts it.

This refusal to address the causes is closely connected to the politics of emotion and ramped-up rhetoric on which populism rests, which as we have seen tends toward the simplified, polarized, and excessive, thus avoiding the complex, layered, and studied. Inconvenient facts (e.g., wealth concentration, climate change, authoritarian tendencies) are dodged in favor of alternative facts (conspiracy theories, simplifications). Decisiveness and bossiness, rather than painstaking and consultative policymaking, are seen as strengths. Slogans are preferred over considered opinions, and difficult truths are tagged as "fake news."

Yet populism's contradictions and weaknesses eventually show up and catch up. Emotional politics and inflammatory rhetoric only last so long, losing their appeal when the populist does not live up to promises, cannot deliver on commitments, or implements faulty policies and programs. The chaos of Brexit, Maduro's bungling, increasing inequality and wealth concentration around the world, Europe's continuing refugee crisis despite anti-immigrant measures, Trump's inability to build his wall or get Mexico to fund it—all these speak to the failings and limits of current populist politics.

So eventually, populism's chickens do come home to roost. But the problem, of course, is that in the meantime it produces a lot of collateral damage: the judiciary is weakened, refugees and minorities are persecuted, journalists and academics are threatened, and drug users are gunned down. All the while, the rich continue to get richer and the poor get poorer.

Walls

On January 11, 2019, U.S. Air Force veteran, triple amputee, and Purple Heart recipient Brian Kolfage set up We Build the Wall, Inc., a nonprofit, advocacy organization with the mission to build segments of the Trump Wall along the U.S.-Mexico border. "Build the Wall!," together with "Lock Her Up!," was one of the iconic rallying cries on the Republican campaign trail in the lead-up to the 2016 U.S. presidential elections. But since President Trump failed to secure federal funding for his wall, this privately funded initiative was meant to fulfill his campaign promise and protect the southern border against undocumented migration and drug smuggling. In June 2019, the first major segment of the wall funded by We Build the Wall was built in Sunland Park, New Mexico. The organization's website declared that the newly constructed barrier "blocked one of the worst human- and drug-smuggling corridors in the El Paso Sector . . . [and] immediately altered the entire region's flow of illegal drugs and illegal migrants coming into the United States."[1]

This enthusiasm for the (new) wall ignores the limitations of the 654-mile-long barrier that already exists on the U.S.-Mexico border. Admittedly, it does not cover the entire span of the nearly 2,000-mile border. But even in locations where there are barriers, they have done little to stop what President Trump and his supporters consider "illegal immigration." This was all the more evident in April 2016 when a Mexican news crew, filming a story along the border in Nogales, Arizona, was interrupted by two young men climbing over the barrier from Mexico with ease. Once on the American side, they were alarmed by the presence of the news crew recording their every move and were seen frantically communicating over a cell phone. Before long the two men climbed back over thirty-foot barrier, and within moments, they were in Mexico again.[2]

Such shortcomings are not unique to the southern border of the United States. The wall in the occupied West Bank was built in 2002 during the Second Intifada, in response to what the Israeli government calls "Palestinian terrorism." It cuts through Palestinian communities, restricts Palestinians' access to clean water and fertile land, and limits their ability to navigate freely the occupied West Bank and

Jerusalem. For Palestinians, this structure represents more of an apartheid wall than, as Israel likes to refer to it, a "security barrier." Expectedly, Israeli authorities insist that the wall works. Writing for *Foreign Policy*, former director general of the Ministry of Foreign affairs Shlomo Avineri argued, "lost amid the international outcry over the legality of the barrier is the undeniable fact that it's working. Israel is more or less returning to normal life, with people no longer afraid to walk the streets."[3] But in 2015–16, when the occupied West Bank and Jerusalem witnessed scores of attacks by young Palestinians armed with knives and scissors, it was all the more apparent that the "security barrier" does not work.

The Great Wall of China did not work either. Undoubtedly a marvel of human engineering, the five-thousand-mile structure was meant to protect the agricultural Chinese population from the nomadic peoples of Central Asia, Mongolia, and Manchuria. It was also supposed to maintain a clear distinction between the "civilized" pastoral (Chinese) communities and their "barbaric" nomadic neighbors to the north.[4] Yet as a *National Geographic* story revealed, the wall did little to discourage attacks by the nomadic population. The underpaid Chinese guards stationed on the wall, working in harsh weather conditions and possessing limited weaponry, rarely resisted the invaders. Chinese troops also "had a great deal of friendly contact with the nomads." The troops "traded with their enemies" and, on occasion, colluded with them as well. In fact, in 1533, Chinese troops acted as "guides for Mongol war parties during their incursions into Chinese territory."[5]

Still, despite such well-documented failures across time and space, we live in an increasingly walled world, littered with anti-terrorist walls, anti-refugee fences, and gated communities. But why? A wall is material. We can see it and touch it. Therefore, it is only instinctive that we often discuss the purpose of a wall in terms of what it is (un)able to accomplish, physically. Yet to understand the enduring popularity of walls, we have to turn our gaze away from their physicality and toward the political narratives that deem their existence necessary. To this end, I argue here that walls are deeply implicated in the rhetoric of war and war making—especially since the urge to build a wall often appears at times of perceived crises and looming threats. As is the case then with the wartime lexicon of collateral language, here "language acts as a determinate factor in the formation of our perceptions of the world."[6] In this case, the often uncomplicated and seemingly commonsensical narrative of who ("illegal immigrants," "smugglers," "terrorists," "barbaric invaders," etc.) needs to be walled out is what gives walls meaning and purpose. Of course, if we consent to the building of a wall, we also consent to the premise of the narrative that deems the wall necessary.[7] And sometimes the narrative is far more important. A politician simply expressing the intention to build a wall is enough to indicate both that he or she agrees with the proposition that there are indeed looming threats that need to be walled out and that he or she is committed to combatting them. So, the physical wall may not be built. But if the narrative persists, the practice of walling will also continue—albeit through other ways and means available in politics and policy-making. In the end, this obsession with walls has real, human consequences. And whether the practice of walling (out) is carried out under the pretext of fighting crime, terrorism, or undocumented migration, walls physically divide (border) communities, prevent those fleeing persecution from reaching safe havens, and ensure that economic opportunities are inaccessible to those looking to build a better life.

The Story of the Wall

The importance of the story was apparent in Thomas Oles's discussion of Robert Frost's poem "Mending Wall." The most commonly cited line from the poem—"good fences make good neighbors"—is often misunderstood and used to justify anti-immigrant measures, including the construction of border walls, barriers, and fences.[8] But it would seem that for Frost the wall had very little physical purpose, seeing as neither the narrator nor his neighbor is a farmer, and the physical barrier has no use "in a place devoid of livestock."[9] Why, then, do both the narrator and his neighbor return every year to mend the wall? The answer, Oles argues, is in the way both men consider the material presence of the wall to be essential. For the neighbor, the wall is "a guarantor of cordial, duly distant relations between two men." For the narrator, however, the purpose of the wall is in its disintegration: by regularly disintegrating, the wall requires "the yearly ritual [of mending the wall] between the two men." Evidently, the narrator and his neighbor have very different understandings of why the wall (and its mending) is necessary. Nonetheless, it is these "stories" that animate the (material) purpose of the wall. And in the case of Frost's poem, good fences don't make good neighbors; "mending them does."[10]

If such is the significance of the story of a wall, let us then consider the narrative that led to the construction of the wall in the occupied West Bank. After the construction of Israel's security barrier, Avineri insisted that it had allowed Israelis to return to normal life. The narrative for why the wall was built in the first place, however, was outlined in a document titled "Saving

Lives: Israel's Anti-Terrorist Fence; Answers to Questions," published by the Israel Ministry of Foreign Affairs. In response to the question "Why is Israel building the Anti-Terrorist Fence?," the document states:

> More than 900 people were murdered in attacks carried out by Palestinian terrorists since late September 2000.
>
> Thousands of Israelis have been injured, many of the victims maimed for life. The terrorists infiltrated Israeli cities and towns and carried out attacks—often in the form of suicide bombings—on buses, in restaurants, shopping malls, and even private homes.
>
> No other nation in the world has before this time faced such an intense wave of terror, especially in the form of suicide bombings.
>
> In almost all of the cases, the terrorists infiltrated from Palestinian areas in the West Bank. The Palestinian leadership has done nothing to stop them and has even encouraged them.
>
> Israel's decision to erect a physical barrier against terrorism was taken only after other options were tried but failed to stop the deadly terrorist attacks. Public opinion in Israel pushed for building a fence that would block the terrorists from entering Israeli population centers. The absence of a barrier makes infiltration into Israel communities a relatively easy task for terrorists. No terrorists have infiltrated from the Gaza Strip into Israel in recent years, because an electronic anti-terrorist fence already exists there.
>
> The Government of Israel has an obligation to defend its citizens against terrorism. This right of self-defense is anchored in international law. The anti-terrorist fence is an act of self-defense that saves lives.[11]

The rationale for the existence of the wall revolves around the sole premise that Palestinian terrorists have carried out attacks. As is often the case with this brand of political discourse, the problem formulation follows an uncomplicated logic that doesn't take into account all of the complexities that define the politics of Palestine/Israel. Instead, the text states very simply that "900 people were murdered," the perpetrators were "Palestinian terrorists," the "terrorists infiltrated from Palestinian areas," and the "physical barrier" is meant to stop the attacks.

To be sure, the language (and vocabulary) used to describe the problem at hand does not just communicate or describe a political reality as is. Instead, as is often the case with wartime political rhetoric, it uses politically loaded terms such as "murder" and "terrorism" to create a sense of an existential crisis and, in the words of Collins and Glover, "generate [a] fear" of the cruel, murderous "Palestinian terrorist."[12] With the crisis established and fear generated, the wall is then presented as the only natural and commonsensical response. The narrative here is straightforward; Israelis face terrorism, and the anti-terrorist wall is meant to "block the terrorists." If one were to take into account the history of the Palestinian *Nakba* (the mass expulsion of Palestinians during and after the 1948 War), the proliferation of the settlement movement, and, in general, the dynamics of Israel's settler colonialism, the problem formulation would not be as uncomplicated as it stands in the above-mentioned document.[13] Furthermore, the solution to the problem (i.e., a physical barrier) would not be as simplistic either, especially when we consider the unsavory consequences this solution has for Palestinian lives and livelihoods in the occupied West Bank. Yet the proponents of the anti-terrorist wall only have a simplistic, dehistoricized characterization of Palestinian terrorism in view. The wall poses as a material consequence of, and an uncomplicated solution to, the problem of "Palestinian terrorists."

131

Expectedly, with the global proliferation of the "war on terror," it would be easy to locate this story of the wall elsewhere. For instance, this kind of narrative was enacted following an attack on Indian security forces in Pulwama in Jammu and Kashmir on February 14, 2019, and used to justify the construction of an anti-terror smart fence in Kashmir. The Indian Ministry of External Affairs responded to the incident by declaring the following in a press release: "This heinous and despicable act has been perpetrated by Jaish-e-Mohammed, a Pakistan-based and supported terrorist organization proscribed by the United Nations and other countries. This terror group is led by the international terrorist Masood Azhar, who has been given full freedom by Government of Pakistan to operate and expand his terror infrastructure in territories under the control of Pakistan and to carry out attacks in India and elsewhere with impunity."[14] Here too, the press release uses polarizing expressions such as "heinous and despicable act" and "terror infrastructure" to create a sense of crisis and generate fear. The overall narrative is also similarly uncomplicated as it entirely ignores the political context in which the attacks took place. It ignores the history of the Kashmiri liberation struggle, the everyday and structural oppression of Kashmiris, and the imperious presence of Indian military personnel in the area.[15] Instead, the problem is simple: India was attacked by Pakistani terrorists. India's response, as the press release goes on to specify, is as follows: "The Government of India is firmly and resolutely committed to take all necessary measures to safeguard national security. We are equally resolved to fight against the menace of terrorism. We demand that Pakistan stop supporting terrorists and terror groups operating from their territory and dismantle the infrastructure operated by terrorist outfits to launch attacks in other countries."[16] The solution is just as simple as the problem: The government of India only seeks to firmly and resolutely safeguard national security. This being the narrative character of the problem/solution, an anti-terror smart fence in Kashmir would seem like a commonsensical response to Pakistani terrorism. During the inauguration ceremony for the fence, the Union home minister Rajnath Singh said simply, "Pakistan has its own nature and we cannot change their nature. They will have to do it. Whatever initiatives India could take, we have taken."[17] Like the Israeli security barrier, the fence in Kashmir also has certain unsavory human and environmental consequences.[18] Yet for the proponents of the fence, the nature of Pakistani terrorism is so heinous and despicable that one is expected to consent to the (presumably) unintended consequences of such initiatives that are meant to secure India's national security.

As Collins and Sen argue in the introduction to this volume, however, the globalization of the "war on terrorism" discourse is not just a matter of other countries taking on the mantle of the fight against terrorism that was first initiated by the United States. It is equally a matter of the discursive tropes that define post-9/11 collateral language being replicated in political projects that ostensibly have nothing to do with the "war on terror." An obvious example is anti-immigration discourse (see Berry, this volume). Once again, this rhetoric involves a decontextualized, uncomplicated conception of the problem that aims to present a crisis at hand, generate fear, and encourage one to consent to unsavory political responses. Such a rhetoric was adopted by Hungarian prime minister Viktor Orbán when campaigning for a third term in office. With the European refugee crisis in view, he warned supporters, "Countries that don't stop immigration will be lost," and added, "Africa wants to kick down our door, and Brussels [i.e., the European Union] is not defending us. . . . Europe is under invasion already, and they are watching with their hands in the air."[19] Only a month earlier Orbán, during his state of the nation speech, had also declared that Europe (and its Christian identity) was threatened by a "decline of Christian culture and . . . Islamic expansion." He said, "We are those who think that Europe's last hope is Christianity. . . . If hundreds of millions of young people are allowed to move north, there will be enormous pressure on Europe. If all this continues, in the big cities of Europe there will be a Muslim majority."[20]

When signing "Executive Order 13767: Border Security and Immigration

Enforcement Improvements," President Trump invoked a similar discourse to raise the alarm over "illegal immigration." Section 1 of the executive order reads:

> Border security is critically important to the national security of the United States. Aliens who illegally enter the United States without inspection or admission present a significant threat to national security and public safety. Such aliens have not been identified or inspected by Federal immigration officers to determine their admissibility to the United States. The recent surge of illegal immigration at the southern border with Mexico has placed a significant strain on Federal resources and overwhelmed agencies charged with border security and immigration enforcement, as well as the local communities into which many of the aliens are placed.
>
> Transnational criminal organizations operate sophisticated drug- and human-trafficking networks and smuggling operations on both sides of the southern border, contributing to a significant increase in violent crime and United States deaths from dangerous drugs. Among those who illegally enter are those who seek to harm Americans through acts of terror or criminal conduct. Continued illegal immigration presents a clear and present danger to the interests of the United States.[21]

The terminology here is hardly apolitical. Like the political rhetoric of the "war on terror," both Orbán's public statements and the text of Trump's executive order use a highly charged vocabulary. Expressions such as "invasion," "Islamic expansion," "surge," "crime," and "danger" are not meant to reassure citizens of the state's ability to protect them, quite the contrary. They paint the current state-of-affairs as hapless, seeking to instill a sense of uncertainty, crisis, and fear. Admittedly, neither the U.S. president nor the Hungarian prime minister care to provide a context or evidence for their sweeping claims. There is no evidence of the impending "Islamic expansion" in Europe, the wholesale alteration of the cultural fabric of European societies, or the criminality of migrants entering the United States from the south. But it is only a straightforward formulation of the problem (of immigration) that pairs well with simple (or simplistic) solutions. For Hungary, the simple solution to the threat of "Islamic expansion" and "invasion" by African migrants was the construction of a border fence with Serbia and Croatia. In an interview five years after the construction of the fence, Hungarian secretary of state for public diplomacy and relations Zoltan Kovacs insisted that it was a means for Europe to defend itself against "global mass migration."[22] The wall was also the preferred (commonsensical) solution for Trump, as the

executive order went on to announce "the immediate construction of a physical wall on the southern border" with Mexico. And confirming that there
was indeed a slippage between the material and discursive tactics employed
in the war on "illegal immigration" and those deployed in the "war on terror," the executive order added that wall would prevent "illegal immigration,
drug and human trafficking, and *acts of terrorism* [emphasis added]."[23]

The Wall Is the Story

So far I have tied the story of the wall to its physical attributes. But can we
also talk about the purpose of a wall in a way that is entirely detached from
its physicality? Recounting the function of medieval walls, archeologist Ross
Samson proposed that the physical structure was nearly defenseless. Yet for
the "rulers, lords, and masters" who built these structures, their purpose was
symbolic, with the walls serving as markers of the "possession, authority,
and power" over those they "ruled or lorded." It is then not without reason
that peasant revolts in this period often led to the destruction of the largely
defenseless "manorial gatehouses."[24] The symbolism (or symbolic potency)
of the Berlin Wall was equally prominent. And for many, it was primarily a
symbol of bitter "publicity battles" that aimed to build "legitimacy and collective identity at home" and undermine "the other Germany."[25]

Returning to President Trump's proposed wall, it also became more of a
wall that operates in the realm of political discourse, rather than a material
presence, due to a lack of federal funding, despite the efforts of private initiatives such as We Build the Wall and Trump having forced the federal government into shutdown when his demand for $5.6 billion in federal fund-
ing was not met. In some parts of the border area, such as in south Texas,
terrain is also too rugged to build a physical barrier.[26] But while all these
factors meant that the entirety of the physical barrier did not materialize,
the wall still served a purpose since the appearance of the term "wall"—or,
more specifically, the intention to build a wall—in speeches and statements
concerning "terrorism" or "illegal immigration" was meant to be politically
poignant. This was the case when Trump announced that he was running
for president in 2016. In his speech, Trump said, "I would build a great wall,
and nobody builds walls better than me, believe me, and I'll build them very
inexpensively, I will build a great, great wall on our southern border. And I
will have Mexico pay for that wall." These lines, in and of themselves, do not
mean much. What is significant, however, is that they were couched between
the following statements:

. . . Our country is in serious trouble. We don't have victories anymore. . . .

. . . When do we beat Mexico at the border? They're laughing at us, at our stupidity. And now they are beating us economically. They are not our friend, believe me. But they're killing us economically. The U.S. has become a dumping ground for everybody else's problems. . . . When Mexico sends its people, they're not sending their best. They're not sending you. They're not sending you. They're sending people that have lots of problems, and they're bringing those problems with us. They're bringing drugs. They're bringing crime. They're rapists. And some, I assume, are good people. Our enemies are getting stronger and stronger by the way, and we as a country are getting weaker. . . .

. . . Now, our country needs—our country needs a truly great leader, and we need a truly great leader now. . . .

. . . Mark my words. Nobody would be tougher on ISIS than Donald Trump. Nobody.

I will find—within our military, I will find the General Patton, or I will find General MacArthur, I will find the right guy. I will find the guy that's going to take that military and make it really work. Nobody, nobody will be pushing us around. I will stop Iran from getting nuclear weapons.[27]

This speech—as is the case with all such announcements—was about Trump. It was meant to portray him as presidential. To this end, expressions such as "serious trouble," "we don't have victories," "the U.S. has become a dumping ground," "They're bringing drugs. They're bringing crime. They're rapists," "Our enemies are getting stronger," and "we as a country are getting weaker" were meant to signify a crisis that affects the country's standing, politically, socially, and economically. More importantly, such a crisis demanded "a truly great leader." Thus, enters the wall. The wall is something physical. But as the *Merriam-Webster Dictionary* definition of "wall" indicates, it also represents something that is resolute and unyielding and helps defend, deter, and protect. It is therefore not surprising that immediately after declaring his intention to build a wall along the southern border, Trump said, "Mark my words. Nobody would be tougher on ISIS than Donald Trump." This sequence was meant to indicate synonymy between something (i.e., a wall) that is physically resolute and unyielding and Trump's own toughness as a leader. Here, the feasibility of Trump's wall didn't matter. But simply uttering the term "wall" was (politically) poignant enough, as it colored Trump as a "tough leader" who, faced with a multiplicity of crises, intended to build something resolute and unyielding to help protect the nation and its people. This means that in the absence of an actual (physical) Trump wall, the mere utterance of the term "wall" in Trump's speeches served as an indicator of who he is as a political leader and what he intended to accomplish—in this case, a leader who plans to wall out "illegal immigrants." Admittedly, the fate of Trump's wall presents us with a unique scenario where we can discuss the wall only as the discourse. Nonetheless, it is still worthwhile to consider the potency of the discourse of walls in places where the physical wall exists. Here, we may wonder, what is the driving force? Is it the physical barrier that does the heavy lifting, or is it the discourse that in fact accomplishes the task of walling?

"Walls Don't Work" . . . So What?

The punchline here could be "walls don't work." In fact, in response to President Trump's plan to wall the entire U.S.-Mexico border, publications such as *Foreign Policy*, *Politico Magazine*, and *Reason Magazine* ran articles where the conclusion was simply, "history shows that walls don't work."[28] Or, as the historian Elisabeth Vallet puts it, "a border fence is the best way of doing nothing while showing that you are doing something."[29] But in a way, walls don't need to work. The Trump administration didn't need the physical wall to deport unaccompanied migrant children in its bid to, as Department of Homeland Security secretary Kirstjen Nielsen explained in her letter to the U.S. Congress, "secure our borders, enforce our immigration laws, and provide appropriate humanitarian protections to those who need it."[30] In the same way, the wall wasn't necessary when President Trump signed Executive Order 13769, "Protecting the Nation from Foreign Terrorist Entry into the United States," which placed a temporary moratorium on the resettlement of Syrian refugees and temporarily banned the entry of travelers from seven Muslim majority countries.[31] When India's Hindu nationalist government ventured to alter the demographic makeup of the country under the pretext of combating "illegal immigration," it didn't look to build a wall either. Instead, it passed the Citizenship Amendment Act of 2019 that effectively restricted Muslims' access to Indian citizenship. In these cases, the takeaway is that while the physical wall didn't exist, the narratives that drive the practice of walling prevailed. And lawmakers who agreed to the premise of these narratives erected other types of walls through laws and policies that persisted with the effort to wall out the perceived scourge of undocumented migration or the alleged threat of terrorism.

Of course, these other ways of walling also remind us that building a physical wall is a massively inconvenient affair. As was also the case with

Trump's wall, it requires the mobilization of exorbitant amounts of material and human resources in ways that are often politically unviable. That said, it would seem that the wall has now gone digital. The availability of biometric technologies such as fingerprinting, DNA testing, facial recognition, and bone marrow x-rays has meant that states don't need to engage with the inconvenience of building the physical wall. These technologies have "automated" the process of identifying "individuals based on their biological and behavioral characteristics." [32] While they are being used to control and limit migration and mobility, such biometric technologies also carry with them the added convenience that they are able to erect the wall within us. For the political leaders and states looking to build walls, this ensures that the inherent biology of certain individuals and communities forms the foundations of the (biometric) wall that keeps them out. So, building the physical wall may be inconvenient. But the practice of walling is now as easy as ever.

Internally Displaced People (IDPs)

Sri Lanka's celebrated victory over terrorism overlooked the implications for internally displaced people (IDPs) and their resettlement.[1] Yet IDPs and their resettlement have origins in the increasingly concentrated control of two factors of production, land and labor, by the third, capital—particularly following the creation of international institutions after World War II under U.S. hegemony. From 1796, following British colonization, this small island was known as Ceylon and in 1972 became Sri Lanka. At independence in 1948, Ceylon was led by a domestic bourgeoisie installed by the British to maintain the island as a Crown Colony and part of the Anglophone world in general. This "comprador bourgeoisie"—local elites who became intermediaries of foreign imperialist capital after independence—used nationalism and social democracy in a volatile mix supported by the Anglo-American-led liberal international system, with Ceylonese governments able to keep socialists and communists from gaining power.[2] The liberal Anglophone powers' historical tolerance for Sri Lanka's drift to nationalism crushed the people's liberation movements from the Sinhala and Tamil communities. Where Tamil people were concerned, the ensuing civil war lasted for more than twenty-five years and ultimately led to the creation of IDPs.[3] The end of civil war would leave the Tamil refugees—those who were not able to flee overseas in the hundreds of thousands—being resettled within the country's borders but not always in their original abodes. In examining the roots of this state of affairs in Sri Lanka, it is possible to make visible Anglo-American hegemonic tolerance of proto-fascism, with its destructive racist norms and vile exclusive nationalism, as a modern formation that is part of capitalism globally.[4]

This chapter addresses the importance of global language and metaphors in the context of social theory related to the fate of human rights under failing capitalism and the subsequent rise of forms of fascism. The first section addresses metaphors of political English language in the context of the material conditions of the liberal international order led by the United States. This sets the context for the use of the terms "IDPs" and "resettlement," considering how these terms serve to obfuscate actual war or conflict that refugees and ethnic cleansing entail. Following the banality of structural violence of the Bretton Woods system, banal use of "IDPs" and "resettlement" means not only ignoring violence but also accepting the land appropriation along with the victims being used as cheap surplus labor. The second section offers a historical analysis of Sri Lanka as it shifts from colonized plantation economy to parliamentary postcolonial state within the liberal international system. It examines how bourgeois capitalism that stratifies the class structure invites a majoritarian Sinhala reactionary system trending toward proto-fascism and resulting in ethnic cleansing and genocide that are given cover by the use of the language of "IDPs" and "resettlement." With the Bretton Woods system and the UN system tolerating the rightward drift, postcolonial Ceylon/Sri Lanka has been about the dominance of the structure of Anglo-America global hegemony disguised through a morass of English language terms central to several academic disciplines.

139

Banality of Liberal Internationalism: From "Development" to "IDPs" and "Resettlement"

Having witnessed the futility of colonialism in Burma and the horrors of the interwar years, George Orwell developed a general disgust for politicians. In his essay "Politics and the English Language," he argues that political language "of all political parties, from Conservatives to Anarchists—is designed to make lies sound truthful and murder respectable," suggesting that "political speech and writing are largely the defense of the indefensible."[5] In making evil essentially normal, colonial era politicians—Tory, Liberal, and Labour—lacked decency and honor as they continued with their practices in places such as Ceylon through institutions of government and society. These included the Ceylonese parliament occupied by the comprador bourgeoisie that the British created though a hundred years of a plantation economy, built on the exploitation of land and labor. Colonies were maintained by British hegemony that operated not only the world's structures of finance controlling credit, production serving free trade, and security in areas including shipping and naval warfare, but also in terms of knowledge, the ideas of bourgeois parliaments and the language of authority to maintain them.[6] When considering Ceylon and later Sri Lanka and language, major terms include "Crown land," "planter," and "coolie," not to mention "riot," "constable of peace," "paddy wagon," and then "insurgency," "emergency rule," "terrorism," and "prevention of terrorism act," leading to the twenty-first-century terms we are concerned with in this chapter, "internally displaced people"/"IDPs" and "resettlement."

It is important to consider the manipulation of language in bourgeois practices of politics. With metaphors central to language, they enable narratives conveyed to a constituency to hide actual practices of uneven capitalist development.[7] While Lakoff and Johnson do not offer a theory of political economy or culture, Orwell points to a plethora of regime types that use language to obfuscate reality. What really is pervasive through Ceylonese/Sri Lankan history in the use of the aforementioned terms is exploitation by imperial powers—exploitation in which Orwell himself participated as a colonial policeman in Burma. Bourgeois rule to benefit Western firms required cheap labor, abundant land, and lucrative markets overseas, all requiring practices of exploitation. In this process, language makes such terrible practices against people and the land banal, in Hannah Arendt's terms, working to defuse, vilify, and extinguish forms of resistance. In the twenty-first century not only the International Monetary Fund (IMF) and World Bank, but also the United Nations High Commissioner for Refugees (UNHCR), go along with the now ubiquitous language of "internally displaced people" or "IDPs" and "resettlement," overlooking how newly settled land in Sri Lanka proves fallow, with conditions forcing these refugees to become commodified as mobile labor without rights, as if they are stateless beings without protection of the state. For Arendt, it goes beyond the banal as statelessness is about a lack of political membership without a state or any institution to guarantee their rights.[8] With the law focused on individual human rights, the refugee is deliberately left in the hands of the violating state. In new postcolonial states, the "IDP" category created with the conveyance of the UN system means that refugees can be subject to any form of detention for their entire life, including in resettlements. Access to citizenship does not mean access to land. While the former colonial states deny refugees state protection, the abusive postcolonial states are left to obfuscate the truth with the aid of the Anglo-American powers.

For List and Polanyi, land and labor were brought under the control of early capital within the feudal system in England for wool export to the Hanseatic League in the fourteenth century, leading to harsh early accumulation. In this context, for Polanyi, the English state was created for the purpose of accumulation to then set the terms for the exploitation of land and labor, with self-protection against excesses reserved for the "white man" while colonizers undermined governments in colonized nations. In England it was through codifying crucial land takeovers via a land registry and accompanying institutions that by the sixteenth century landless people were internally displaced as "paupers" so numerous that they had to be resettled in urban workhouses to become part of abundant labor for the factories. These excesses were challenged by strikes in the nineteenth century, forcing new codes of rights and processes of self-protection for the "white man" via institutions allowing gradual improvements in England.[9] Laws for those in the colonized spaces, however, imposed the writ of Western industrial capital globally, decimating precapitalist structures in the colonies and providing Britain and the Western world a surplus army of labor—slaves and indentured labor—for material gains, with Ceylon (and later Sri Lanka) a prime case in almost every phase of colonialism and postcolonialism.

Shaping language for over five hundred years, the English experience, protected by the English Channel and the British flotilla without having to devote resources to maintain a large standing army, absorbed ideas and used overseas markets to surpass continental powers and impose its own order in *Pax Britannica*. Britain's version of global capitalism in the nineteenth century based on the domination of the seas and settler plantations displaced the more transactional commerce-oriented Dutch system. With it the English language become instrumental in normalizing exploitation of land and labor—making it banal as it might for Arendt—across the world, but particularly in postcolonial places such as Ceylon.

When the British arrived in Ceylon in 1797, there were three kingdoms: Jaffna in the north, and Kandy and Kotte in the south. These were forced into one centrally governed entity by 1815 though military might and that classic British chicanery that Orwell documented. The chicanery extended to the loss of native land to British control—as Crown land—but also the normalization of "volunteers" from the local population for road works, clearing of undesirable jungles, and so forth for the benefit of British firms. When more labor was needed and with locals unwilling to work while neglecting their traditional holdings, the British brought in indentured labor, even after the 1833 Slavery Abolition Act of the British Parliament. Faced with local rebellion, and thus an acute shortage of labor, the British began the settlement of Indian Tamil *coolies* in Ceylon to provide socially reproduced labor in turning Crown land into plantations connected by the railways being built.

To bolster the British settler population and their power, the colonial authorities provided land to the eager remnants of the Dutch and Portuguese colonial elite from the sixteenth to the eighteenth centuries, creating a land-owning Govigama caste in service of Britain.[10] This new Anglophile comprador bourgeoisie sustained the lucrative plantation economy of tea, rubber, and so on in Ceylon in perpetuity. Its utmost banality was symbolized by cricket played in whites on carefully groomed green fields over days punctuated by pleasant afternoon teas, while colonial subjects slaved in the hot sun on the plantations to create surplus for the shareholders in Great Britain. This was not without deep resentment among the local population, often led by materialist Buddhist monks toward violence.

142   Buddhist revivalism was initiated in the late nineteenth century by Anagarika Dharmapala, a Ceylonese Buddhist from a prominent family educated at the island's elite Royal College. Sponsored by American purists, this revivalist Buddhism was initially worldly and universal, rather than the crass perversion of materialist Buddhist nationalism Orwell observed in Burma. Yet it was not this scientific approach to Buddhism from colonial Ceylon, but rather the form that Orwell saw in Burma, that began to dominate Ceylon and later Sri Lanka. Intensively involved in the material world, in direct contravention of Dharmapala's Buddhist revivalism, the English-educated reactionary sentiments in modern Sri Lanka have origins in Europe in the English educations obtained by so many Sinhala leaders of the time. It would defy imagination that Sinhala leaders educated in England in the 1920s were not attentive to the activities of reactionaries in Italy and Germany turning to fascism, as well as the aggressive imperialism of Japan's version of "Asia for Asians."

The English common-law approach of appropriating land for monoculture for cultivation by labor in slave-like conditions underpinned the empire's success. The surpluses from the colonies guaranteed peace within the United Kingdom, where the working population rapidly gained middle-class status and people achieved some self-protection. Yet overseas it was an evil system made banal, for instance, by the mythos of a liberal Oxford and Cambridge education, despite protests in London by Fabians backed by the lectures at upstart London School of Economics. The banality became entrenched with actions such as trading of shares of colonial firms in London, with each having a berth and headquarters along the Thames with the expressions of pride in the British Empire conveyed by flags and coats of arms unique to British firms. In Ceylon, reactionary sentiments emerged with the rise of a virulently Sinhala Buddhist nationalism led by Oxbridge-trained S. W. R. D. Bandaranaike while the working class was organized by Trotskyites trained at the University of London and the London School of Economics.[11]

British liberalism had failed as a global project of the colonial powers because as an economic system it created and relied on uneven capitalist development. It operated by transferring wealth to the Anglo-American core to induce liberalism within, while it excluded Italy and Germany, leading to the rise of reactionary parties in those countries. In Japan, reactionaries abandoned the Taisho democracy, constructed within the Anglo-Japanese alliance signed in 1902, to return to extreme nationalist imperialism once Western powers imposed limits on Japan in the Four-Power Pacific Treaty in 1921. During this interwar period nationalists in colonized countries, including Ceylon, could not have helped but see the logic of the global trend toward reactionary parties countering Britain and its liberal politics. In this context, Bandaranaike created the reactionary Sinhala Maha Sahaba (Great Sinhala Council) in 1932 with an eye on Indian nationalism that was influenced by Italy and Germany—this, while the more reactionary Subhas Chandra Bose was falling under the sway of the Japanese project of the Greater Co-prosperity Sphere that emerged in reaction to the Four-Power Pacific Treaty. In influencing the "common man" the Bandaranaike trajectory looked to use Sinhala culture and to combine "populism and Sinhala chauvinism" as the Trotskyite Lanka Sama Samaja Party (LSSP) compared it with "brown fascism."[12]

The resort to reactionary politics globally was only halted by the Holocaust, which, for a time, made fascism a stillborn project and liberalism the only alternative. The subsequent Cold War ensured socialism was not tolerated even as forms of social democracy operated in parts of Western Europe under Christian Democrats, Socialists, and so on. However, at the core of the emerging United States hegemony, the continuations of New Deal policies were challenged by limiting Roosevelt's influence and openly rolling back these ideas via the Republican party's "Southern strategies" of proto-fascism. The implications of United States hegemony for postcolonial states such as Ceylon (at the time) were then profoundly tragic.

IDPs Being Resettled: Appropriation of Land and Emergence of Proto-Fascism

Understanding uses of ideology and language requires historical treatment of the spread of capitalism in its totality into Sri Lanka—that is, examining the material conditions under which metaphors are used in particular ways for particular purposes. In addressing general strikes of the early twentieth century, Leon Trotsky noted "power is indubitably in question: the revolutionary proletariat or fascism—which?"[13] World War II settled the question of fascism in material terms for the period, leaving history to settle the contest between failed liberalism and yet-to-be-established socialism. Rather than follow a more radical course to address liberal failure as suggested by John Maynard Keynes, the United States, led by Treasury official Harry Dexter, imposed an even more obviously exploitative system. At Bretton Woods in 1944, Dexter replaced the failed British imperial model with a formal global governance system in which the United States dominated, leading to resistance across the new "Third World," including Ceylon. The United States set up the IMF and World Bank in Washington, D.C., along with the General Agreement on Tariffs and Trade (GATT) in Geneva. With trade resuscitated and tariffs to be rolled back, this brought an embedding of uneven development into the postcolonial era. The system continued to provide cheap raw materials from the former colonies such as Ceylon to the colonial center in a continuous transfer of surplus value to the rich nations, thereby immiserating development in the postcolonial states. Meanwhile, with the politics of domination a dangerous game, the United Nations was set up with headquarters in New York City to ensure peace among the great powers but with license to continue war in the periphery, allowing Western powers means to contain organized opposition with even the weaponization of food.

This was the setting into which Ceylon emerged to be independent in 1948. The Crown Colony period from 1948 to 1972 meant two more decades of Western capitalist dominance that maintained existing production and continued the appropriation of new land and labor for new plantations. Within this banal liberal international system dominated by Anglo-American interests and run by Washington, the comprador bourgeoisie were willing partners. At independence the plantation industry was run by private firms locally, known as Rupee and Sterling companies with "a substantial continuity in terms of how the island's plantations were operated and managed."[14] The new U.S.-led global system meant that by 1951 the IMF imposed an end to social support programs for the poor, where most recipients were Sinhalese. Meanwhile the best-organized parties of the left, especially the LSSP with its Trotskyite zeal, were trending away from the gradualism of the Fabians. They led the counterhegemonic/counter-imperialist forces, facing Western governments that encouraged anticommunist actions.[15] With the reduction of subsidized food for the masses, the newly elected national socialist Bandaranaike government appropriated U.S. petroleum interests in Ceylon in the 1960s to save foreign currency and pay for imports of food. Washington responded by imposing sanctions, resulting in deepening crises as the Bretton Woods system pushed the electorate in the struggling postcolonial state over the next decade toward bourgeois notions of a free market.[16]

The actions of the colonial/imperial powers in Ceylon bordered on paranoia that resulted in proto-fascism. This led the comprador bourgeoisie to use Sinhala nationalist propaganda and the legitimation of the extremist monks that Orwell disliked in the Burmese context. The Sinhala masses were deprived of social support programs, and their poverty and increasing desperation meant they were easily co-opted by ultranationalist monks who hijacked a peaceful religion to construct a homogenous Sinhala identity and impose Sinhala Buddhism as the sole historical reality for the island. The mix of this nationalism with a notion of state socialism of the Stalinist patronage model meant a heady and corrupt nationalization of British-owned plantations was made worse as it was carried out without adequate consideration of others, especially minority Tamils who lost land to state-owned farms in the northeast region of the country.[17]

Ultranationalism meant that Sri Lanka's new national socialists—this is what they arguably were, given the heavy hand of the state over workers in addition to other policies—ignored the millennia of intermixing of peoples (aboriginal, Sinhala, Tamil, Moor, and so on) in favor of sinister proto-fascist notions of an Aryan Sinhala Buddhist nation threated by "50 million" Dravidian/Tamil peoples in India. Given space in the anticommunist fervor of the times, the ideological evil of proto-fascism spread cancerously in Sri Lanka while the Western powers ignored its rise in favor of crushing labor unionism. The comprador politicians obfuscated the true nature of exploitation as they violently quelled rebellions using terms such as "riots" to underplay Sinhala violence against minorities including the 1956–58 pogrom against Tamils, "insurgency" to crush Sinhala class-based opposition, and "terrorism" to delegitimate Tamil resistance while taking over Tamil land, particularly in the strategic northeast region of the island closest to India that also connects the Northern province with the Eastern province. As the drift became extreme with Buddhist Sinhala nationalism gaining momentum, Christian officers of the Ceylonese Army attempted a coup, and with Ceylon still a Crown Colony, the British delivered what amounted to a pardon, and arguably it served as a catalyst for deeper Sinhala Buddhist nationalism to then take over the country that then became the Republic of Sri Lanka in 1972.[18] The acceleration toward proto-fascism saw the Sinhala language and Buddhist religion promoted by successive governments led by both major parties, in a race to appease the chauvinistic forces led by Buddhist monks gaining power throughout the post-independence period.

As Sri Lankan political parties pandered to nationalist forces, the West's modus operandi increasingly shifted to using the far right, giving full support to the comprador classes using Buddhist Sinhala nationalism, as opportunity came in 1977 with the reimposition of a market economy that led to the privatization of nationalized plantations. The reimposition of the capitalist system in the late Cold War—following the Kirkpatrick Doctrine of U.S. alliances with far-right regimes—spawned new patterns of post–World War II proto-fascism featuring the displacement of minorities expelled from their land. This was also the case in Sri Lanka, especially in lands with access to water. Post-independence governments saw an opportunity for developing commercial-scale agriculture, fed by diverting the Mahaweli, the largest river. This meant the strategic displacement of Tamil people. Nonetheless, the Accelerated Mahaweli Development Project in Sri Lanka is supported by the UN agencies and Western powers.[19]

With movement further to the right as inequity increased, the reimposition of market economics on the Third World could only occur via an appeal to nationalist growth to signify a break with the colonial period. In essence, the comprador bourgeoisie had to become the nationalist bourgeoisie, exploiting their own people with Western capitalists supporting this arrangement using the structures of power to provide the necessary cover for human rights abuses. The shift to ultranationalism allowed the pro-market United National Party (UNP) to win, and so too with the Sri Lanka Freedom Party (SLFP) that shifted to the right from its social democratic coalition with the LSSP to carry on with market economics. Both parties competed further and further to the right in the 1980s all the way to proto-fascism. It meant that while NGOs and Western governments made the requisite discourse about human rights, Sri Lanka was being helped in the civil war against the Tamil separatists by many powers behind the scenes, especially the United States, India, and China.

The Tamil separatism of the 1980s came in part due to land takeovers and the loss of language rights following Sri Lankan independence in 1948.[20] With victory in the resulting civil war in 2009, the Sri Lankan government, with the active support of the United States and India, among others, prevented the creation of an independent Tamil Eelam state. From there emerged an extreme form of Sinhala Buddhist nationalism. With separatism denied to terrorists by government forces, tens of thousands of Tamil IDPs have been resettled in places other than their original hamlet, village, town, or city, on their own land.[21] Human rights violations continued in peace time. This included the appropriation of land and fearful minorities working for low wages, as Buddhist priests led violent mobs against them and their property while the police and military often just watched.

With refugees narrowly seen to be those outside their home country, the term "IDP" has come to be used instrumentally by the Sri Lankan state in collaboration with state and nonstate actors internationally. In reality, Tamil people displaced by war are actually UN Convention refugees unable to return to their land by an occupying force. In this situation the UN and the Sri Lankan government are denying UN Convention protection for Tamil people even when they have no state to appeal to for protection (in Arendt's terms). This follows over two decades of use of the term "terrorism" to prevent recognition of a civil war within territorial Sri Lanka. Such negligence allowed the nationalist bourgeoisie state and the liberal Anglophone partners running both international organizations and NGOs to ignore the nature of the conflict—and thus to continue to allow the extraction of surpluses from the still active plantation economy in Sri Lanka, when we consider use of cheap Tamil estate labor and valuable products such as tea and services such as tourism. Meanwhile an accepting international society, even if critical discursively, overlooked ethnic cleansing and even what could be described as micro-genocides, while those journalists and academics pointing to it have disappeared or been murdered.[22]

Rather than IDPs being merely displaced by unmentioned forces and conditions, these were refugees fleeing the violence of poverty or violence itself that came from targeted prosecution. For Arendt, the refugee to be resettled is a victim of totalitarian beliefs—whether fascism or Bolshevism—though the former has proved to be far more common within liberal spaces after World War II than scholars who dominate the scene care to admit. In examining the Third World, liberal scholars have often characterized proto-fascist moments as merely barbaric ethnic conflict, overlooking systematic prosecution via a modern state led by an ideology in the service of capital.[23] What liberal scholars have missed is that with the exclusion and delegitimization of the victims via language rife with clever use of metaphors, far-right governments have provided an overarching narrative to tie together national, political, and linguistic-religio-cultural elements to create a narrative of victimhood for themselves—a classic fascist strategy.

With greater contextualization offered by his longue durée critique, Polanyi saw the rise of fascism with the failure of liberalism. Arendt sees that when governments lose legitimacy and power, they resort to violence. For her, a (violent) totalitarian system—Bolshevism or fascism—signifies a lack of power, thus illegitimate, with followers unaware that this overarching ideology (filled with promises) ultimately sacrifices them. Arendt's insight into fascist ideology as an expression of weakness of the state brings her closer to Polanyi. Ultimately, for both, the loss of legitimacy leads to violence, including crimes against humanity that fascism yields.[24] As Butler and Spivak note of Arendt: "If a crime against humanity had become in some sense 'banal' it was precisely because it was committed in a daily way, systematically, without being adequately named and opposed. In a sense, by calling a crime against humanity 'banal,' she was trying to point to the way in which the crime had become for the criminals accepted, routinised, and implemented without moral revulsion and political indignation and resistance."[25] As for Arendt, the banality of clichés and the mundane are ways to account for the role of language, but Polanyi points to material interests of capital.

The Sinhala Buddhist majority community in Sri Lanka has been made to feel victimized despite their dominance in local politics. Sinhala Buddhist dominance was never in question even through the colonial years with the rise of Dharmapala and return to worldly Buddhism in the late nineteenth century. Sinhala Buddhists under the influence of a victim narrative overlook the vulnerability and victimization of minority populations in Sri Lanka who would be protected in a society operating according to actual Buddhist principles. The civil war began after the 1983 pogrom against Tamils in which thousands died. It was brutally ended in 2009 with tens of thousands massacred in a short period of months, leading to the subjugation of historically Tamil areas of the country in full view of the international community and the language it has accepted.

Following use of the language of "riots," "insurgency," and "terrorism" by Ceylonese leaders through the twentieth century, it was perhaps not surprising that the Sri Lankan state would favor the language of "internal displacement" and "resettlement" following the logic of capitalism that created Western colonialism and a global capitalist system reliant on land and labor well into the twenty-first century. In the interest of reactionary Sinhala nationalism and colonization of Tamil lands, the state was targeting minority resistance with charges of "terrorism" in the 1980s. Tamil separatists sought to protect their land by any means necessary. They were labeled "terrorists" to be "eradicated" or exiled for the purpose of "national unity" and "national security." The resulting human tragedy visited on the Tamil population in the three-decade-long civil war led to hundreds of thousands of IDPs, who were placed in high-security camps and strategically located new settlements provided by Western aid.

Despite rights of minorities enshrined in the UN, the historically compromised bourgeois state–dominated UN system means that when it comes to the interests of minorities—including in Sri Lanka, where Tamils and Moors were ethnically cleansed at a minimum, if not also targets of at least cultural genocide—there is no mechanism of actual prevention, with action made next to impossible through the use of language to convey the opposite of what is taking place. Simply stated, the cover of the sanitized terminology of "IDPs" and "resettlement" allows the capitalist state to dominate minorities. While in Sri Lanka the total number of IDPs dropped from over half a million at the peak, those who have been moved permanently are often resettled in model villages not far from military camps and away from their ancestral lands. These refugees have been resettled on lands that are not productive or are in locations vulnerable to drought. Others are being forced into cheap labor in the city, fearfully driving cabs, working in restaurants, and so forth.

The language of "IDPs" in the new century is useful for hegemonic actors—British, U.S., Indian, and Chinese—as they seek to contain the damage, avoid responsibility, and incorporate the Tamil parts of the island not yet part of any corporate supply chain due to the three-decade civil war. Despite public displays to the contrary in the issue of war crimes in Sri Lanka, these major actors do not just tolerate but actually sponsor new forms of Sri Lankan state violence for the sake their interests, and thus they have created together a new global proto-fascist turn in competition with each other.[26] It is in this larger historical frame that post-independence Ceylon and then republican Sri Lanka, with successive UNP- and SLFP-centered governments in competition with each other, have operated in zones beyond humanitarian norms by strategically working between and with the major powers of the world, particularly Britain, India, the United States, and China, all with interests in the Indian Ocean. Within this complex global capitalist context, shaped by centuries of colonial rule, the term "IDP" has become ubiquitous in the reporting of masses of people being forced from their homes from war, systematic rape, ethnic cleansing, and genocide in multiple locations in the world.

Confronting Proto-Fascism

The oldest Asian democracy and one of the earliest with market systems in place has failed to live up to its promise. This chapter points to the degree of material interest driven by global capitalism and its institutions that has underpinned the trajectory of Sinhala Buddhist nationalism in Sri Lanka from the 1920s onward inexorably toward conflict with minorities, civil war, and proto-fascism. This situation is completely against the tenets of Buddhism that Anagarika Dharmapala, the leading nineteenth-century Buddhist revivalist, would understand.[27] In that spirit of Buddhist principle, Tamils of Indian origin—the so-called Indian Tamils—should be full citizens having essentially contributed to Sri Lanka for two hundred years as slave labor providing their surplus to the island as a whole.

Given the importance of Sri Lanka to liberalism, this chapter contends that the contemporary use of the language of "IDPs" and "resettlements," in full view of the world, has normalized not just ethnic cleansing but also the exploitation of Tamil refugees in precarious work carried out under perpetual fear. The establishment of proto-fascism means civil society is silenced by Sinhala "Buddhist" vigilantes led by priests at times. The proto-fascist state with narratives of Sinhala Buddhist victimhood victimizes othered minority communities of Tamils and Moors. This invites important questions not only about domestic history and conditions in Sri Lanka today, but also about the structural setting created especially by British colonization and U.S. hegemony and the subsequent impact of Indian and Chinese influence that has systematically imposed market relations and ignored human rights.

The late twentieth-century formation of Sinhala Buddhist domination of the country takes place with the full complicity of Western powers still seeking to maintain a presence on the island in competition with China and India. Appropriated land is being deployed at a global commercial scale for the benefit of capitalists and new Sinhala settlements forming a historical vanguard in minority areas. Land has been taken over by the military—reflecting the current example of the Chinese proto-fascist military with direct corporate interests. Chinese proto-fascism as a formation supports the Sri Lankan regime in competition with the Indian government that has also taken a proto-fascist turn. For their part, Western nations waver over concerns for human rights, while supporting interests of capitalists and seeking to contain China; in a way, they reflect how their own far right has gained traction toward proto-fascism.

At the present historical juncture, it is difficult not to reach the conclusion that capitalism's most advanced stage is, in fact, a form of fascism. Within its narrative of victimhood for the dominant community, this formation allows land takeovers via ethnic cleansings and land takeovers with impunity. It is enabled by the use of the language of "IDPs" that leaves the legal responsibility for human rights squarely in the hands of the sovereign nation state, itself a creation of capitalism. The twenty-first-century formation of proto-fascist capitalism is normalized by language. It leaves only the emancipatory social democratic alternative, that Lenin ironically crushed to address uneven capitalist development, as a way of preventing the root cause of proto-fascism. The irony deepens as parties such as the LSSP did offer a multiethnic/multilinguistic path—away from violence—in Ceylon but never found support in the West, which was transfixed by Bolshevism and instead tolerated the emerging Sinhala Buddhist nationalism that became proto-fascist.

CHAPTER 13

JOHN COLLINS,
PALOMA ELVIRA RUIZ,
AND MARINA LLORENTE

Victims

On October 2, 2014, the leader of the Spanish Socialist Party (PSOE), Pedro Sánchez, issued a tweet addressing gender-related killings of women. Rather than speaking of *violencia de género* (gender violence) or *violencia doméstica* (domestic violence), both of which already had broad currency within civil society and public discourse, the future Spanish president chose a relatively new term: *terrorismo machista*. Borrowing from progressive movements that had worked to bring the concept of *machismo* (male chauvinism) into public discussions of violence in order to emphasize the structural nature of violence against women, Sánchez connected *violencia machista* (male chauvinist violence) rhetorically with the concept of "terrorism." Further, he proposed recognizing the victims of *terrorismo machista* with state funerals, which previously had been granted to some victims of political terrorism in Spain.

The tweet came roughly a decade after some Spanish news outlets had begun reporting regularly on intimate partner violence. By 2014, viewers of Spanish state TV would not have been surprised to see the death of a woman at the hands of her husband, partner, or ex-partner reported as a national story rather than simply a local one, with each new case statistically recognized as part of a larger pattern. Sánchez's suggestion of state funerals went further, taking the pain suffered by victims of intimate partner violence and giving that pain the ultimate form of national recognition.

Sánchez's proposal spoke to the growing attention paid to violence against women in Spain, and it revealed the impact of decades of grassroots organizing. The long-overdue arrival of this issue to the public stage is cause for celebration. At the same time, Sánchez's decision to draw on the concept of terrorism suggests that there is more to the story. As the "global war on terrorism" (GWOT) has surely taught us, any invocation of terrorism by the state calls for critical analysis. In Spain, the spread of this concept into broader areas of social and political life reveals a need to examine the closely related discourse of victimization and its particular significance in a society that still struggles to come to terms with its own violent history.

In this chapter, we argue that the use of the term "victims" (in Spanish, *víctimas*) in the contemporary Spanish context reveals its instrumentalization by the state, with two far-reaching consequences. First, it contributes to the ongoing collective amnesia surrounding the country's Civil War (1936–39) and the violence of the subsequent Francoist dictatorship (1939–75). Second, it empowers the state in its neoliberal project of defending the privileged against the demands of the global majority at a time of escalating global crisis.

Our purpose in offering this analysis is not to cast doubt on particular claims of victimization, nor is it to suggest that the term "victims" needs to be abandoned. Indeed, acknowledgment of victimization is an essential step toward diagnosing structural injustices and making them more visible. Nonetheless, we seek to illuminate what happens when national discussions of victimization are sequestered within the rhetorical frame of terrorism and anti-terrorism.

Tracing the Concept of "Victim"

One function of official discourses of victimization is to specify what the dead are allowed to teach us. Under the state-supported logic of the GWOT, a death at the hands of terrorists teaches us that we must empower the state to take measures to fight terrorism. Presumably, the effort to label *violencia machista* as a form of terrorism is designed to impart a similar lesson. But what of the victims of capitalism, or fascism, or state violence in general? What do they teach us? What are we allowed to learn from them?

Writing of the struggle against fascism, Walter Benjamin predicted in 1940 that "even the dead will not be safe from the enemy if he wins. And this enemy has not ceased to be victorious."[1] Composed shortly before he died in the border town of Portbou, Spain, while trying to flee the advance of fascism, Benjamin's haunting words remind us that the concept of victimization is always bound up in the politics of social memory—that is, the power dynamics that shape how we understand the relationship between past and present. In an era of mass violence, the power to decide who is a victim and who is not is an especially potent form of symbolic power, one that customizes victimhood for the purpose of writing official histories. For this reason, it matters greatly which deaths are given the official status of victim in the eyes of the state.

Spain in the era of the GWOT provides us with an excellent case for exploring what is at stake in the naming of victims. Popular voices criticizing the instrumentalization of victims by the state have a long background within Spanish civil society. In the case of terrorism, several associations of victims have already denounced political parties' attempts to take advantage of their cause. Similarly, some Spanish feminists have long defended the autonomy of grassroots feminist movements in relation to structures of formal institutional power. We see our intervention as a contribution to this broader discussion through a critical exploration of the strategies that the state has articulated to produce such "national victims" in recent Spanish democratic history. Following the main thread of the book, we organize our analysis around two broad temporal periods: "Before 9/11" and "After 9/11".

Before 9/11

The concept of terrorism has a significant pre-9/11 history in Spain. As in many other contexts, its usage in Spain has always been deeply ideological, focusing attention on official enemies—in this case, ETA (Euskadi Ta Askatasuna—Basque Homeland and Freedom)—and away from the state's own violence. The selectivity of this process has direct implications for how the concept of victimhood is politically organized in the country. Prior to 9/11, important patterns had already established which victims would be granted national recognition and which would be systematically forgotten.

Created in 1959, ETA was an armed separatist organization that joined other Basque groups in seeking national independence for the Basque Country, which straddles the border between Spain and France. Beginning in the late 1960s, ETA employed tactics of political violence, including shootings and bombings that killed more than eight hundred people. In keeping with the dominant definition of terrorism that emerged globally during this period, a definition reserved almost exclusively for nonstate actors, the Spanish state declared ETA a terrorist organization and sought to disrupt the group's activities through arrests, covert operations, and other tactics. ETA declared a permanent ceasefire in 2011.

For several decades, the victims of ETA's attacks were the only recognized and celebrated victims of terrorism in Spain. Initially the majority of these victims were military and police personnel and their families, but soon the group began to target individuals from the business sector as well as Basque parliamentarians. After Franco's death in 1975, ETA expected to get independence for the Basque Country. When the group's demand was not addressed, they escalated their tactics. On July 28, 1979, three bombs in Madrid's airport and train stations killed seven people and injured a further one hundred. This came a day after attacks in Bilbao and San Sebastian had killed four people. These initial attacks on civilians generated a strong outcry from the Spanish public. In 1981, the Terrorism Victims Association (Asociación de Víctimas del Terrorismo or AVT) was created with the goal of supporting people affected by terrorist acts. The AVT pioneered the civil movement against terrorism in Spain, leading to the establishment of many other similar associations in the following decades. The AVT received extensive support from the state, particularly after ETA killed Miguel Angel Blanco, a Basque parliamentarian from the governing right-wing Popular Party (PP), on July 13, 1997.

The Blanco killing represented a unifying moment for Spain, sparking many protests and other gatherings held throughout the country to condemn ETA and memorialize the victims, who were honored at the national level with state funerals and financial compensation for families. This was a key moment when broader Spanish political discourse and the discourse of terrorism intersected, revealing the state's effort to instrumentalize the concept of terrorism. Equally important, it is a clear example of how the status of victims has been politicized for right-wing ideological purposes. While the conservative government used state television to make statements against ETA, many citizens at demonstrations in cities throughout Spain began raising "white hands" (*manos blancas*) as a symbol, following the example of Spanish students who had used maneuver in 1996 as a sign of innocence and of their revulsion at ETA's murder of law professor Francisco Tomás y Valiente.

At the same time, another grassroots movement was gaining visibility at the national level: the struggle by families to recognize the victims of the Spanish Civil War (1936–39) and the subsequent Francoist dictatorship. The Association for the Recuperation of Historical Memory (ARMH) was created in 2000, responding to the needs of these families. The active response of the government and Spanish society in general to the needs of ETA's victims had raised obvious questions: What about Francoism's victims? What about those who had lost their lives in the struggle against fascism? Shouldn't these victims and their families receive national acknowledgment and support?

To answer these questions, we have to go back to Franco's death in 1975 and examine the incomplete manner in which the transition from dictatorship to democracy (generally known in Spain as "the Transition") was carried out. On the one hand, the deep structures of the dictatorship were never broken and remain active in some key state institutions. On the other hand, the country never carried out a process of national reconciliation that would have represented a real confrontation with the past. In this sense, the Civil War itself could be viewed as unfinished, especially given that it was erased from the national imaginary during the Transition through a rhetoric claiming that revisiting the country's violent past would only provoke divisions and that it was better to look to the future. Equally important, the 1977 Amnesty Law freeing all political prisoners had sought to put an end to the armed conflict that had divided the country into winners and losers throughout the dictatorship.

What was also forgotten, however, is that the Civil War was a class struggle as well as a struggle between modernism and conservatism. The fascist victory in 1939 alienated all those who had participated in the democratizing process of the Second Spanish Republic between 1931 and 1936 and subsequently defended it during the war. The gains won by reformers during the Republican period, such as the abolition of the monarchy, the subordination of the military to civilian authority, the law of agrarian reform, the secularization of the state, and the 1932 divorce law, had made Spain one of the world's most progressive countries. With its victory in the Civil War, Francoism sought to demonize these advances and to create a grim and dangerous image of the Republican years and the anti-fascist struggle. The fear of leftist ideologies, combined with the fear of reprisals against those who had different ideas during the long Francoist years, worsened after 1975 and produced the erasure of the past. This narrative effectively made it possible for the Transition to break with the period of the Republic in order to construct a new Spain, a European Spain disconnected from the past. The Amnesty Law closed the door on any revisionist efforts, legal or otherwise.

The norm in Spain has been to refer to the Transition as a model process in which no blood was spilled. In September 2019, for example, top PSOE official Carmen Calvo told Spanish newspaper *El País* that the country had emerged from the dictatorship "in a brilliant manner, without even a touch of violence except from ETA."[2] As many Twitter users quickly pointed out, Calvo was forgetting what investigators had previously established: that political violence of "institutional origin" and from right-wing terrorism resulted in the deaths of more than seven hundred people during the years of the Transition. Calvo's error, however, inadvertently revealed how the example of ETA has served as a convenient bogeyman for a state seeking to hide the long history of fascist violence.

Spanish historians and sociologists have offered sharp critiques of the political class's idealized picture of the Transition. Juan Carlos Monedero,

Paloma Aguilar, and Víctor Pérez Díaz note that even before Franco's death, the Left itself helped ensure that the Transition would take place in the way that it did. Monedero highlights how the PSOE, in its famous thirteenth Congress held in exile near Paris in 1974, began a process of reform that sparked a major ideological change in the party. It was there that a group of young socialists led by Felipe González proposed a shift away from Marxism and toward European-style social democracy, eventually succeeding in getting González elected as secretary-general.

157

This moment would shape the country's political future and the development of the Transition. On the cultural level, a thick veil was thrown over the memories of the Second Republic, the Civil War, and the Francoist years, and the 130,000 Spaniards buried in mass graves throughout the country were forgotten. The Transition presented itself as a division between conservatives and reformers or democrats, and because the Left didn't want to be accused of being reactionary, it had to accept the rules of the game introduced by the young socialists and the inheritors of Francoism now disguised as liberal centrists.

The amnesia imposed on the Spanish social fabric covered the trauma of the Civil War, preventing a process of national reconciliation and erasing the class struggle by presenting it as obsolete and anachronistic. In this "new" Spain, there was no room for Marxist paradigms; there would be no working classes because all would be "modern" and "European," belonging to an immense and powerful middle class. This rhetoric was quite successful. The majority of Spaniards accepted the "pact of silence" and took the euphoric European train, leaving behind a past of which they had become ashamed or which they viewed as an obstacle. Today, however, many Spaniards recognize that the Transition remains incomplete and that a process of national reconciliation is still needed along with a dismantling of the Francoist traces in public institutions and society in general.

The families belonging to the ARMH believe that their victims have a right to the same recognition as any other victims. Their efforts initially met strong opposition from the right-wing PP government during the 1990s. The PP's interest in the victims of ETA terrorism and disinterest in victims of the Civil War and the dictatorship is not surprising given the party's origins as the inheritor of the Francoist tradition. Acknowledging Francoism's victims would have brought to the surface an obvious tension between the PP's commitment to neoliberal policies and the progressive ideology of the Spanish Republic. Crucially, however, the PSOE and United Left (Izquierda Unida) provided support to the ARMH and related social movements by presenting parliamentary proposals that condemned Francoism and honored its victims after twenty years of inactivity on this subject.

The PP defended its argument of not wanting to "reopen old wounds," insisting that national reconciliation had already been reached with the democratic Constitution of 1978. In reality, what was happening was a calculated process of burying the past once again. Acknowledging and addressing this history would have encouraged Spaniards to recognize that Francoism's victims were killed precisely because of their progressive values and their love of the Republic. It would have forced a reckoning with the mass violence, including state terrorism, that was integral to the Francoist project. We needed to wait until the attacks of September 11, 2001, and the subsequent 2004 attacks in Madrid to see how the concept of terrorism would shape Spanish public discourse in a new and complex way.

After 9/11

The September 11 attacks mark a "before" and an "after" in this chapter as an allusion to the shift in global policies against terrorism and to the role that terrorism's victims played after that date. As illustrated in the original *Collateral Language* volume, powerful media corporations were collaborators in the launching of the GWOT, deploying language that made a global war against terrorists—the enemies of the state—seem necessary and inevitable. The same applies to the main international political forums, such as the United Nations Security Council, which passed a resolution to globally "fight against terrorism" a few weeks after 9/11. The resolution addressed the expectations placed on member states to participate actively in the nascent GWOT by preventing, detecting, and condemning terrorist attacks and to adopt additional measures in their territories.

In Spain, the GWOT discourse established a strong foothold in political debates when Spain chose to ally itself with the U.S. war on Iraq in 2003. The threat of jihadist terrorism became a new mantra for the ruling PP as it sought to justify its international posture. Following the March 11, 2004, Madrid train bombings (referred to in Spanish as 11M), however, frictions emerged within the PP between the invocation of the emerging post-9/11 global discourse on terrorism—in which jihadists are the unequivocal agents of terrorist attacks—and the allusion to the historical Spanish discourse on ETA as perpetrators of terrorist acts.

Immediately after the 11M attack, Spanish society was confronted with an urgent question: was the attack a consequence of the government's decision to become an ally of the GWOT? The question acquired a special relevance as general elections were about to take place just three days later. A positive answer to that question would foreseeably hurt the PP's electoral chances, as people might blame the party for the death of nearly two hundred people and the injury of another two thousand in Madrid. Finding itself at a political crossroads, the PP chose the easy way: pointing to ETA as the alleged perpetrator. ETA denied its involvement, and al-Qaeda claimed responsibility, but the PP stuck to its initial theory for two days, with the support of important right-leaning media groups.

Meanwhile, the opposition PSOE stuck to the evidence, condemned the attack, and pointed out al-Qaeda as the perpetrator. On March 14, the PSOE won the general elections, and soon after he took office as president, party leader José Luis Rodriguez Zapatero visited Madrid's "ground zero" and several hospitals where victims were resting. During one visit, Zapatero had a chance meeting with the mother of a gender violence victim who had been admitted to the same hospital. According to media reports, Zapatero expressed the PSOE's commitment to fighting against gender violence by pushing forward legislation that had been stuck in parliament for years.[3] Thus, a single visit served the new president to subtly outline two of the main social issues that would mark the PSOE's political agenda: gender violence and (inter)national terrorism. Moreover, by taking the side of the victims, the PSOE set a "moral" distance from previous PP social policies.

During Zapatero's nearly eight years in office, the parliament passed three important laws connected with attempts to define victims and victimizers. A review of the new laws and the sociopolitical contexts in which they were passed gives us a general picture of how the state understands the status of "victim" as well as the ideological reasons behind the condemnation of certain social conflicts over others. Two of the laws are directly related to the political agenda shown in Zapatero's hospital scene after 11M. The first is the Organic Law 1/2004 of Comprehensive Protection Measures against Violence against Women, passed in December 2004 after lengthy negotiations. Here it is worth noting that on September 11, 2002, the left-wing Izquierda Unida (IU) had presented a motion urging the PP to tackle "gender terrorism."[4] The second law, passed in 2011, concerns "recognition and protection of victims of terrorism." It derives from the application of the aforementioned 2001 UN Security Council resolution but also addresses the victims of national terrorism by groups such as ETA or GRAPO (an armed antifascist group). Between the approval of these two laws, parliament also passed the 2007 Law on

Historical Memory, which aimed to recognize "those who suffered political persecution and violence during the civil war and the dictatorship."[5]

With these three laws and their respective contexts in mind, two key points emerge regarding how the state regulates the status of victim. First, looking at the texts of the laws themselves, it is remarkable that the only explicit and recurring references to the condition of the victim are in relation to ETA/jihadist terrorism and gender violence, and never in relation to the crimes committed by Franco's regime. Instead, these crimes are embodied by an abstract, collective, and homogeneous subject (*aquellos que sufrieron* [those who suffered]) situated in the blurred temporal borders between the Civil War and the subsequent dictatorship.

The point here is not to insist on the right to be called "victims"—a measure that many Marxist and anarchist militants would reject. Instead, we are pointing out that the legislation and the attribution (or not) of the condition of victim carries ideological rereadings of certain episodes of the Spanish history and specifies a certain role for the state. For instance, referring explicitly to (national) victims within the frame of gender violence and terrorism might be a fruitful political strategy for empowering the state as the savior that protects us from the victimizers—the enemies of the state. On the other hand, talking about victims when referring to those murdered after Franco's military coup might be a dead end for the state, since it would also presume the existence of a victimizer state—a taboo subject after the passage of the 1977 Amnesty law. In this vein, it is important to remark that we are not seeking to discredit the victims who have been recognized by the state. On the contrary, our argument stands with the victims who have passed through different forms of violence; but it does not stand with the state's manipulation of history and the instrumentalization of victims for its own benefit and for the benefit of the elites that it serves.

Second, the overlapping of the debates on the fights against terrorism and gender violence after 9/11 does not seem to be a one-time coincidence but something recurrent and normalized within political discourses over time. The examples discussed here show how the liberal political class started to incorporate that metaphorical association in its own rhetorical arsenal. While the origins of the metaphor are unclear, it seems the references to (victims of) *terrorismo machista* within activist spaces might be aimed at pushing this issue under the umbrella of the state while providing the assaulted with social recognition. Given what we know about the rhetoric of the GWOT and its broader influence since 9/11 (e.g., an expansion of executive power and security apparatuses, growing ethnic and religious persecution, the strengthening of regimes of punishment), the entrance of this rhetoric into debates on gender violence should raise alarm bells.

More than a decade separates the IU's motion to tackle "gender terrorism," Zapatero's hospital encounter, and Pedro Sánchez's tweet. These examples reveal the nature of the conceptual leap that is taking place, but the story does not finish there. While other discursive frames have become obsolete over the years, this one seems to have fossilized in Spanish political rhetoric. Furthermore, its symbolic value appears to have been substituted for a material one. Such is the case of the August 2019 statement by Compromís (a left-leaning party based in the Spanish region of Valencia) calling on the Senate to declare a state of emergency—a measure typically restricted to situations of armed conflict or natural disaster—against "gender terrorism" and to criminalize the denial or banalization of "gender terrorism."

Resisting Neoliberal Securitization

The analysis presented here reveals that the two consequences listed in the introduction to this chapter—national amnesia and the carrying out of the neoliberal project—are really two parts of an interrelated whole. The Spanish state's selective use of the discourse of victimization results not only in the failure to acknowledge those who were harmed by Francoism, but also in a deeper failure: the failure to create a space in the current political landscape for the socially progressive and anti-fascist ideals that emerged during the Republican years and the Civil War. These twin failures suggest that the legacy of the anti-fascist movements of that period—a legacy of popular empowerment and solidarity against entrenched economic interests—poses a direct threat to the neoliberal order that the state seeks to uphold.

This process of neoliberal forgetting has further consequences that bear on the larger process through which the GWOT has fed a global machinery of racial exclusion and securitization. When Spanish news outlets began to increase their coverage of gender violence in the early 2000s, they often employed language that foregrounded the ethnic, religious, or national identity of certain perpetrators—those who could be described as *de origen marroquí* (of Moroccan origin), for example. The use of such language signaled how easily the racist logic of the GWOT can slide into discussions of domestic issues, with the male chauvinist immigrant occupying the same space in the discourse as the jihadi or Basque terrorist. These constructions, in turn, echo ideological constructions of the anti-fascist "losers" of the Civil War as criminal, mentally ill, and not fully Spanish. In other words, the discursive intersection of anti-terrorism, Francoism, and the struggle against gender violence illustrates a common strategy of convincing the people that the enemy is not the state or the ruling class, but the Other: immigrants, Muslims, anarchists, and *rojos* (reds).

162

The refusal to recognize these groups as victims coincides with an additional element of the GWOT: the construction of anyone who opposes the state as a potential terrorist. While the individual victim of jihadist or Basque terrorism may be rhetorically useful for the state, the logic of the GWOT constructs the state itself as the ultimate victim even as it seeks to reconsolidate its power after more than a decade of post-1989 talk about the "decline" of the state. The passage of Spain's infamous 2015 law on public security, widely known as "La Ley Mordaza (the Gag Law)," represented a draconian expansion of state power to criminalize dissent at a time when grassroots mobilization was on the rise. This use of exceptional measures reminds us of why calls to declare a state of emergency against gender violence must be viewed with considerable skepticism.

Finally, recent developments in Spanish politics demonstrate how state efforts to manipulate the discourse of victimization can open the door for far-right groups to weaponize that discourse for their own purposes. With the neoliberal project and the securitizing machine of the GWOT producing popular resistance in the form of the anti-austerity *indignados* movement and mobilizations on behalf of global migrants, Spain's most conservative political forces began referring to themselves as victims—of multiculturalism, of feminism, of political correctness, and of anti-fascist groups. As the PP disintegrated amid a devastating corruption scandal and the country lurched from one inconclusive election campaign to the next, these far-right forces—those for whom the demise of Francoism had represented an ideological defeat—coalesced in the form of Vox, a new political party whose misogynistic and racist rhetoric echoed that of Donald Trump. During the January 2020 parliamentary debate on Sanchez's investiture as president following an agreement to form a coalition with the leftist Unidas Podemos party, Vox leader Santiago Abascal accused the PSOE of enabling the sexual assault of Spanish women by opposing life sentences for convicted offenders. More than a cynical invocation of women's victimization for right-wing purposes, it was also a transparent attempt to construct all of Spanish society as a victim of progressive leaders whose approach to fighting terrorism is somehow never harsh enough.

In this light, the decision of liberal and even leftist parties in Spain to adopt the language of terrorism when advocating for action against gender violence calls for further analysis. Certainly, for the PSOE, the growing embrace of neoliberal managerialism has resulted in an attempt to rule through the foregrounding of social policies that appeal to mainstream feminism rather than *indignados*-style populism or militant anti-fascism. At the most basic level, one is reminded of Audre Lorde's famous observation that "the master's tools can never dismantle the master's house." More specifically, this emerging discourse of victimization represents a denial of the structural nature of the very suffering it seeks to eliminate. Rather than focusing attention on patriarchy as something that must be eliminated through education, community organizing, and a focus on fundamental human rights, the discourse of *terrorismo machista* seeks liberation through the repressive power of the state. This troubling approach finds its analogue in the refusal to name Francoism as a structural reality that continues to operate throughout Spanish society, leaving a trail of victims in its wake. Thus, in the face of these two ways of instrumentalizing victims, we would see a common resistance strategy among feminist movements and those struggling for historical memory: defending a notion of victimhood that reminds us of our right to truth, justice, reparation, and liberation.

163

Catherine Tedford, *Virus*. Reprinted with permission of the artist.

Afterword: Wounds

VIJAY PRASHAD

These are miserable times. Everywhere you look the news is startling. The keywords for the present are straightforward—"COVID-19" and the "Great Lockdown." If you walk slightly away from mainstream discourse, you might add "hunger," "police brutality," and the "atrocious hybrid wars" that suffocate certain parts of the planet. The statistics of deprivation and death are gruesome. Many of us journalists and writers have become actuaries of suffering. The general mood is despair; the general conditions of life are bare. The rhetoric of hope sounds less like inspiration and more like a rebuke. The gap between the rhetoric of hope and the condition of despair is vast. There is no bridge between them. We live in the wound.

Where does one even begin? Not to do an investigation of the wound alone, but to look around it—see how it is talked about, how it is understood. Who gets to define the wound, select what aspects of the human disaster should be seen as a wound? We would have to do a long detour into the way the ruling ideas are shaped—a journey into the world of the ideological apparatus, namely the way ruling elites own and shape the media, forge consensus through the clever arrangement of vocabulary and concepts. We would have to consider how what is seen as true is often not produced through a great deal of effort—an immense amount of energy going toward making some questions (and answers) seem off the wall, absurd, even crazy. For example, to trace the consistent drive to push out any questions about U.S. complicity in the production of the social conditions for 9/11; to toss these kinds of concerns into the dustbin of 9/11 Truth conspiracy theories: sensible questions raised about U.S.-Saudi social forces that endowed jihadis with respectability in the Afghan War shelved as disruptive and beside the point. We would have to consider how certain sharp associations make certain kinds of political claims very hard to sustain—the sword of anti-Semitism used to cut through the allegations of human rights violations by Israel, for instance. All this would have to be done.

We would have to ask why certain wounds are more important than others—why not the wound of the Congo, several million dead in a civil war around—among other things—coltan, the main ingredient to help store energy in capacitors in our cellphones and laptops. Or we can ask why it is so much easier to paint the president of Venezuela—Nicolas Maduro—or the president of Bolivia—Evo Morales Ayma—as illegitimate, when there is no noise about the actual violations of international law by people such as George W. Bush, Dick Cheney, Donald Rumsfeld, and Tony Blair for their war of aggression against Iraq? There is no evidence that Libya's Muammar Qaddafi killed half a million children, yet he was overthrown in a UN-backed invasion by France and the United States of America; U.S. ambassador to the UN Madeleine Albright, meanwhile, admitted on U.S. television that her government was responsible for the death of half a million Iraqi children in the 1990s due to its sanctions regime, and yet neither she nor her government—led by U.S. president Bill Clinton—appeared before any international tribunal or find their reputations permanently dented. What makes certain wounds easier to see as wounds? What makes the shockingly high rates of violence against women in the United States something fixable within U.S. culture while the violence against women in Sudan or Afghanistan seems inevitable because of that culture? We would have to ask these questions.

It is hard to see through crises, to look beneath the surface of anxiety and fear; it is hard to find a way around the metaphors of helplessness and the oxymoron of liberal intervention. Hard enough to watch the news, harder yet to find a critical voice against it. The bureaucrats of the news industry smugly put their stamp on reality and call it the truth. To go around them, to see through them, to slip the banana peel of interpretation underneath them—all this is harder than it seems. Or rather, it is easy to analyze their platitudes, but hard to make them seem as such in the wide landscape of what passes for the truth.

The cheapest explanation is to make the origin of the crisis eternal. Coronavirus? That comes from Asia, a "Chinese virus," a product of old Asian barbarity. The wound cannot be healed. It is too old and too dangerous. Walls must be built against its pus. Quarantines are necessary; Sinophobia becomes about security. If a crisis emerges periodically but with an eternal origin, the crisis can only be cauterized—it is too much to expect it to be vanquished. It is enough to protect civilization from its others.

When the cholera of 1832 flickered at the outskirts of France, a Frenchman suggested that on the "uncultivated arid plains of Asia" the cholera morbus "ferments and warms itself amidst the residue of poisonous plants burned by the sun"; meanwhile, "in the placid climate and productive soils of Europe the morbus would perish."[1] It did not perish. It actually was the vengeful spirit of death. But its entry did not change the idea of eternal crises elsewhere; it produced a new argument—God had sent a message to the

Europeans to change their behavior, who could do so unlike, as the Englishman Edwin Chadwick put it, "the resignation of Turkish fatalists."[2] Europe might have fallen prey to an Asiatic disease, but this was not Europe's fate. It could introduce a religion of hygiene. This was preordained for Europe.

For Asia and for Africa, such inoculation was of no use. Writing in 1955, the celebrated anthropologist Claude Levi-Strauss wrote of my city, Calcutta: "Filth, chaos, promiscuity, congestion; ruins, huts, mud, dirt; dung, urine, pus, humours, secretions and running sores; all the things which we expect urban life to give us organised protection, all the things we hate and guard against at such great cost, all these by-products of cohabitation do not set any limitation on it in India. They are more like a natural environment which the Indian town needs in order to prosper."[3] They are fated to this. Let it be so. No need to ask questions of why the string of ills—from filth to running sores—exist. No need to raise questions of colonialism and the drain of wealth. Far better to let this be the fate of what Levi-Strauss called the "martyred continent." Europe is not martyred. It has been active.

Chadwick, our Englishman, urged his government not to "sit still amidst the population . . . under the supposed destiny of the prevalent ignorance, sloth and filth."[4] Englishmen could not succumb to the fatalism of the Turks. Public health movements had to begin, public bathing movements had to be enforced, and sanitation had to become a national priority. In light of Ebola, why bother asking of Liberia, Sierra Leone, and Guinea—where is your public health infrastructure? What has happened to your medical system, your access to pharmaceuticals? Why bother to remind us of Sierra Leone's eightfold reduction in recurrent health expenditures per capita in real terms between 1980/81 and 1992/93 under IMF mandate, which caused "a near breakdown of essential government health services"?[5] Why bother with the fact that while Liberia is a major rubber producer and exporter, the country has a cataclysmic shortage of rubber gloves? Why bother with these facts when the time of the eternal, racist time, is a sufficient explanatory factor?

The wound that erupts because of explanations that exist on the time of the eternal can be fenced in—the cordon sanitaire established—but no permanent solution can be found. Timelessness has its own logic. It is beyond the human imagination.

At the other end of the time of the eternal is the time of the hero. If there is a crisis somewhere—a bank collapsing, a people dying—the hero shakes off lassitude and rushes to the rescue. Suddenly we hear that in Iraq a community most people had never heard of before—the Yazidis—are in danger for their lives from the Islamic State in Iraq and Syria (ISIS)—a group also shielded from the U.S. public despite having taken large parts of Iraq and Syria in 2013—a whole year before the U.S. fulminations. The U.S. president takes to the airwaves; "America is coming to help," Barack Obama says. How will the United States help? With its military, of course. The bugle has sounded; the blue jackets mount up and gallop out of the fort—led by none other than John Wayne. But by the time they get to Jabal Sinjar they find other armed men and women on the mountain, from where they had opened up a rescue corridor for the tens of thousands trapped on the hillside. But these are the Kurdish Workers' Party (PKK) fighters, terrorists in the U.S. State Department's annals, and so impossible to acknowledge. The PKK and its Syrian ally, the People's Protection Units (YPG), cannot be the hero. That role is reserved for the U.S. armed forces, the "finest military in the history of the world," as U.S. president Barack Obama put it. Coalitions are useful screens, for everyone knows that it is the U.S. armed forces that are in the lead, and everyone knows that the others are only useful as a shield against criticism of what is really happening, namely unilateral, heroic action. The hero comes in to treat the problem. This is the time of the hero, to swoop in and save the day. There are no illusions that the help is only provisional. It would be too much to expect the hero to do more than that. The natives— bathed from filth to running sores—cannot be expected to be lifted by mere mortals from their eternal crises. It is enough for the hero to cauterize the wound.

These are the times that should be unremarkable to you—the time of the eternal and the time of the hero, the narrative that suggests that crises are ahistorical and without context, and that solutions are epic but partial. No one is culpable for these immortal crises, for, after all, they have no human author. These things happen. They are in the nature of things. No one is at fault. And even if the hero cannot force the termination of the crisis, the hero's intervention is sufficient. It also means that if the hero exacerbates the problem, no one can blame the hero. The hero is irreproachable.

This is the view from the wound.

Notes

INTRODUCTION

1. John Collins and Ross Glover, eds., *Collateral Language: A User's Guide to America's New War* (New York: New York University Press, 2002), 2.

2. Collins and Glover, *Collateral Language*, 2.

3. While the term "war on terror" has become standard usage in much public discourse, many analysts have noted that the term itself is an ideological one that requires critical examination. Given that the term occupied a central role in the broader collateral language lexicon, we have allowed space in this book for authors to use their own preferred terminology in the context of their own critical arguments.

4. Roland Barthes, *Mythologies: The Complete Edition in a New Translation*, trans. Richard Howard and Annette Lavers (New York: Hill and Wang, 2013).

5. Ibid., 240.

6. Anthony Lane, "This Is Not a Movie," *New Yorker*, September 17, 2001, https://www.newyorker.com/magazine/2001/09/24/this-is-not-a-movie.

7. Jeff Lewis, *Language Wars: The Role of Media and Culture in Global Terror and Political Violence* (London: Pluto Press, 2005), 2.

8. Sandra Silberstein, *War of Words: Language, Politics, and 9/11* (London: Routledge, 2002), xii–xiii.

9. Noam Chomsky and David Barsamian, *Imperial Ambitions: Conversations with Noam Chomsky on the Post-9/11 World* (New York: Metropolitan Books, 2005), 18–19.

10. Ibid., 19.

11. Adriana Cavarero, *Horrorism: Naming Contemporary Violence* (New York: Columbia University Press, 2011), 2.

12. Douglas Kellner, "9/11, Spectacles of Terror, and Media Manipulation," *Critical Discourse Studies* 1, no. 1 (2004): 41–64. See also Bruce Lincoln, *Holy Terrors: Thinking about Religion after September 11* (Chicago: University of Chicago Press, 2002).

13. Stephen Graham, "Cities and the 'War on Terror,'" *International Journal of Urban and Regional Research* 30, no. 2 (2006): 255–76; Richard Jackson, "Language, Policy, and the Construction of a Torture Culture in the War on Terrorism," *Review of International Studies* 33, no. 3 (2007): 353–71; Patricia L. Dunmire, "'9/11 Changed Everything': An Intertextual Analysis of the Bush Doctrine," *Discourse & Society* 20, no. 2 (2009): 195–222.

14. Walter Lippmann, *Public Opinion* (New York: Harcourt, Brace, 1922), 204.

15. Walter Benjamin, "The Work of Art in the Age of Mechanical Reproduction," in *Illuminations*, ed. Hannah Arendt, trans. Harry Zohn (New York: Schocken Books, 1968), 241.

16. Naomi Klein, *No Is Not Enough: Resisting Trump's Shock Politics and Winning the World We Need* (Chicago: Haymarket Books, 2017), 9.

17. Umberto Eco, "Ur-Fascism," *New York Review of Books* 42, no. 11 (1995).

18. Chris Hedges, *American Fascists: The Christian Right and the War on America* (New York: Free Press, 2006), 14.

CHAPTER 1. HOMELAND SECURITY

1. Elizabeth Becker, "Washington Talk; The Prickly Roots of 'Homeland Security,'" *New York Times*, August 31, 2002, https://www.nytimes.com/2002/08/31/us /washington-talk-prickly-roots-of-homeland-security.html.

2. Ibid.

3. Ibid.

4. More astute minds than Tom Ridge have pointed out that the etymological roots of "homeland" can be traced back as far as the Book of Genesis. The Hebrew word for homeland, *Moledet*, it is claimed, comes out of God's mouth as he commands Abraham to lead his people back home. The Zionist movement appropriated this notion, and it is a measure of its success that the idea of a "homeland" for the Jewish people was reiterated by the Balfour Declaration and Woodrow Wilson as he spoke of the concept of self-determination.

5. Benedict Anderson, *The Spectre of Comparisons: Nationalism, Southeast Asia and the World* (London: Verso, 1998): 58–74.

6. Shawn Reese, "Defining Homeland Security: Analysis and Congressional Considerations," Congressional Research Service, January 8, 2013.

7. Janet Napolitano, DHS secretary, cited in "The U.S. Department of Homeland Security Strategic Plan: Fiscal Years 2012–2016," https://www.dhs.gov/xlibrary/assets /dhs-strategic-plan-fy-2012-2016.pdf.

8. Department of Homeland Security, "FY 2020: Budget-in-Brief," https://www.dhs .gov/sites/default/files/publications/19_0318_MGMT_FY-2020-Budget-In-Brief.pdf; emphasis added.

9. See, for instance, Bill Ong Hing, "Misusing Immigration Policies in the Name of Homeland Security," *CR: The New Centennial Review*, 6, no. 1 (2006): 195–224.

10. Ibid., 199.

11. "Remarks by President Trump in Joint Address to Congress," February 28, 2017, https://www.whitehouse.gov/briefings-statements/remarks-president-trump -joint-address-congress/.

12. In August 2019, the DHS moved $155 million from FEMA (and a further $116 million from other agencies under its purview) to fund ICE and Border Patrol Operations. This was, incidentally, just before tropical storm Dorian was threatening Puerto Rico, a U.S. territory that had still not recovered from the devastation of Hurricane Maria three years earlier.

13. "Remarks by President Trump to the Venezuelan American community," February 18, 2019, https://www.whitehouse.gov/briefings-statements /remarks-president-trump-venezuelan-american-community/.

14. The CPAC conference, as has been reported, was unusually fixated on the threat of socialism, with speeches by Vice-President Mike Pence and Senator Ted Cruz also playing on the theme. The most bizarre statement, however, came from former White House adviser Sebastian Gorka, who, while insisting that he and the audience were at the frontlines of the "war against communism," declared: "They want to take your pickup truck, they want to rebuild your home, they want to take away your hamburgers. . . . This is what Stalin dreamt about but never achieved."

15. "Remarks by the President to the 74th Session of the United Nations General Assembly," September 24, 2019, https://www.whitehouse.gov/briefings-statements /remarks-president-trump-74th-session-united-nations-general-assembly/.

CHAPTER 2. MUSHROOM CLOUD

1. Peggy Rosenthal, "The Nuclear Mushroom Cloud as a Cultural Image," *American Literary History*, 3, no. 1 (1991): 63–66.

2. Ibid., 70.

3. Yaung Thoroughbread, "Navy Veterans Speak about Being Close to the Nuclear Explosion." YouTube, online video clip, September 17, 2018, https://youtu.be /B8O8sBIsKHI.

4. WatchMojo.com, "Top 10 Nuclear Bomb Scenes in Movies," YouTube, online video clip, March 31, 2015, https://youtu.be/FB-Ghg8aRj8.

5. The complete list includes (1) *Dr. Strangelove* (1964); (2) *Terminator 2: Judgement Day* (1991); (3) *The Day After* (1983); (4) *Threads* (1984); (5) *The Sum of All Fears* (2002); (6) *Armageddon* (1998); (7) *Independence Day*; (8) *The Dark Knight Rises* (2012); (9) *Indiana Jones and the Kingdom of the Crystal Skull* (2008); and (10) *The Wolverine* (2013).

6. *The Siege* (1998) with Denzel Washington and Bruce Willis certainly better captures these emerging anxieties about Islamic terrorism.

7. *The Peacemaker*, directed by Mimi Leder, performances by George Clooney and Nicole Kidman, DreamWorks Pictures, 1997.

8. Ervand Abrahamian, *The Coup: 1953, the CIA, and the Roots of Modern U.S.-Iranian Relations* (New York: New Press, 2013), 2.

9. Ibid., 171.

10. Ibid.

11. Mary Ann Heiss, "Real Men Don't Wear Pajamas: Anglo-American Cultural Perceptions of Mohammad Mossadeq and the Iranian Oil Nationalization Dispute," in *Cold War Constructions: The Political Culture of United States Imperialism, 1945–1966*, ed. Christian G. Appy (Amherst: University of Massachusetts Press, 2000), 187.

12. Matthew Alford, *Reel Power: Hollywood, Cinema, and American Supremacy* (New York: Pluto Press, 2010), 99.

13. *The Peacemaker*.

14. Ibid.

15. Ibid.

16. *The Sum of All Fears,* directed by Phil Alden Robinson, performances by Ben Affleck and Morgan Freeman, Paramount Pictures, 2002.

17. David A. Altheide, *Terrorism and the Politics of Fear,* 2nd ed. (Lanham, Md.: Rowman and Littlefield, 2017), 24.

18. Box Office Mojo, "Domestic Box Office for 1997," https://www.boxofficemojo .com/yearly/chart/?yr=1997&p=.htm.

19. Alford, *Reel Power,* 92.

20. Tom Secker and Matthew Alford, "EXCLUSIVE: Documents Expose How Hollywood Promotes War on Behalf of the Pentagon, CIA and NSA," *Medium,* July 4, 2017, https://medium.com/insurge-intelligence/exclusive-documents-expose-direct -us-military-intelligence-influence-on-1-800-movies-and-tv-shows-36433107c307.

21. Ibid.

22. Ibid.

23. Ibid.

24. Ibid.

25. Ibid.

26. John Schwartz, "U.S. to Drop Color-Coded Terror Alerts," *New York Times,* November 24, 2010, https://www.nytimes.com/2010/11/25/us/25colors.html.

27. Ibid.

28. Jeanne Meserve, "Duct Tape Sales Rise amid Terror Fears," CNN, February 11, 2003. http://www.cnn.com/2003/US/02/11/emergency.supplies/.

29. Ibid.

30. See Robert S. Snyder, "Hating America: Bin Laden as a Civilization Revolutionary," *Review of Politics* 65, no. 4 (2003); and Farwaz A. Gerges, *The Far Enemy: Why Jihad Went Global* (Cambridge: Cambridge University Press, 2009).

31. Altheide, *Terrorism and the Politics,* 28.

32. Ibid., 28–29.

33. Michael Isikoff and David Corn, *Hubris: The Inside Story of Spin, Scandal, and the Selling of the Iraq War* (New York: Crown, 2006), 108.

34. Ibid., 38–39; Michael R. Gordon and Judith Miller, "Threats and Responses: The Iraqis; U.S. Says Hussein Intensifies Quest for A-Bomb Parts," *New York Times,* September 8, 2002, https://www.nytimes.com/2002/09/08/world/threats-responses -iraqis-us-says-hussein-intensifies-quest-for-bomb-parts.html.

35. "Interview With Condoleezza Rice; Pataki Talks about 9-11; Graham, Shelby Discuss War on Terrorism," CNN, September 8, 2002, http://transcripts.cnn.com /TRANSCRIPTS/0209/08/le.00.html.

36. *Wall Street Journal,* "The Iraq War: George W. Bush's Speech 10 Years Later," YouTube, online video clip, March 19, 2013. https://youtu.be/WejYdT3Lof8.

37. Peggy Rosenthal, "The Nuclear Mushroom Cloud as a Cultural Image," *American Literary History* 3, no. 1 (1991), 74.

38. Richard Benedetto, "Poll: Most Back War, but Want U.N. Support," *USA Today,* March 16, 2003, https://usatoday30.usatoday.com/news/world/iraq /2003-03-16-poll-iraq_x.htm.

CHAPTER 3. ECOTERRORISM

1. Quoted in Liz Ruskin, "Stevens, Murkowski and Young Vow Retribution," *Anchorage Daily News*, September 12, 2001.

2. Edward Abbey, *The Monkey Wrench Gang* (New York: Avon Books, 1992).

3. Eugene Hargrove, "Ecological Sabotage: Pranks or Terrorism?" *Environmental Ethics* 4, no. 4 (Winter 1982): 291–92.

4. Edward Abbey, "Earth First! and The Monkey Wrench Gang," *Environmental Ethics* 5, no. 1 (Spring 1983): 94–95.

5. Ron Arnold, "Eco-Terrorism," *Reason*, February 1, 1983, https://reason.com/1983/02/01/eco-terrorism/.

6. Ron Arnold, *EcoTerror: The Violent Agenda to Save Nature—The World of the Unabomber* (Bellevue, Wash.: Free Enterprise, 1997), 12.

7. Antiterrorism Act of 1990, *U.S. Code* 18 (1994) §2331; emphasis added.

8. Arnold, *EcoTerror*, ix.

9. House Committee on the Judiciary, *Hearings on Acts of Ecoterrorism by Radical Environmental Organizations*, 105th Cong., 2nd sess., June 9, 1998.

10. Evan Mecham was briefly governor of Arizona in 1987–88 until he was impeached for obstruction of justice and the misuse of public funds.

11. Quoted in Martha F. Lee, *Earth First! Environmental Apocalypse* (Syracuse, N.Y.: Syracuse University Press, 1995), 132.

12. Dean Kuipers, *Operation Bite Back: Rod Coronado's War to Save American Wilderness* (New York: Bloomsbury, 2009), 231.

13. Animal Enterprise Protection Act of 1992, *U.S. Code* 18 (1994) §43.

14. U.S. Department of Agriculture and U.S. Department of Justice, *Report to Congress on the Extent and Effects of Domestic and International Terrorism on Animal Enterprises*, 103rd Cong., 1st sess., 1993.

15. Arnold, *EcoTerror*, 120.

16. Will Potter, *Green Is the New Red: An Insider's Account of a Social Movement under Siege* (San Francisco: City Lights Books, 2011), 56.

17. USA PATRIOT Act of 2001, *U.S. Code* 18 (2001) §2331.

18. House Committee, *Eco-terrorism and Lawlessness on the National Forests*, 107th Cong., 2d sess., 2002.

19. Ibid.

20. Federal Bureau of Investigation, *Terrorism 2002–2005* (Washington, D.C.: U.S. Department of Justice, 2007), 18.

21. Ibid., 29.

22. House Committee, *Eco-terrorism and Lawlessness*.

23. U.S. Department of Justice, Office of the Inspector General, Audit Division, *The Federal Bureau of Investigation's Efforts to Improve the Sharing of Intelligence and Other Information* (Washington, D.C., 2003), 50, 85, 94.

24. Senate Committee on Environment and Public Works, *Eco-terrorism Specifically Examining the Earth Liberation Front and the Animal Liberation Front*, 109th Cong., 1st sess., 2005, 2.

25. Eric Lipton, "Homeland Report Says Threat From Terror-List Nations Is Declining," *New York Times*, March 31, 2005, https://www.nytimes.com/2005/03/31/politics/homeland-report-says-threat-from-terrorlist-nations-is-declining.html.

26. Senate Committee, *Eco-terrorism*, 42.

27. American Legislative Exchange Council, *Animal & Ecological Terrorism in America* (Washington, D.C.: ALEC, 2003), 21, 23, 8, 15.

28. Animal Enterprise Terrorism Act of 2006, *U.S. Code 18* (2006) §43.

29. Federal Bureau of Investigation, "Operation Backfire: Searching for Two Final Fugitives," December 6, 2015, https://www.fbi.gov/contact-us/field-offices/portland/news/stories/operation-backfire.

30. Potter, *Green Is the New Red*, 214.

31. William Petroski, "Dakota Access Pipeline Developer Sues Greenpeace, Others for $1 Billion," *USA Today*, August 23, 2017, https://www.usatoday.com/story/news/nation-now/2017/08/23/dakota-access-pipeline-lawsuit/595413001/.

32. Alleen Brown, Will Parrish, and Alice Speri, "Leaked Documents Reveal Counterterrorism Tactics Used at Standing Rock to 'Defeat Pipeline Insurgencies,'" *The Intercept*, May 27, 2017, https://theintercept.com/2017/05/27/leaked-documents-reveal-security-firms-counterterrorism-tactics-at-standing-rock-to-defeat-pipeline-insurgencies/.

33. Quoted in Miranda Green, "Zinke Blames 'Environmental Terrorist Groups' for Scale of California Wildfires," *The Hill*, August 8, 2018, https://thehill.com/policy/energy-environment/401736-zinke-environmental-terrorist-groups-responsible-for-california.

34. Quoted in Alleen Brown, "The Green Scare: How a Movement That Never Killed Anyone Became the FBI's No. 1 Domestic Terrorism Threat," *The Intercept*, March 23, 2019, https://theintercept.com/2019/03/23/ecoterrorism-fbi-animal-rights/.

35. Quoted on *The Situation Room*, CNN, March 15, 2019, http://www.cnn.com/TRANSCRIPTS/1903/15/sitroom.02.html.

36. Quoted in Allan Smith, "Mulvaney after New Zealand Massacre: Trump 'Not a White Supremacist,'" *NBC News*, March 17, 2019, https://www.nbcnews.com/politics/donald-trump/mulvaney-after-new-zealand-massacre-trump-not-white-supremacist-n984191.

CHAPTER 4. WOMEN

1. Maha El Said, Lena Meari, and Nicola Pratt, eds., *Rethinking Gender in Revolutions and Resistance: Lessons from the Arab World* (London: Zed Books, 2015).

2. Edward Said, *Orientalism* (London: Penguin Books, 1978).

3. Saba Mahmood, "Feminist Theory, Embodiment, and the Docile Agent: Some Reflections on the Egyptian Islamic Revival," *Cultural Anthropology* 16, no. 2 (2001): 202–36.

4. Lila Abu-Lughod, *Writing Women's Worlds: Bedouin Stories* (Berkeley: University

of California Press, 2008); Abu-Lughod, *Do Muslim Women Need Saving?* (Cambridge, Mass.: Harvard University Press, 2013).

5. Talal Asad, *On Suicide Bombing* (New York: Columbia University Press, 2007).

6. Nigel Julian Rapport, *Cosmopolitan Love and Individuality: Ethical Engagement beyond Culture* (Lanham, Md.: Lexington Books, 2018).

7. Said, *Orientalism.*

8. See Andrew Brandel and Marco Motta, eds., *Living with Concepts: Anthropology in the Grip of Reality* (New York: Fordham University Press, forthcoming).

9. El Said, Meari, and Pratt, *Rethinking Gender in Revolutions.*

10. Margit Warburg, Birgitte Schepelern Johansen, and Kate Østergaard, "Counting *niqabs* and *burqas* in Denmark: Methodological Aspects of Quantifying Rare and Elusive Religious Sub-cultures," *Journal of Contemporary Religion* 28, no. 1 (2013): 33–48.

11. Ibid.

12. El Said, Meari and Pratt, *Rethinking Gender in Revolutions.*

13. Mahmood, "Feminist Theory, Embodiment," 203.

14. Lena Meari, "*Sumud*: A Palestinian Philosophy of Confrontation in Colonial Prisons," *South Atlantic Quarterly* 113, no. 3 (2014): 547–78.

15. Ilana Feldman, "Looking for Humanitarian Purpose: Endurance and the Value of Lives in a Palestinian Refugee Camp," *Public Culture* 27, no. 3 (2015): 427–47.

16. Brandel and Motta, *Living with Concepts.*

17. Meari, "*Sumud*"; Laleh Khalili, *Heroes and Martyrs of Palestine: The Politics of National Commemoration* (Cambridge: Cambridge University Press, 2007).

18. Somdeep Sen, *Decolonizing Palestine: Hamas between the Anticolonial and the Postcolonial* (Ithaca, N.Y.: Cornell University Press, 2020).

19. Lila Abu-Lughod, "Do Muslim Women Really Need Saving? Anthropological Reflections on Cultural Relativism and Its Others," *Current Anthropology* 104, no. 3 (2002): 783.

CHAPTER 5. INSURGENCY

1. I covered these protests at the time in a series of articles published at *Counterpunch.*

2. Puck Lo, "Oakland Cops Decide to Not Use Sound Cannon on Protesters," *East Bay Express*, July 7, 2010, https://www.eastbayexpress.com/SevenDays /archives/2010/07/07/oakland-cops-decide-to-not-use-sound-cannon-on-protesters.

3. Etymologically speaking, "insurgency" appears in English in 1745, where "in-surge" indicates both resistance *against* and a gathering of forces. Earlier French usage shows that this is not "surge" as we understand it (which appears only with the English deriva- tion), however, but an older meaning of "surge" as indicating an attack.

4. See, on the one hand, the pseudonymous account of the 1798 Irish Insurgency by Solomon Secondsight, *The Insurgent Chief; or, O'Halloran* (Philadelphia: Carey & Lea, 1824); on the other, the reclamation of insurgency in ballad form in "Song of the Wexford Insurgent," *Catholic Miscellany* (Dublin: J. Robins, 1828), 46. On the

borderline nature of the Irish in particular, see Noel Ignatiev, *How the Irish Became White* (New York: Routledge, 1995).

5. Balibar continues, observing that in a colonial order "where the 'center' rules over the 'periphery,' revolutions were supposed to be *political processes typical for the center* because they involve a participation of 'citizens' who exist only in the nation-states." Étienne Balibar, "The Idea of Revolution: Yesterday, Today and Tomorrow," *Uprising 13/13* (New York: Columbia Center for Contemporary Critical Thought, 2016), http://blogs.law.columbia.edu/uprising1313 /etienne-balibar-the-idea-of-revolution-yesterday-today-and-tomorrow/.

6. This colonial divide maps imperfectly onto, while introducing a racial-colonial element into, debates over constituent versus constituted power that from Hobbes to contemporary thinkers such as Paolo Virno, Michael Hardt, and Antonio Negri, are characterized by "the Citizens against the City . . . the Multitude against the People"— the chaotic rebellion of disparate individuals versus the unification of wills toward a shared sovereign project. Thomas Hobbes, *De Cive*, vol. 12 (London, 1651), 8. Virno, Hardt, and Negri of course valorize the multitude over the people, but they do so by maintaining intact Hobbes's distinction.

7. Dupré did not hide his political aims, openly celebrating the revolution of language alongside the revolution of politics, and the text was predictably attacked in the *Anti-Jacobin Review and Magazine* in these same terms: whereas the French had once upheld linguistic purity, the post-Revolutionary "French have now become as profuse in their coinage of new words and phrases, as they were formerly parsimonious." Dupré's text is "a dictionary of that jargon, which is the creature of the French Revolution, the bantling of French philological pruriency" (nos. 35–38, 397–98). *The European Magazine and London Review* quoted Edmund Burke's derision (in *Letters on a Regicide Peace*) of such "Gypsy Jargon" and notes that the book "presents a memorial of the folly, madness, and ferocity of a people freed from the restraints of law and the obligations of religion" (vol. 40, 44).

8. William Dupré, *Lexicographia-neologica Gallica: The Neological French Dictionary* (London: Baylis, 1801), 150–52. This tension was not merely formal but also substantive, since it was precisely the Jacobins who came closest among the French Revolutionary milieu to the anti-colonial abolitionism of the Haitian insurgents (see C. L. R. James, *The Black Jacobins: Toussaint L'Ouverture and the San Domingo Revolution*, 2nd ed. [New York: Vintage, 1989]). Writing in defense of two men accused of sedition in 1820, none other than Jeremy Bentham would argue: "The citizens of the United States, ere they became acknowledged citizens, were they not *insurgents*, and insurgent traitors? So likewise the men in Spanish America? In Spain and every where else on the Continent, *insurgent traitors*; in England, *insurgents* every where." See Jeremy Bentham, *The King against Sir Charles Wolseley, Baronet, and Joseph Harrison, Schoolmaster* (London: M'Creery, 1820), 32.

9. Gerald Horne, *The Counter-Revolution of 1776: Slave Resistance and the Origins of the United States of America* (New York: NYU Press, 2014).

10. Nathan Leites and Charles Wolf Jr., *Rebellion and Authority: An Analytic Essay on Insurgent Conflicts* (Santa Monica, Calif.: RAND/ARPA, 1970), 2–3.

11. Roberto González, Hugh Gusterson, and David Price, introduction to *The Counter-Counterinsurgency Manual: or, Notes on Demilitarizing American Society*, ed. Network of Concerned Anthropologists (Chicago: Prickly Paradigm Press, 2009), 12–13.

12. Ibid.

13. Chris Kyle, with Chris McEwen and Jim DeFelice, *American Sniper: The Autobiography of the Most Lethal Sniper in U.S. Military History* (New York: HarperCollins, 2012), 250. Both Kyle's book and the *American Sniper* script loosely based on the book repeatedly use the term "savages" to describe Iraqi insurgents.

14. In the words of army general Jack Keane, "After the Vietnam War, we purged ourselves of everything that had to do with irregular warfare or insurgency, because it had to do with how we lost that war. In hindsight, that was a bad decision." Cited in John A. Nagl, foreword to *The U.S. Army/Marine Corps Counterinsurgency Field Manual* (Chicago: University of Chicago Press, 2007), xiv.

15. Ibid., xvii.

16. Frantz Fanon, *The Wretched of the Earth*, trans. R. Philcox (New York: Grove Press, 2004), 4.

17. Patrick Gillham, "Securitizing America: Strategic Incapacitation and the Policing of Protest since the 11 September 2001 Terrorist Attacks," *Sociology Compass* 5, no. 7 (2011), 637–38.

18. Ibid., 640. I have shown how this transformation of COIN doctrine and protest policing fueled the "strategic incapacitation" and repression of the Occupy Movement: see George Ciccariello-Maher, "Counterinsurgency and the Occupy Movement," in *Life during Wartime: Resisting Counterinsurgency*, ed. Kristian Williams, Will Munger, and Lara Messersmith-Glavin (Oakland, Calif.: AK Press, 2013).

19. David Hunn and Kim Bell, "Why Was Michael Brown's Body Left There for Hours?" *St. Louis Post-Dispatch*, September 14, 2014, https://www.stltoday.com/news/local/crime-and-courts/why-was-michael-brown-s-body-left-there-for-hours/article_0b73ec58-c6a1-516e-882f-74d18a4246e0.html.

20. Terrence McCoy, "Ferguson Shows How a Police Force Can Turn into a Plundering 'Collection Agency,'" *Washington Post*, March 5, 2015, https://www.washingtonpost.com/news/morning-mix/wp/2015/03/05/ferguson-shows-how-a-police-force-can-turn-into-a-plundering-collection-agency/. Despite a promising title, Chris Hayes manages to miss the fundamental point in "Policing the Colony: From the American Revolution to Ferguson," *The Nation*, March 29, 2017, https://www.thenation.com/article/archive/policing-the-colony-from-the-american-revolution-to-ferguson/. This is because by "colony," Hayes means the white British settlers of the original thirteen colonies. With this sleight-of-hand, substituting colonizer for colonized, race disappears almost entirely from the equation.

21. Jamelle Bouie, "The Militarization of the Police," *Slate*, August 13, 2014, https://

slate.com/news-and-politics/2014/08/police-in-ferguson-military-weapons-threaten
-protesters.html.

22. The argument that Black America constitutes an internal colony of the United States has a long pedigree from the Black Belt thesis to works by Martin Delaney, W. E. B. Du Bois, and Harold Cruse and was subsequently popularized by the simultaneous publication of Robert Blauner's "Internal Colonialism and Ghetto Revolt," *Social Problems* 16, no. 4 (Spring 1969), 393–408; and Robert Allen's *Black Awakening in Capitalist America* (Trenton: Africa World Press, 1969). The concept was later used to similarly describe Chicano communities in Mario Barrera, Carlos Muñoz, and Charles Ornelas, "The Barrio as an Internal Colony," in *People and Politics in Urban Society*, ed. Harlan Hahn (Beverly Hills, Calif.: Sage, 1972).

23. While COINTELPRO is the most obvious recent example of this, Angela Davis has also underscored how "the slave master's sexual domination of the black woman contained an unveiled element of counter-insurgency. See Davis, "Reflections on the Black Woman's Role in the Community of Slaves," *Black Scholar* 3, no. 4 (December 1971): 11.

24. Rania Khalek, "Israel-Trained Police 'Occupy' Missouri after Killing of Black Youth," *Electronic Intifada*, August 15, 2014, https://electronicintifada.net/blogs/rania-khalek/israel-trained-police-occupy-missouri-after-killing-black-youth.

25. Nick Estes, *Our History Is the Future: Standing Rock versus the Dakota Access Pipeline, and the Long Tradition of Indigenous Resistance* (London: Verso, 2019), 10. In Canada, too, the 1990 Oka Crisis is a stark reminder of the same. In the largest internal military operation in Canadian history, the Mohawk blockades at Oka, Quebec, were met with more than four thousand troops in armored personnel carriers and helicopters.

26. Ibid., 2.

27. Ibid., 3.

28. Ibid., 251.

29. George Ciccariello-Maher, *We Created Chávez: A People's History of the Venezuelan Revolution* (Durham: Duke University Press, 2013), 72–76.

30. Dawn Paley, *Guerra Neoliberal y Contrainsurgencia Ampliada: Vida en El Holocausto en Torreón, Coahuila* (Puebla, México: Bénemerita Universidad Autónoma de Puebla, 2018).

31. González, Gusterson, and Price, introduction, 17.

32. Susan Buck-Morss, *Hegel, Haiti, and Universal History* (Pittsburgh: University of Pittsburgh Press, 2009), 134.

33. Ibid., 143–44.

34. Slavoj Žižek, *In Defense of Lost Causes*, 2nd ed. (London: Verso, 2009), 471.

35. Antonio Negri, *Insurgencies: Constituent Power and the Modern State*, trans. M. Boscagli (Minneapolis: University of Minnesota Press, 1999).

36. James Holston, *Insurgent Citizenship: Disjunctions of Democracy and Modernity in Brazil* (Princeton, N.J.: Princeton University Press, 2009).

37. Massimiliano Tomba, *Insurgent Universality: An Alternative Legacy of Modernity* (Oxford: Oxford University Press, 2019).

38. Kléber Ramírez Rojas, *Historia documental del 4 de febrero*, 4th ed. (Caracas: El Perro y la Rana, 2017), 57.

CHAPTER 6. DEMOCRACY

1. The Levellers, *The Putney Debates*, ed. Geoffrey Robertson (London: Verso, 2007), 69.

2. Leon Trotsky, "Karl Marx," in *The Living Thoughts of Karl Marx* (London: Cassell, 1946), 10.

CHAPTER 7. FAKE NEWS

1. *New York Times*, "FROM THE EDITORS; The Times and Iraq," May 26, 2004, sec. World, https://www.nytimes.com/2004/05/26/world/from-the-editors-the-times -and-iraq.html.

2. David Corn, "Jeb Bush Says His Brother Was Misled into War by Faulty Intelligence. That's Not What Happened," *Mother Jones*, May 19, 2015, https://www .motherjones.com/politics/2015/05/jeb-bush-marco-rubio-iraq-war-intelligence/; Bryan Wright, "Iraq WMD Timeline: How the Mystery Unraveled," *National Public Radio* (blog), November 15, 2005, https://www.npr.org/templates/story/story .php?storyId=4996218.

3. Jacqueline E. Sharkey, "The Television War," *American Journalism Review*, May 2003, 18–27.

4. Associated Press, "Text of Bush Speech," May 1, 2003, https://www.cbsnews.com /news/text-of-bush-speech-01-05-2003/.

5. Yochai Benkler, Robert Faris, and Hal Roberts, *Network Propaganda: Manipulation, Disinformation, and Radicalization in American Politics* (New York: Oxford University Press, 2018).

6. Ibid.

7. Edward S. Herman and Noam Chomsky, *Manufacturing Consent: The Political Economy of the Mass Media* (New York: Pantheon, 2002).

8. Data available at Google Trends, https://trends.google.com/trends /explore?date=all&q=%22fake%20news%22.

9. "Trump Twitter Archive," http://www.trumptwitterarchive.com.

10. "Fake News Definition and Meaning," in *Collins English Dictionary*, https://www .collinsdictionary.com/us/dictionary/english/fake-news; Alison Flood, "Fake News Is 'Very Real' Word of the Year for 2017," *The Guardian*, November 2, 2017, https://www .theguardian.com/books/2017/nov/02/fake-news-is-very-real-word-of-the-year-for-2017.

11. Edson C. Tandoc Jr., Zheng Wei Lim, and Richard Ling, "Defining 'Fake News,'" *Digital Journalism* 6, no. 2 (2018): 137–53, https://doi.org/10.1080/21670811.2017.1360143.

12. Glenn Kessler, Salvador Rizzo, and Meg Kelly, "Analysis: President Trump Made

18,000 False or Misleading Claims in 1,170 Days," *Washington Post*, April 14, 2020, https://www.washingtonpost.com/politics/2020/04/14/president-trump-made-18000-false-or-misleading-claims-1170-days/.

13. Chris Cilizza, "Donald Trump Just Claimed He Invented 'Fake News,'" *CNN* (blog), October 26, 2017, https://www.cnn.com/2017/10/08/politics/trump-huckabee-fake/index.html.

14. Claire Wardle and Hossein Derakhshan, "Information Disorder: Toward an Interdisciplinary Framework for Research and Policymaking," Freedom of Expression, Council of Europe, https://www.coe.int/en/web/freedom-expression/information-disorder, 5.

15. Shibani Mahtani and Regine Cabato, "Why Crafty Internet Trolls in the Philippines May Be Coming to a Website near You," *Washington Post*, July 26, 2019, https://www.washingtonpost.com/world/asia_pacific/why-crafty-internet-trolls-in-the-philippines-may-be-coming-to-a-website-near-you/2019/07/25/c5d42ee2-5c53-11e9-98d4-844088d135f2_story.html/

16. "Philippines: Reject Sweeping 'Fake News' Bill," *Human Rights Watch* (blog), July 25, 2019, https://www.hrw.org/news/2019/07/25/philippines-reject-sweeping-fake-news-bill.

17. Kate Conger, "Facebook and Twitter Say China Is Spreading Disinformation in Hong Kong," *New York Times*, August 19, 2019, https://www.nytimes.com/2019/08/19/technology/hong-kong-protests-china-disinformation-facebook-twitter.html.

18. Kevin Roose, "U.S.-Funded Broadcaster Directed Ads to Americans," *New York Times*, July 19, 2018, https://www.nytimes.com/2018/07/19/technology/facebook-ads-propaganda.html.

19. Anthony Boadle, "Facebook's WhatsApp Flooded with Fake News in Brazil Election," *Reuters*, October 20, 2018, https://www.reuters.com/article/us-brazil-election-whatsapp-explainer-idUSKCN1MU0UP, para. 15.

20. Max Fisher and Amanda Taub, "How YouTube Radicalized Brazil," *New York Times*, August 11, 2019, https://www.nytimes.com/2019/08/11/world/americas/youtube-brazil.html.

21. Ibid.

22. Herman and Chomsky, *Manufacturing Consent*.

23. Mark Danner, *Stripping Bare the Body: Politics Violence War* (New York: Nation Books, 2009), 555.

24. Ron Suskind, "Faith, Certainty and the Presidency of George W. Bush," *New York Times*, October 17, 2004, sec. U.S., https://nytimes.com/2004/10/17/magazine/faith-certainty-and-the-presidency-of-george-w-bush.html.

25. Ed Pilkington, "'Truth Isn't Truth': Giuliani Trumps 'Alternative Facts' with New Orwellian Outburst," *The Guardian*, August 19, 2018, https://www.theguardian.com/us-news/2018/aug/19/truth-isnt-truth-rudy-giuliani-trump-alternative-facts-orwellian.

26. David Smith, "'Enemy of the People': Trump's War on the Media Is a Page from Nixon's Playbook," *The Guardian*, September 7, 2019, https://www.theguardian.com/us-news/2019/sep/07/donald-trump-war-on-the-media-oppo-research.

27. W. Lance Bennett, Regina G. Lawrence, and Steven Livingston, *When the Press Fails: Political Power and the News Media from Iraq to Katrina* (Chicago: University of Chicago Press, 2007).

28. Jason Stanley, *How Propaganda Works* (Princeton, N.J.: Princeton University Press, 2015).

29. George Orwell, *Nineteen Eighty-Four* (London: Martin Secker & Warburg Ltd., 1949), 38–39.

30. "News: Definition and Meaning," in *Collins English Dictionary*, https://www .collinsdictionary.com/us/dictionary/english/news; "Information: Definition and Meaning," in *Collins English Dictionary*, https://www.collinsdictionary.com/dictionary /english/information

31. Megan Brenan, "Americans' Trust in Mass Media Edges Down to 41%," *Gallup. Com* (blog), September 26, 2019, https://news.gallup.com/poll/267047 /americans-trust-mass-media-edges-down.aspx.

32. Charlotte Clifford, "Concern over 'Fake News' Has Decreased Global Trust in Media," YouGov, June 11, 2019, https://yougov.co.uk/topics/media /articles-reports/2019/06/11/concern-over-fake-news-has-decreased-global-trust-.

33. Jay Rosen, "It's Time for the Press to Suspend Normal Relations with the Trump Presidency," *PressThink* (blog), June 25, 2018, http://pressthink.org/2018/06 /its-time-for-the-press-to-suspend-normal-relations-with-the-trump-presidency/.

34. Maggie Haberman, "Trump Assails Ilhan Omar with Video of 9/11 Attacks," *New York Times*, April 13, 2019, sec. U.S., https://www.nytimes.com/2019/04/13/us/politics /trump-ilhan-omar-sept-11.html. Omar was among the first Muslim women elected to Congress.

35. Bobby Lewis, "After White Nationalist Gun Massacre, Major Newspapers' Headlines Give Trump a Pass for His Racism," Media Matters for America, August 6, 2019, https://www.mediamatters.org/new-york-times /after-white-nationalist-gun-massacre-major-newspapers-headlines-give-trump-pass-his.

36. Mike Levine, "'No Blame?' ABC News Finds 54 Cases Invoking 'Trump' in Connection with Violence, Threats, Alleged Assaults," *ABC News* (blog), May 30, 2020, https://abcnews.go.com/Politics/blame-abc-news-finds-17-cases-invoking-trump /story?id=58912889. The report, which was initially published on August 14, 2019, found no such references to either of the previous two presidents, Barack Obama or George W. Bush.

37. Sasha Ingber and Rachel Martin. "Immigration Chief: 'Give Me Your Tired, Your Poor Who Can Stand On Their Own 2 Feet'," *National Public Radio*, August 13, 2019, https://www.npr.org/2019/08/13/750726795/immigration-chief -give-me-your-tired-your-poor-who-can-stand-on-their-own-2-feet.

CHAPTER 8. LIFE

1. Camille LeGrand, "Rape and Rape Laws: Sexism in Society and Law," *California Law Review* 61, essay 3, article 3 (May 1973).

2. The names of all private individuals interviewed for this chapter have been changed to protect their privacy.

3. See Kimberlé Crenshaw, "Demarginalizing the Intersection of Race and Sex: A Black Feminist Critique of Antidiscrimination Doctrine, Feminist Theory and Antiracist Policies," *University of Chicago Legal Forum* 1989, no. 1 (1989); and Crenshaw, "Why Intersectionality Can't Wait," *Washington Post*, September 24, 2015, https://www .washingtonpost.com/news/in-theory/wp/2015/09/24/why-intersectionality-cant-wait/.

4. "Mission and Principles," Women's March, https://womensmarch.com /mission-and-principles.

5. Natalia Singer, "The Come as You Are Not Party," *American Scholar* 70, no. 3 (2001): 91–101.

6. Jill Filipovic, "Planned Parenthood Forced to Make an Impossible Choice," *CNN Opinion*, August 20, 2019, https://edition.cnn.com/2019/08/20/opinions/planned -parenthood-title-x-impossible-choice-filipovic/index.html; and Filipovic, "A New Poll Shows What Really Interests 'Pro-lifers': Controlling Women," *The Guardian*, August 22, 2019.

7. "New Report Highlights Worldwide Variations in Abortion Incidence and Safety," Guttmacher Institute, March 20, 2018, https://www.guttmacher.org/news-release/2018 /new-report-highlights-worldwide-variations-abortion-incidence-and-safety.

8. Planned Parenthood, "Timeline of Attacks on Abortion," https://www .plannedparenthoodaction.org/issues/abortion/timeline-attacks-abortion.

9. Nicole Gaudiano, "At Anti-Abortion Rally, Mike Pence Is a Beacon of Hope," *USA Today*, January 27, 2017, https://www.usatoday.com/story/news /politics/2017/01/27/anti-abortion-rally-mike-pence-beacon-hope/97151584/.

10. Ilhan Omar, "It Is Not Enough to Condemn Trump's Racism," *New York Times*, July 25, 2019, https://www.nytimes.com/2019/07/25/opinion/ilhan-omar-trump-racism.html.

11. Rebecca Traister, *Good and Mad: The Revolutionary Power of Women's Anger* (New York: Simon & Schuster, 2018).

12. David Choi, "Hate Crimes Increased 226% in Places Trump Held a Campaign Rally in 2016, Study Claims," *Business Insider*, March 23, 2019.

13. Neal Gabler, "Farewell, America," *Moyers on Democracy*, November 10, 2016, https://billmoyers.com/story/farewell-america/.

14. Naomi Klein, *No Is Not Enough: Resisting Trump's Shock Politics and Winning the World We Need* (Chicago: Haymarket Books, 2017).

CHAPTER 9. INVADERS

1. Brian Crevente, "Artist Explains WTC Space Invaders Exhibit at Games Convention," *Kotaku*, August 20, 2008, https://kotaku.com /artist-explains-wtc-space-invaders-exhibit-at-games-con-5039580.

2. Chris Kohler, "Controversial *Space Invaders* Remix Raises Square Enix's Ire," *Wired*, August 22, 2008, https://www.wired.com/2008/08/controversial-s/.

3. "President Bush Addresses the Nation," *PBS*, September 7, 2003, https://www.pbs
.org/newshour/show/president-bush-addresses-the-nation.

4. "Pittsburg Shooting and Other Cases Point to Rise in Domestic Terrorism,"
NPR, October 30, 2018, https://www.npr.org/2018/10/30/662233666
/pittsburgh-shooting-and-other-cases-again-point-to-domestic-extremism.

5. Thomas Nast, "The American River Ganges," *Harpweek* (repr. from *Harper's
Weekly*, May 8, 1875), https://www.harpweek.com/09cartoon/BrowseByDateCartoon
.asp?Month=May&Date=8.

6. Jean Raspail, *The Camp of the Saints*, 4th ed., trans. Norman Shapiro (Petosky,
Mich.: Social Contract Press, 1987), 222.

7. Ibid., 310.

8. Ibid., 311.

9. Ibid., afterword.

10. Ibid., xiii.

11. Ibid., afterword.

12. Jean Raspail, "'Our Civilization Is Disappearing': An Interview with Jean
Raspail," *Counter-Currents Publishing*, November 4, 2013, https://www.counter-currents
.com/2013/11/our-civilization-is-disappearing-interview-with-jean-raspail/.

13. Stephen Bannon, "Breitbart News Daily—Jason Richwine—January 6, 2016,"
Soundcloud, January 6, 2016, https://soundcloud.com/breitbart
/breitbart-news-daily-jason-richwine-january-6-2016.

14. Stephen Bannon, "Breitbart News Daily—Dr. Thomas D. Williams—January 19,
2016," *Soundcloud*. January 19, 2016, https://soundcloud.com/breitbart
/breitbart-news-daily-dr-thomas-d-williams-january-19-2016?in=breitbart/sets
/breitbart-news-daily-43.

15. Sindre Bangstad, "Bat Ye'or and Eurabia," in *Key Thinkers of the Radical Right:
Behind the New Threat to Liberal Democracy*, ed. Mark Sedgwick (New York: Oxford
University Press, 2019), 170–71.

16. Bat Ye'or, *Eurabia: The Euro-Arab Axis* (Madison, N.J.: Farleigh Dickinson
University Press, 2005), 9.

17. Renaud Camus, *Le Grande Remplacement: Introduction au remplacisme global*
(Plieux, France: self-pub., 2017).

18. Renaud Camus, *You Will Not Replace Us!* (Plieux, France: self-pub., 2018), 19, 21.

19. Ibid., 185.

20. *Åsne Seierstad, One of Us: The Story of Anders Breivik and the Massacre in Norway*,
trans. Sarah Death (New York: Farrar, Strauss and Giroux, 2013), 339.

21. Mark Memmott, "Mass Killer in Norway Declares 'I Would Have Done It
Again,'" *NPR*, April 27, 2012, https://www.npr.org/sections/thetwo-way
/2012/04/17/150790728/mass-murderer-in-norway-declares-i-would-have-done-it-again.

22. Andrew Berwick [Anders Behring Breivik], "2083: A European Declaration of
Independence," https://fas.org/programs/tap/_docs/2083_-_A_European_Declaration
_of_Independence.pdf.

23. Brenton Tarrant, *The Great Replacement: Towards a New Society We March Ever Forwards*, https://www.academia.edu/38562522/The_Great_Replacement.

24. "French 'Great Replacement' Writer Denounces 'Appalling' New Zealand Attack," *France24*, March 15, 2019, https://www.france24.com/en /20190315-french-great-replacement-writer-denounces-appalling-nzealand-attack.

25. The United States Attorney's Office, Western District of Pennsylvania, *US v. Robert Bowers*, October 31, 2018, https://www.justice.gov/usao-wdpa/vw/us-v-bowers.

26. "Analyzing a Terrorist's Social Media Manifesto: The Pittsburgh Synagogue Shooter's Posts on Gab," Southern Poverty Law Center, October 28, 2018. https://www.splcenter.org/hatewatch/2018/10/28/analyzing-terrorists-social -media-manifesto-pittsburgh-synagogue-shooters-posts-gab.

27. "History," HIAS, https://www.hias.org/who/history.

28. "Analyzing a Terrorist's Social Media Manifesto."

29. "Tucker Carlson: Washington 'Experts' Would Rather Help Morocco and Mozambique Than Protect U.S. Border," *RealClear Politics*, April 10, 2019, https://www .realclearpolitics.com/video/2019/04/10/tucker_carlson_washington_experts_would _rather_help_morocco_and_mozambique_that_protect_us_border.html.

30. United States District Court, Southern District California, *United States of America v. John Timothy Earnest*, https://www.justice.gov/opa/press-release/file /1161421/download.

31. John Timothy Earnest, "The Manifesto," April 28, 2019, https://archive.org/ stream/john-t-ernest-manifesto-8chan-pol-april-27-2019-an-open-letter /John-T-Earnest-April-27-2019-An-Open-Letter_djvu.txt.

32. The State of Texas, *Warrant of Arrest for Crusius, Patrick Wood*, https://int.nyt .com/data/documenthelper/1628-el-paso-affidavit/8b178ce3c1b380ac1b7d/optimized /full.pdf.

33. *"Walmart Shooter Manifesto,"* The Drudge Report, August 3, 2019, https://drudgereport.com/flashtx.htm.

34. Will Steakin and Rachel Scott, "Trump Campaign Defends Thousands of Facebook Ads Warning of Migrant 'Invasion' as 'Accurate,'" *ABC News*, August 7, 2019, https://abcnews.go.com/Politics/trump-campaign-defends-thousands-facebook-ads -warning-migrant/story?id=64829322.

CHAPTER 10. POPULISM

1. See Paul Lewis, Seán Clarke, Caelainn Barr, Niko Kommenda, and Josh Holder, "Revealed: One in Four Europeans Vote Populist," *The Guardian*, November 20, 2018, http://www.theguardian.com/world/ng-interactive/2018/nov/20 /revealed-one-in-four-europeans-vote-populist.

2. Note that several countries (e.g., Germany, Norway, Chile, Canada, Uruguay) do not have a history of populism in recent decades, although, of course, elements of populism (e.g., nationalist rhetoric) can be found in most political parties and movements, even in these countries.

3. The exception appears to be centrist politics, which, precisely because it tends to be moderate, does not lend itself to populism's more black-and-white, friend-or-foe, political rhetoric. Note as well that what was perhaps most striking in the 2016 U.S. election was that both the Right (Trump) and the Left (Sanders) tapped into the same well of popular frustration and rage (although arguably, Sanders is much less of a populist than Trump).

4. These statistics are from "Facts: Global Inequality," Inequality.org, https://inequality.org/facts/global-inequality/.

5. These statistics are from part 2, "Trends in Global Income Inequality," *World Inequality Report 2018*, https://wir2018.wid.world/part-2.html.

6. Scandals revealed by the likes of Wikileaks, the Paradise Papers, the Panama Papers, Edward Snowden, Bradley/Chelsea Manning, etc.

7. It is perhaps this cultural dimension that explains why populism has had traction not just in places where there has been obvious socioeconomic decline or instability (the United States, Russia, Turkey, Brazil, and India), but also places such as Denmark, Austria, Norway, and the Czech Republic, the first three of which are more socially egalitarian than the rest of Europe (with a significant presence of the welfare state despite neoliberal austerity) and the last of which has not recently experienced major economic problems or been significantly touched by the European refugee crisis.

8. Of course, each of these populist leaders leverages different social anxieties differently, with the left-wing ones tending to focus more on fear and paranoia than xenophobia and racism (unlike their right-wing counterparts, who resort to racist and jingoistic discourse more often than not). The political discourse of Chávez and Maduro, for example, has often engaged in fearmongering and paranoia through the identification of both internal and external threats/enemies (judges, journalists, corporate elites, "Yankee imperialism," oil multinationals) as a way of uniting their regime's popular base. See Iñaki Sagarzazu and Cameron G. Thies, "The Foreign Policy Rhetoric of Populism: Chávez, Oil, and Anti-Imperialism," *Political Research Quarterly* 72, no. 1 (2019): 205–14.

9. See Slavoj Žižek, *Žižek's Jokes (Did You Hear the One about Hegel and Negation?)* (Cambridge, Mass.: MIT Press, 2014), 56.

CHAPTER 11. WALLS

1. We Build the Wall, "Plans and Programs," https://webuildthewall.us/plans-programs/.

2. Peter Holley, "Trump Proposes a Border Wall. But There Already Is One, and It Gets Climbed Over," *Washington Post*, April 2, 2016, https://www.washingtonpost.com/news/morning-mix/wp/2016/04/02/shocking-video-shows-suspected-drug-smugglers-easily-crossing-u-s-mexico-border/.

3. Shlomo Avineri, "Straddling the Fence," *Foreign Policy*, October 23, 2009, https://foreignpolicy.com/2009/10/23/straddling-the-fence/.

4. Owen Lattimore, "Origins of the Great Wall of China: A Frontier Concept in Theory and Practice," *Geographical Review* 27, no. 3 (1937): 529–49.

5. Borja Pelegero Alcaide, "The Great Wall of China's Long Legacy," *National Geographic*, December 31, 2018, https://www.nationalgeographic.com/history /magazine/2016/03-04/the-great-wall-of-china/.

6. John Collins and Ross Glover, introduction to *Collateral Language: A User's Guide to America's New War*, ed. John Collins and Ross Glover (New York: New York University Press, 2002), 4.

7. Ibid., 3–4.

8. Thomas Oles, *Walls: Enclosures & Ethics in the Modern Landscape* (Chicago: University of Chicago Press, 2015), 1.

9. Ibid., 6.

10. Ibid., 8.

11. Israel Ministry of Foreign Affairs, *Saving Lives: Israel's Anti-Terrorist Fence; Answers to Questions* (Jerusalem: Israel Information Center, 2004), 5–6.

12. Collins and Glover, introduction, 2.

13. Somdeep Sen, *Decolonizing Palestine: Hamas between the Anticolonial and Postcolonial* (Ithaca, N.Y.: Cornell University Press, 2020), 20–34.

14. "India Strongly Condemns the Cowardly Terrorist Attack on Our Security Forces in Pulwama, Jammu & Kashmir," Ministry of External Affairs, Government of India, February 14, 2019, https://mea.gov.in/press-releases.htm?dtl/31053 /India_strongly_condemns_the_cowardly_terrorist_attack_on_our_security _forces_in_Pulwama_Jammu_amp_Kashmir.

15. See Tariq Ali, Arundhati Roy, Hilal Bhatt, Pankaj Mishra, and Angana P. Chatterji, *Kashmir: The Case for Freedom* (London: Verso, 2011).

16. "India Strongly Condemns the Cowardly Terrorist Attack."

17. Shashwati Das, "Rajnath Inaugurates 'Smart' Border Fence in J&K," *Live Mint*, September 17, 2018, https://www.livemint.com/Politics/8npqi5ITVPTJx5zR60G12H /Rajnath-inaugurates-smart-border-fence-in-JK.html.

18. Osama Bin Javaid, "Kashmir Border Fence, Forest Fires Endanger Wildlife," Al Jazeera, August 25, 2019, https://www.aljazeera.com/news/2019/08 /kashmir-border-fence-forest-fires-endanger-wildlife-190825155952780.html.

19. Shaun Walker, "Hungarian Leader Says Europe Is Now 'under Invasion' by Migrants," *The Guardian*, March 18, 2018, https://www.theguardian.com/world/2018 /mar/15/hungarian-leader-says-europe-is-now-under-invasion-by-migrants.

20. Daniel Boffey, "Orbán Claims Hungary Is the Last Bastion against 'Islamisation' of Europe," *The Guardian*, February 18, 2018, https://www.theguardian.com/world/2018 /feb/18/orban-claims-hungary-is-last-bastion-against-islamisation-of-europe.

21. Donald J. Trump, "Executive Order: Border Security and Immigration Enforcement Improvements," *The White House*, January 25, 2017, https://www.federalregister.gov/documents/2017/01/30/2017-02095 /border-security-and-immigration-enforcement-improvements.

22. "How the Hungarian Border Fence Remains a Political Symbol," *CBC News*, February 27, 2020, https://www.cbc.ca/radio/ideas /how-the-hungarian-border-fence-remains-a-political-symbol-1.5476964.

23. Trump, "Executive Order."

24. Ross Samson, "Knowledge, Constraint, and Power in Inaction: The Defenseless Medieval Wall," *Historical Archaeology* 26, no. 3 (1992): 37.

25. Pertti Ahonen, "The Berlin Wall and the Battle for Legitimacy in Divided Germany," *German Politics and Society* 29, no. 2 (2011): 41.

26. Stuart Leavenworth, "Biggest Hurdle for Trump's Border Wall Is Rugged Terrain," *Seattle Times*, January 22, 2018, https://www.seattletimes.com/nation-world /biggest-hurdle-for-trumps-border-wall-is-rugged-terrain/.

27. The transcript of the entire speech is available at "Donald Trump's Presidential Announcement Speech," *Time*, June 16, 2015, https://time.com/3923128 /donald-trump-announcement-speech/.

28. See Pamela Kyle Crossley, "Walls Don't Work," *Foreign Policy*, January 3, 2019, https://foreignpolicy.com/2019/01/03/walls-dont-work/; Michael Dear, "The World Is Full of Walls That Don't Work," *Politico Magazine*, August 16, 2016, https://www .politico.com/magazine/story/2016/08/donald-trump-2016-wall-wont-work-214167; and David J. Bier, "Why the Wall Won't Work," *Reason*, March 31, 2017, https://reason .com/2017/03/31/why-the-wall-wont-work/.

29. Sean Neumann, "Six Historians on Why Trump's Border Wall Won't Work," *Rolling Stone*, January 22, 2019, https://www.rollingstone.com/politics/politics-features /why-border-walls-dont-work-782449/.

30. Julia Ainsley, "DHS to Ask Congress for Sweeping Authority to Deport Unaccompanied Migrant Children," *NBC News*, March 28, 2019, https://www .nbcnews.com/politics/immigration/dhs-ask-congress-sweeping-authority -deport-unaccompanied-migrant-children-n988651.

31. Vahid Niayesh, "Trump's Travel Ban Really Was a Muslim Ban, Data Suggests," *Washington Post*, September 26, 2019, https://www.washingtonpost.com /politics/2019/09/26/trumps-muslim-ban-really-was-muslim-ban -thats-what-data-suggest/.

32. Karen Fog Olwig, Kristina Grunenberg, Perle Møhl, and Anja Simonsen, *The Biometric Border World: Technologies, Bodies and Identities on the Move* (New York: Routledge, 2020), 7.

CHAPTER 12. INTERNALLY DISPLACED PEOPLE (IDPS)

1. The Internal Displacement Monitoring Centre (IDMC) is "the world's authoritative source of data and analysis on internal displacement." Set up in 1998 to be part of the Norwegian Refugee Council (NRC), the IDMC note their "rigorous, independent and trusted service to the international community. Our work informs policy and operational decisions that improve the lives of the millions of people living in internal displacement, or at risk of becoming displaced in the future" ("About Us," IDMC, https://www.internal-displacement.org/about-us). The notion of IDPs gained was supported by member states with the United Nations General Assembly, Resolution 58/177 of 2004, para. 7; and United Nations Commission on Human Rights, Resolution

2004/55 of 2004, para. 6. The formal support within the liberal policy community becomes clear in the work by the Brookings Institute (see Brookings-Bern Project on Internal Displacement, "Addressing Internal Displacement: A Framework for National Responsibility," April 2005, available at: https://www.refworld.org/docid/4d357f4f2.html [accessed 28 February 2021]).

2. Frantz Fanon, *The Wretched of the Earth*, trans. R. Philcox (New York: Grove Press, 2004); Nicos Poulantzas, *Classes in Contemporary Capitalism* (London: New Left Books, 1974). The term "comprador bourgeoisie" as used here relates to Franz Fanon, Mao, and Poulantzas at least. Fanon saw that postcolonial governments are still driven by the interests of the comprador elites who assimilated the features of the former colonial power, while for Mao, "The landlord class and the comprador class are wholly append-ages of the international bourgeoisie, depending upon imperialism for their survival and growth." Poulantzas diagnosed that the *comprador* "is a fraction of the bourgeoisie which does not have its own base for capital accumulation, which acts in some way or other as a simple intermediary of foreign imperialist capital." Poulantzas, *Classes in Contemporary Capitalism*, 71.

3. One of the early mentions of the IDP in Sri Lanka was in a review conducted September 6–14, 2001, "to gain an insight into UNHCR's [United Nations High Commissioner for Refugees] policies and performance in the country." It was also the first joint review of a UNHCR program by the UK's DFID (Department for International Development) and the UNHCR's Evaluation and Policy Analysis Unit (EPAU). At the time, there were eight hundred thousand refugees within Sri Lanka (about one in twenty-five people). Hundreds of thousands of Sri Lankans fled to Britain and the West. See UN High Commissioner for Refugees, "UNHCR CDR Background Paper on Refugees and Asylum Seekers from Sri Lanka," March 1, 1997, available at: https://www .refworld.org/docid/3ae6a6470.html [accessed 23 February 2021].

4. Due its discomfort for liberal Westerners, the path to fascism (or proto-fascism) has been difficult to define by looking at a few countries considering ideology rather than the material conditions. Thus, a multitude of Europeans are implicated, from anti-Semite Theodor Fritsch to biblical scholar and orientalist Paul Anton de Lagarde to Romanic art historian and philosopher Julius Langbehn, *only* to some mention German reactionaries. It is far more fruitful to consider the *materiality of colonial practice as fascism* as part of the pseudosciences driven by what was assumed to be Darwinian thinking of human evolution such that races are parted in hierarchical ways by technol-ogies of violence, even though Darwin himself did not present his case that way. It was thus that assumptions of "racial" superiority accompanied European colonialism, whose ideological component was fascism. The key analysis comes from Martinique-born Aimé Césaire. For him, "It would be worthwhile to study clinically, in detail, the steps taken by Hitler and Hitlerism and to reveal to the very distinguished, very humanistic, very Christian bourgeois of the twentieth century that without his being aware of it, he has a Hitler inside him, that Hitler inhabits him, that Hitler is his demon, that if he rails against him, he is being inconsistent and that, at bottom, what he cannot forgive Hitler for is not crime in itself, the crime against man, it is not the humiliation of man

as such, it is the crime against the white man, the humiliation of the white man, and the fact that he applied to Europe colonialist procedures which until then had been reserved exclusively for the Arabs of Algeria, the coolies of India, and the blacks of Africa." Césaire, *Discourse on Colonialism*, trans. Joan Pinkham (1955; rpt., New York: Monthly Review Press, 1972), 3.

5. George Orwell, "Politics and the English language," *Horizon* 13, no. 76 (1946): 252–65, available at Public Library UK, http://www.public-library.uk/ebooks/72/30.pdf, 7–8.

6. For these structures of power as it applies to the United States see Susan Strange, *States and Markets* (London: Pinter, 1988).

7. George Lakoff and Mark Johnson, *Metaphors We Live By* (Chicago: University of Chicago Press, 1980).

8. Hannah Arendt, *The Origins of Totalitarianism* (New York: Schocken Books, 1951).

9. Georg Friedrich List, *National System of Political Economy* (London: Longmans, Green, 1841); Karl Polanyi, *The Great Transformation* (Boston: Beacon Press, 1944).

10. Colvin R. De Silva and R. Weerakoon, *Sri Lanka's New Capitalism and the Erosion of Democracy: Political Writings of Dr. Colvin R. de Silva in the Period 1977–1988* (Colombo: Ceylon Federation of Labour, 1988); Kumari Jayawardena, *Nobodies to Somebodies: The Rise of the Colonial Bourgeoisie in Sri Lanka* (Colombo: Social Scientists' Association, 2009).

11. De Silva and Weerakoon, *Sri Lanka's New Capitalism.*

12. World Socialist Web Site, Editorial Board, "Sri Lanka: The Life and Legacy of Sirima Bandaranaike," October 26, 2000, https://www.wsws.org/en/articles/2000/10 /band-026.html.

13. Leon Trotsky, "In the Middle of the Road," *New International* 2, no. 7 (1935): 215–20.

14. Sunil Poholiyadde, "The Evolution of Sri Lanka's Plantation Sector," *Ceylon Today*, August 5, 2018, https://www.historyofceylontea.com/ceylon-publications /ceylon-tea-articles/the-evolution-of-sri-lankas-plantation-sector.html.

15. Andrew Defty, *Britain, America and Anti-Communist Propaganda, 1945–53: The Information Research Department* (London: Routledge, 2013).

16. Sidney Weintraub, *Economic Coercion and U.S. Foreign Policy: Implications of Case Studies from the Johnson Administration* (London: Routledge, 2019).

17. John Martin Richardson, *Paradise Poisoned: Learning about Conflict, Terrorism, and Development from Sri Lanka's Civil Wars* (Kandy, Sri Lanka: International Center for Ethnic Studies, 2005), 265.

18. Rehan Abeyratne, "Uncertain Sovereignty: Ceylon as a Dominion, 1948–1972," *International Journal of Constitutional Law* 17, no. 4 (2019): 1258–82.

19. Mahaveli Authority of Sri Lanka, http://mahaweli.gov.lk/index.html.

20. Patrick Peebles, "Colonization and Ethnic Conflict in the Dry Zone of Sri Lanka," *Journal of Asian Studies* 49, no. 1 (1990): 30–55.

21. "'Sinhala Gammana' Colony Gets Expanded in Ko'ndaichchi, Mannaar," TamilNet, March 2, 2018, https://www.tamilnet.com/art.html?catid=13&artid=38979;

"Widespread Logging Backed by sl Military in Mannaar Continues to Escape Scrutiny," TamilNet, August 26 2019, https://www.tamilnet.com/art .html?catid=13&artid=39556.

22. Ann Neistat, *Recurring Nightmare: State Responsibility for "Disappearances" and Abductions in Sri Lanka* (New York: Human Rights Watch, 2008), 183; Dinesh De Alwis, "Sri Lanka: Waves of Protests after University Students Shot Dead," *University World News*, October 28, 2016, https://www.universityworldnews.com/post .php?story=20161028072115119.

23. Barbara Harff and Ted Robert Gurr, *Ethnic Conflict in World Politics,* 2nd ed. (London: Routledge, 2018).

24. Polanyi, *Great Transformation*; Hannah Arendt, *On Violence* (Houghton Mifflin Harcourt, 1970), 240–43. Thus, ultimately Arendt's conformance with the notion that modern states are instruments of capital that seeks domination at any cost. Even though she has been skeptical of Marx, her antipathy is with Bolshevism ("larger" in Russian, with Lenin's "dictatorship of the proletariat"), compared with Mensheviks ("smaller" in Russian, who proposed an open democratic constitution and a proletarian party working with the liberals). It is thus possible to make the case that Arendt was a victim of the dominance of Bolshevism, thus missing the social democratic path and bringing her work into conflict with non-European-origin liberation movements whose social democratic leanings she missed, for example, in Sri Lanka.

25. Judith Butler and Gayatri Chakravorty Spivak, *Who Sings the Nation-State: Language, Politics, Belonging* (Kolkata: Seagull Books, 2007), 58–61.

26. Maria Abi-Habib and Dharisha Bastians, "U.S. Bars Sri Lankan Army Chief Accused of War Crimes," *New York Times*, February 15, 2020, https://www .nytimes.com/2020/02/15/world/asia/sri-lanka-us-sanctions.html; Phil Miller, "Exclusive: Secret Documents Reveal How Britain Funded Possible War Crimes in Sri Lanka," *Vice News*, March 31, 2016, https://www.vice.com/en_uk/article/dp5beq /sri-lanka-british-police-training-phil-miller.

27. Steven Kemper, *Rescued from the Nation: Anagarika Dharmapala and the Buddhist World* (Chicago: University of Chicago Press, 2015), 117.

CHAPTER 13. VICTIMS

1. Walter Benjamin, "Theses on the Philosophy of History," in *Illuminations*, ed. Hannah Arendt, trans. Harry Zohn (New York: Schocken Books, 1968), 255.

2. "La Vicepresidenta y el mito de la transicón pacífica," *Público*, September 23, 2019, https://www.publico.es/tremending/2019/09/23/carmen-calvo-dice-que-salimos-de-la -dictadura-sin-un-solo-roce-de-violencia-salvo-eta-y-twitter-recuerda-los-600-muertos/.

3. Agencia efe, "Zapatero visita a los heridos del 11-m en su primer acto como presidente," *Cadena Ser*, April 17, 2004, https://cadenaser.com/ser/2004/04/17/espana /1082159414_850215.html; Agencia efe, "Zapatero se estrena como presidente visitando a víctimas del 11-m y de la violencia doméstica", *El País*, April 17, 2004, https://

elpais.com/elpais/2004/04/17/actualidad/1082189817_850215.html; Enric Hernández, "Zapatero rinde tributo a las víctimas del 11-M al debutar como president," *El Periódico de Aragón*, April 18, 2004, https://www.elperiodicodearagon.com/noticias/temadia /zapatero-rinde-tributo-victimas-11-m-debutar-presidente_113536.html.

4. Gobierno de España, Cortes Generales, *Diario de Sesiones del Pleno del Congreso de los Diputados del 11 de septiembre de 2002*, VII Legislatura, no. 184 (Madrid: Congreso de los Diputados, 2004).

5. Gobierno de España, *Ley 52/2007, de 26 de diciembre, por la que se reconocen y amplían derechos y se establecen medidas en favor de quienes padecieron persecución o violencia durante la guerra civil y la dictadura*, Boletín Oficial del Estado, no. 310, Madrid, 2007.

AFTERWORD. WOUNDS

1. Francois Delaporte, *Disease and Civilization: The Cholera in Paris, 1832* (Cambridge, Mass.: MIT Press, 1986), 17.

2. Edwin Chadwick, *Report to Her Majesty's Principal Secretary of State for the Home Department, from the Poor Law Commissioners on an inquiry into the Sanitary Conditions of the Labouring Populations of Great Britain* (London: W. Clowes and Sons, Stamford Street), 44.

3. Claude Levi-Strauss, *Tristes Tropiques* (New York: Criterion Book, 1984), 134.

4. Chadwick, *Report*, 44.

5. World Bank, *Sierra Leone: Public Expenditure Policies for Sustained Economic Growth and Poverty Alleviation* (Western Africa Department Country Operations Division, 1994), v, http://documents1.worldbank.org/curated/en/439141468759850724 /pdf/multi-page.pdf.

Contributors

POUYA ALIMAGHAM is a historian of the modern Middle East at Massachusetts Institute of Technology. He focuses on such themes as revolutionary and guerrilla movements, U.S. foreign policy and imperialism, Orientalism, "Political Islam" and post-Islamism, women and gender studies, and the intersections therein. He won the Association for Iranian Studies Mehrdad Mashayekhi Dissertation Award in 2016. His first book, *Contesting the Iranian Revolution: The Green Uprisings*, was published in 2020.

STEPHEN R. BARNARD is associate professor of sociology at St. Lawrence University. His research and teaching focus on the role media and communication technologies play in relations of power, practice, and democracy. He is the author of *Citizens at the Gates: Twitter, Networked Publics, and the Transformation of American Journalism* and coauthor of *All Media Are Social: Sociological Perspectives on Mass Media*. His work has been published in *New Media & Society, Journalism, Cultural Studies ↔ Critical Methodologies, Hybrid Pedagogy*, and several edited volumes. He has also written for broader audiences in publications such as *The Hill, RealClearPolitics*, and *Contexts*.

DAMON T. BERRY is assistant professor of American religions and contemporary issues in religion at St. Lawrence University in Canton, New York. His work focuses on the intersections between religion, racism, and violence. He has published in *Politics & Religion, Security Journal*, and *Nova Religio*. He is the author of *Blood & Faith: Christianity in American White Nationalism* (2017) and *Christianity & The Alt-Right: Exploring the Relationship* (2021).

CHRIS BUCK is an associate professor in the Department of Government at St. Lawrence University. He specializes in environmental political theory and has published work on "post-environmentalism" as well as on Theodor Adorno's critique of the concept of nature. He is currently working on a book project that examines crises related to environmental politics from a critical theory perspective.

GEORGE CICCARIELLO-MAHER is a Philadelphia-based writer, organizer, and educator, and a visiting associate professor of global political thought at Vassar College, having taught previously at Drexel University, San Quentin State Prison, and the Venezuelan School of Planning in Caracas. He is coeditor of the Radical Américas book series and author of three books: *We Created Chávez* (2013), *Building the Commune* (2016), and *Decolonizing Dialectics* (2017).

JOHN COLLINS is professor of global studies at St. Lawrence University, where he teaches courses on globalization, Palestine, critical media literacy, cultural studies, and political activism. He is the author of *Global Palestine* (2011) and *Occupied by Memory: The Intifada Generation and the Palestinian State of Emergency* (2004) and the coauthor (with Eve Stoddard) of *Social and Cultural Foundations in Global Studies* (2015). In 2002, he coedited with Ross Glover the original *Collateral Language: A User's Guide to America's New War* volume. He is also a founder of Weave News (www.weavenews.org), an independent citizen journalism platform, and currently serves as its editorial director.

194 PALOMA ELVIRA RUIZ is a PhD candidate in psychology at the Autonomous University of Madrid, in collaboration with the Centre of Discourse Studies, Barcelona. Her research interests span youth political participation, territorial struggles, and politics of the commons. Her work is mainly informed by feminist, decolonial, and critical theory, as well as by the field of applied linguistics and discourse studies.

JAYANTHA JAYMAN has led a life of learning that has taken him from Asia and Africa to Europe and North America, with formal work at Denison University (BA in physics and political science), the University of Toronto (MA in international development/political economy), and the London School of Economics (PhD in international relations/political economy). He has witnessed armed insurrection and famine and writes on problems of global leadership, hegemony, imperialism, and fascism, seeking progressive change by deploying overlooked non-Western theory. He draws on Murakami Yasusuke's work to acknowledge Japan's post–World War II global public goods provision for a more peaceful Asian order. With crisis in the liberal international system in the late twentieth century, his work examines the potential of Ali Mazrui's African "triple heritage" ethics of inclusion as a realistic approach to global problems, challenging myopic expropriation of E. H. Carr's realism. Recognizing Mao's insight on comprador control of China, Jayman's work illuminates Beijing's authoritarian capitalist challenge to the liberal international system via its world-leading *qi ye ji tuan* (conglomerates). Jayman is currently exploring how the response to China and Russia's kleptocracy is split between a turn toward fascism and a hopeful shift to the progressive politics of the New Deal.

ILAN KAPOOR is professor of critical development studies at the Faculty of Environmental and Urban Change, York University, Toronto. His research focuses on psychoanalytic and postcolonial theory and politics, participatory development and democracy, and ideology critique. He is the author of *The Postcolonial Politics of Development* (2008), *Celebrity Humanitarianism: The Ideology of Global Charity* (2013), and *Confronting Desire: Psychoanalysis and International Development* (2020); coauthor with Zahi Zalloua of *Universal Politics* (2021); and editor of the collected volume *Psychoanalysis and the GlObal* (2018).

MARINA LLORENTE is Charles A. Dana Professor of Hispanic Studies at St. Lawrence University. She has published two monographs, *Palabra y deseo: Espacios transgresores en la poesía Española, 1975–1990* and *Poesía en acción: Poemas críticos en la España contemporánea*, and has coedited two anthologies, *Abuelas Hispanas: Desde la memoria y el recuerdo* and *Activism through Poetry: Critical Spanish Poems in Translation*. She has also coedited the volume *Sites of Memory in Spain and Latin America: Trauma, Politics, and Resistance*, a collection of essays exploring historical memory at the intersection of political, cultural, social, and economic forces in the contexts of Spain and Latin America. Her new book project explores traces of the Francoism time in contemporary Spanish poetry, focusing on poems dealing with violence against women.

VIJAY PRASHAD is an Indian historian and journalist. He is the author of thirty books, including *Washington Bullets, Red Star over the Third World, The Darker Nations: A People's History of the Third World,* and *The Poorer Nations: A Possible History of the Global South.* He is the chief correspondent for *Globetrotter* and a columnist for *Frontline* (India). He is the chief editor of LeftWord Books (New Delhi). He has appeared in two films, *Shadow World* (2016) and *Two Meetings and a Funeral* (2017).

EMANUELE SACCARELLI teaches political theory at San Diego State University. He is the author of two books, *Gramsci and Trotsky in the Shadow of Stalinism* (2008) and *Imperialism, Past and Present* (2015, coauthored with Latha Varadarajan). He has also published articles on Plato, Rousseau, Marx, Gramsci, Silone, and Hardt and Negri.

LOTTE BUCH SEGAL is a lecturer in social anthropology at the University of Edinburgh. Her research is animated by questions of violence, relatedness, everyday life, and knowledge, as well as issues pertaining to gender and voice. Her first book, *No Place for Grief: Martyrs, Prisoners and Mourning in Contemporary Palestine* (2016), is an ethnographic monograph about the porous boundary between endurance and exhaustion and, importantly, how kinship is the site in which such exhaustion is felt. Methodological questions of how to do ethnography among people in precarious situations informs the ethical sensibility with which she approaches ethnography and collaboration more broadly. Through her research, she has worked closely with NGOs and academic colleagues globally and committed to different modes of engaged anthropology in and beyond her current research areas.

SOMDEEP SEN is associate professor in international development studies at Roskilde University, Denmark. His research focuses include spatial politics, liberation movements, critical race theory, international relations, and postcolonial studies. He is the author of *Decolonizing Palestine: Hamas between the Anticolonial and Postcolonial* (2020). He is the coauthor of *The Palestinian Authority in the West Bank: The Theatrics of Woeful Statecraft* (2019) and the coeditor of *Syrian Refugee Children in the Middle East and Europe: Integrating the Young and Exiled* (2018). He has also published in *Foreign Policy*, the *Huffington Post, Jacobin, Open Democracy, London Review of Books, The Palestine Chronicle, Al Ahram Weekly, World Development, Social Anthropology, Middle East Critique, Arab Studies Quarterly,* and *Interventions: International Journal of Postcolonial Studies.*

NATALIA RACHEL SINGER is the author of a political memoir, *Scraping By in the Big Eighties.* Her fiction and nonfiction have appeared in *Speculative Nonfiction, Harper's, Ms., O: The Oprah Magazine, The Nation, New Flash Fiction Review, Alternet.org, Iowa Review, Redbook, American Scholar, Chronicle of Higher Education,* and many others. Her work has been short-listed for *The Best American Travel Essays* and *The*

Pushcart Prize and anthologized widely. She is completing a new essay collection, *Stubborn Roots*, and is at work on a novel. A professor of creative writing and environmental literature at St. Lawrence University, she has led study-abroad programs in France and India.

CATHERINE TEDFORD is gallery director at St. Lawrence University. As Ted C. Ford, she helped create illustrations for the first *Collateral Language* publication in 2002. Since 2008, she has been writing about street art stickers on her research blog *Stickerkitty*. Her most recent exhibition on this topic, *Paper Bullets: 100 Years of Political Stickers from around the World*, was featured at Neurotitan Gallery in Berlin, Germany, in 2019.

LATHA VARADARAJAN is a professor of political science and the director of the Center on International Security and Conflict Resolution at San Diego State University. She is the author of *The Domestic Abroad: Diasporas in International Relations* (2010) and *Imperialism Past and Present* (2015, coauthored with Emanuele Saccarelli). Her articles on transnationalism, nationalism, and imperialism have been published in journals such as the *European Journal of International Relations, International Relations, New Political Science*, and *Review of International Studies*.

Printed in the United States
by Baker & Taylor Publisher Services